1994 Lannan Literary Awards

Simon Armitage
POETRY

Eavan Boland
POETRY

Jack Gilbert
POETRY

Linda Hogan
POETRY

Richard Kenney
POETRY

Edward P. Jones
FICTION

Steven Millhauser
FICTION

Caryl Phillips
FICTION

Stephen Wright
FICTION

Jonathan Kozol
NONFICTION

Lannan Foundation honors writers of
distinctive literary merit with an award of $50,000 each.

ANDRE EMMERICH GALLERY

41 EAST 57TH STREET

NEW YORK, NEW YORK 10022

TELEPHONE (212) 752-0124

FAX (212) 371-7345

CONJUNCTIONS

Bi-Annual Volumes of New Writing

Edited by
Bradford Morrow

Contributing Editors
Walter Abish
John Ashbery
Mei-mei Berssenbrugge
Guy Davenport
Elizabeth Frank
William H. Gass
Susan Howe
Robert Kelly
Ann Lauterbach
Patrick McGrath
Nathaniel Tarn
Quincy Troupe
John Edgar Wideman

Bard College   *distributed by Random House, Inc.*

EDITOR: Bradford Morrow
MANAGING EDITOR: Dale Cotton
SENIOR EDITORS: Martine Bellen, Peter Cole
ART EDITOR: Anthony McCall
ASSOCIATE EDITORS: Eric Darton, Ben Marcus, Pat Sims
EDITORIAL ASSISTANTS: Sharon Becker, Nomi Eve, Joan Reilly

CONJUNCTIONS is published in the Spring and Fall of each year by Bard College, Annandale-on-Hudson, NY 12504. This issue is made possible in part with the generous funding of the Lannan Foundation, the National Endowment for the Arts and the New York State Council on the Arts. Major new marketing initiatives have been made possible by the Lila Wallace–Reader's Digest Literary Publishers Marketing Development Program, funded through a grant to the Council of Literary Magazines and Presses. A generous project grant from Z Press offset translating costs of the work in this issue.

SUBSCRIPTIONS: Send subscription order to CONJUNCTIONS, Bard College, Annandale-on-Hudson, NY 12504. Single year (two volumes): $18.00 for individuals; $25.00 for institutions and overseas. Two years (four volumes): $32.00 for individuals; $45.00 for institutions and overseas. Patron subscription (lifetime): $500.00. Overseas subscribers please make payment by International Money Order. Back issues available at $10.00 per copy. For subscription and advertising information, call or fax 914-758-1539.

Editorial communications should be sent to 33 West 9th Street, New York, NY 10011. Unsolicited manuscripts cannot be returned unless accompanied by a stamped, self-addressed envelope.

Distributed by Random House.

Cover painting © 1991 by Komar & Melamid. "Psalms" (detail) (1991; tempera, oil and varnish on canvas; triptych, 72 inches by 198 inches). Photograph by Dennis Cowley. Reproduced courtesy Ronald Feldman Fine Art, New York.
Cover design by Anthony McCall Associates, New York.

Printers: Edwards Brothers.
Typesetter: Bill White, Typeworks.

ISSN 0278-2324
ISBN 0-679-75820-8

Manufactured in the United States of America.

TABLE OF CONTENTS

Unless otherwise noted, each contribution includes
an afterword by the translator.

William Everson
1912–1994

EDITOR'S NOTE

FRANCE, PERU, MEXICO, Italy, Israel, China, Pakistan, Nigeria, Argentina, Spain, Russia, Egypt, Austria, Bosnia, Australia, Uruguay, Japan — the countries where these writings were written — do not the world make. Which is to say that this little anthology neither makes the claim nor ever held the hope of being exhaustive. Indeed, we ran out of space with more than a hundred further pages of work typeset and proofed.

Yoel Hoffmann's luminous, lapidary novella "The Christ of Fish" will be included in the spring issue, his first appearance in print in this country. The Indian writer Githa Hariharan, whose stories Michael Ondaatje recommended to me, will also appear in the spring. Her work displays a psychological and even technical kinship with that of Mary Caponegro, Can Xue, Paola Capriolo, even Angela Carter (how the world begins to shrink). A passage from Louis-Ferdinand Céline's *Guignol's Band*, translated by Dominic Di Bernardi, too, will appear in the next issue. The Congolese writer Tchicaya U'Tamsi; Kateb Yacine; a story by the Sri Lankan Jean Arasanayagan — and there are others, many others — might have appeared but that illness and deadlines prevented it.

What we have here is a beginning, the commencement of a more deliberate pushing out into the wider world. World writing, cousin through the auspices of translation to world music.

Guiding principle for inclusion was the same as always in the pages of this workbook — that the writing embrace form and tale in a single gesture, seeing them as head and tail, say, of the same beautiful beast. Is *innovative* an exhausted polysyllabic? Maybe, but I believe each of these pieces displays a certain freshness of approach both toward subject and locution, which makes it "new." And so, *new* world writing. Beyond that, as always, from where I sit the work is its own manifesto and needs no critical garnish to be delectable.

Also, as always, there are many friends to thank. The majority of writers published here were new to me, and I would never have found my way to them but for the generosity of other writers willing to point me in right directions.

Forrest Gander must be acknowledged above all for sending me to Japan and Mexico, not to mention places like Cuba and Bulgaria where I might have come back empty-handed this first go-around, but know the road there better than before. Peter Cole gathered the materials from Israel. Ammiel Alcalay, John Ashbery, Charles Bernstein, John Cayley, Stacy Doris, William Gass, James Laughlin, Ann Lauterbach, John Taggart, Nathaniel Tarn, Larry Venuti, Rosmarie Waldrop and Paul West sent work my way and made invaluable suggestions. To my knowledge this issue marks the first appearance in print in this country of a number of these writers — Abd al-Hakim Qasim, Araki Yasusada, Carlos Germán Belli, Ishihara Yoshiro, J. Rodolfo Wilcock, perhaps one or two of the others — and I am especially grateful to those who helped with these discoveries.

The translators, above all, deserve credit not just for bringing into English these often-resistant texts, but for providing afterwords which are meant to help the reader who is not acquainted with background and work of these practitioners of invigorating contemporary writing.

— October 30, 1994
New York City

8

Chinese Travelogue
Olga Sedakova

— Translated from Russian by Andrew Wachtel

> *If you could dull its perspicuity, free it from*
> *chaos, limit its gleam, liken it to a grain of dust,*
> *then it would seem to exist clearly.*
>
> — Lao-Tse

1.

These things amazed me:
    the still waters,
    the familiar sky,
    the junk floating slowly within stone banks.
Homeland! my heart shouted at the sight of willow:
there are willows in China
that erase their ovals with great eagerness,
since only our generosity
will meet us in the next world.

2.

The pond says:
had I hands and a voice
I would love and cherish you.
People, you see, are greedy and frequently sick
and they tear other's clothes
to make bandages.
While I need nothing:
after all, tenderness is healing.
I'd place my hands on your knees
as if I were a toy dog,
and through my voice I'd descend
from above like the heavens.

3.

In falling, they fall not
the long sleeves of trees
     dip into the water but don't get wet.
My ancient trees —
pagodas, roads.
How many times have we seen each other,
yet each time's like the first,
as I gasp, my heart heaving hard
with a completely empty pack,
along the trunk, over the hills and valleys of branches,
into the long wide eyes of temples
toward the mirror on the altar,
over the green floor.
Haven't we wandered enough
to set off together at last
along the only pleasant
     invisible
        path
that bothers no one?
Cap conferring invisibility,
godly garment, garment of eyes,
in falling it falls not, dips into the water but isn't wet.
Trees, for you only "I love you" will do.

4.

There — on a mountain
at whose knees is a last hut,
and no one's gone higher;
whose brow can't be seen behind the storm clouds
so you can't say whether it's frowning or smiling —
someone comes and doesn't, is and isn't.
He's the size of a swallow's eye,
     of a crumb of dry bread,
of a ladder on a butterfly's wings,
of a ladder thrown down from heaven,
of a ladder that
no one wants to climb;
smaller than what wasps see,
smaller than the word is.

5.

Do you know
the dwarf pines, the weeping willows?
An untied boat
doesn't hug the bank for long —
and there's no joy
in what's past
nor sorrow:
we're all here today, but who can speak
for tomorrow?
and no reason:
only the blameless spirits are
modest, fearless and charitable —
simple rapture can't be stopped,
simple rapture setting like the sun.
An untied boat
floats without a thought,
a broken bough
takes root, but not in this world.

6.

Just as soon as I'd see
a traveler brightly clad, in white —
what can we do, how can we escape?

Just as soon as I'd see
white clothing, old shoulders —
better that my eyes were made of stone
                my heart of water.

Just as soon as I'd see
what happens to a man —
I'd follow him, weeping:
wherever he'd go, I'd go, walking
with the same measured walk.

7.

A boat's floating across the wet flattened azure.
The sky darkens quickly and glances out
with the alien eyes of that other sapphire.
Do you know what? no one ever believed me
(like a child tells another,
dying from his own audacity:
yea, and then they buried him
by the third pine). I'll tell you the same way:
no one ever believed me,
and neither will you,
just don't tell anybody
that while the boat floats, and the sun gleams
heavenly joy is playing in the sapphire.

8.

Roofs raised at the edges
like amazed eyebrows:
Really? you don't say? I'm so glad.
Terraces, from which you can always see
everything a person loves to see:
dry banks, silvery-yellow rivers,
a broken line of bushes — like a love letter.
Two passersby bow low to one another on a pontoon bridge
and a swallow brings you
a teaspoon of height:
heart medicine, a healing potion.
By the way, in China no one gets sick:
the heavens know how to strike at the right time
        with a long needle.

9.

Unhappy
is he who speaks with a guest and thinks about tomorrow's task;
    unhappy
is he who does a task and thinks about completing it
that it's not the air and the rays that control him,
like a brush, a butterfly or bee;
    he who strikes a chord and thinks
    what the next one will be
is unhappy, afraid and miserly.

Even more unhappy
is he who does not forgive;
he's insane and does not know
how tame storks come out of the bushes,
or how the golden sphere
flies up all alone
into the precious sky above the precious earth.

10.

Great is the artist who knows no task
but the task of the playing brush:
his brush penetrates the heart of mountains,
penetrates the happiness of leaves,
with a single strike, merely through humility,
elation, merely through embarrassment
he penetrates immortality itself
and immortality plays with him.

But he whom the spirit leaves, from whom
rays are deflected,
who searches a silty spot the tenth time
for a pure spring,
who fell from the hands of miracles, but who'd never say:
miracles are silly —
Before him the heavens bow with esteem.

11.

With tenderness and depth —
since only tenderness is deep,
and only depth possesses tenderness —
out of a thousand faces I'd know;
whoever has seen it, on whomever it has glanced
from stone things as if from glass,
tender depth and deep tenderness.

So light up,
warm lantern of the west,
lamp, moth trap.
Speak once more
with our everyday light
sun of tenderness and of depth,
sun which is quitting the earth,
first and final sun.

12.

Maybe you're the soul's ring,
the blue water's stone,
a muffled voice murmuring
about a terraced garden —
But why has the winged chariot raced with a moan,
wind, shore, a sand dune,
empty sea —
you can't say adieu
there's nowhere to part from you.
A simple man —
like salt in sea sprays,
without word, or face, or phrase,
with only the tide, salt and iodine —
having no one in whom to confide
incants internally:
Perhaps you're the soul's ring,
the blue water's stone,
a muffled voice murmuring
about an unimaginable garden.

13.

Must we, too, like all others,
really part?

Knowing something
about passion that's quicker than finality,
knowing something
about the world that's smaller than a penny —
let whoever needs take —
know that this shell has no pearl,
that there's no match, candle or lantern
other than the flash of rapture,
knowing whence come
sound and light —
must we, too, part, like simple fools?

Loving to be together
no less than willows love to grow by the water,
or than waters to follow a star's magnet,
or than the drunken Li Bo to stare
at the yellow, moonlike wine,
or than a stone to sink to the bottom —
must we, too, part, like simple misers and boors?

14.

Flute responds to flute —
not ivory or wooden,
but the one that the mountains hold
in their caves and crevasses.
Strings respond to strings,
and words respond to words.

And the supplication of my heart
responds to the quickly rising evening star:

you breed thousands of stars,
evening star,
and thousands of supplications burn my heart,

myriad supplications about one and the same thing:
wake up,
glance at me, my inspired friend,
see how the night sparkles . . .

15.

By the white way, by the cold and starry cloud they strode,
it is said, and we, too, will go:
fording the water from boulder to boulder,
fording separation from planet to planet,
like a singing voice going from note to note.
It is said that we'll all meet there, bleached
                    by the milky road.
How often — I'll admit — has my heart, beating heavily,
approached the forbidden threshold
promising I don't know whom:
no one is searching for me, no one will mourn
no one will beg: remain with me!
It's not earthly grief that makes miraculous what waits
                    behind the earth's door,
it's because we don't want, don't want our trespassing,
because the time has arrived
to ask forgiveness for all, since
none can survive
without this bread of radiance.
It's time to go where
everything is compassion.

16.

You know, I love you so much
        that should there come a day
when I am taken from you,
        it will not take me away —
as if anyone could forget fire?
        as if anyone could forget
that happiness wants to be
        and unhappiness wants not to be?

You know, I love you so much
    that I can't separate it from
the wind's whistle, a branch's rustle, the rain's life,
    or a path that looks candle-like,
the alien dark that mumbles,
    my mind that has flashed like a match,
or even the sad dry sound of a butterfly's
    knock against glass.

17.

Whenever we decide to drift,
    not knowing what awaits us,
on inspiration's empty ship,
    on the poorly moored raft,
on the scaly wing, or on a boat without oarsmen,
imagining the best
    and the worst of ends,
and searching for nothing inside:
    that's when, in exchange for everything
the divining dice are thrown for the I Ching.
Who invented the emptiness of water? who discovered
    that up above there is war?
who decreed
    that gardens grow from fiery seed?
that a nightingale would rather die
    than not sing what he sings,
than not write out on the silk of time
    that which the people can't.
Each time you blow into your whistle,
    inspiration, each time
between earth and our soul your springs
    climb —
if only you knew, whirlwind of death
    and you empty surface,
how I want to kiss your feet and beg forgiveness.

Olga Sedakova

18.

Let us praise our earthly sphere,
    the moon on the water,
and that which is with none and all
    here and not here —
the size of a swallow's eye
    of a crumb of dry bread
of a ladder on a butterfly's wings,
    of a ladder thrown down from heaven.
My heart is bridled
    not just by woe and by pity
but also by the miraculous water's smile.
Let us praise the swimming of dark
    precious branches in living glass,
and, above each grain in the earth,
    the sleepless souls of all who have passed,
and the fact there are rewards,
    that we can ward off evil
that there is praise in the world,
    like a gardener in a garden.

———————————

Understated, restrained, delicate — these are hardly the first words that come to mind when the subject is Russian literature. After all, the general impression is that Russian literature consists primarily of powerful but somewhat misshapen novels, the "loose and baggy monsters" of Tolstoy and Dostoevsky. Even when the topic is limited to Russian poetry, non-Russian readers are most likely to know the erudite, complex lyrics of Mandelstam and Pasternak, the futurist experiments of Mayakovsky and Khlebnikov or the wrenching emotional verse of Tsvetaeva, Akhmatova and Brodsky. There is, however, another tradition of Russian literature, less well known in translation perhaps, and less "exotic" but no less cherished by Russian readers. It begins, as does most modern Russian literature, with the perfect classical balance of Alexander Pushkin's lyric verse, and includes in addition the poetry of Afanasy Fet, Mikhail Kuzmin and Vladislav Khodasevich. It is to this tradition that the poetry of Olga Sedakova belongs.

Sedakova was born in Moscow in 1949 and came to poetic maturity during the late Brezhnev years, the "period of stagnation" of the early 1970s. Although Stalinist terror was already a thing of the past, this was a time of widespread apathy and dejection. It was clear to all that the Soviet system was decaying, yet it seemed destined to last indefinitely. For young and independent poets, publication was almost out of the question, although poetic life went on quite actively behind the closed doors of poets' apartments. In this milieu, Sedakova's work quickly stood out. As opposed to most of her contemporaries, who continued and continue to employ "classical" meters and rhyme schemes, Sedakova favored free verse. She cultivated a conversational, seemingly prosaic diction and a dialogic form (enhanced by her preference to compose thematically connected cycles rather than individual lyrics), but her intensely personal verse was always tinged with elements of the eternal and mystical. As a colleague of mine, Stephanie Sandler, has observed: "Sedakova writes about processes of thought, about the emotions that surge when one turns an idea over in the mind, rather than the discoveries that thinking can yield. She is a metaphysical poet whose lyrics circle the eddying currents of mental change."

In parallel with her prosaic cycles, and perhaps as a way to balance the "low" impression they produce, Sedakova has cultivated a "high" neo-classical style, producing elegant and unexpected "imitations" in the style of eighteenth-century poetry. Thus, her magnificent "Mountain Ode" of 1984 employs the stanzaic form and poetic diction of the greatest Russian eighteenth-century poet, Gavrilo Derzhavin. The poetic themes, however, remain the same: death, immortality, God, poetry's power to cheat mortality. Here for example, are the final lines of Sedakova's "Ode":

> O speak, o speak, the tongue of accolades
> the language that descends into the world of darkness:
> there is a fife that opens treasure caves
> recalling somehow sounds of grace,
> and treasure, meaning, models of likeness.

In many respects, the cycle "Chinese Travelogue" represents a composite of Sedakova's entire oeuvre to date. The poems are primarily in free verse, although rhyme is occasionally used. The loosely connected cyclical form used as an organizing principle is

Olga Sedakova

familiar. Yet stylization is also present — in this case the verse clearly and appropriately imitates the elliptical gnomic forms of classical Chinese poetry. The simple, conversational tone which conceals far greater depth is, of course, Sedakova's trademark. But finally it is the images — of multiple reflections, of the parting death brings, of the poet's wonder in the face of God's creation and her own — presented in a luminous, yet understated idiom, that mark Sedakova as one of the great contemporary Russian-language poets.

— Andrew Wachtel

From Al-Mahdi
Abd al-Hakim Qasim

— Translated from Arabic by Peter Theroux

IT WAS MIDAFTERNOON, the sun was gentle and the air was fresh and pure. The canal water reflected the blue sky and cooled the lapping breezes. Master Awadallah Awadallah, the umbrella maker, carried his provisions on his shoulder, a small bag in one hand, and in the other the hand of his son, Hantas. Behind him walked his wife, Fula, with a bundle on her head. In one hand she held a little basket and in the other her daughter, Lawza.

The breeze on Awadallah's brow cooled his sweat and lightened his weariness, or rather turned it into a feeling of winy tipsiness. Walking through the stems and stalks filled him with delight and freed his soul from worry. Yes, Master Awadallah's heart had been heavy with the situation with his landlady, Mrs. Gabuna. She was a kindly and animated lady who enjoyed the respect of the people and the honor of the neighborhood, but times had been very hard recently, and there was no money. For long months they had paid her no rent for the room they occupied in the ground floor of her house. The lady made not a single complaint. Whenever she went down, she would knock on their door and stand off a little, timid.

"Master? Abu Hantas?"

He knew, when he went out every day carrying his provisions, making his rounds through the streets to repair umbrellas or make new ones and returning in the evening, that he would have barely enough in his pocket to keep his family alive. His wife, Umm Hantas, did her utmost and scrimped as much as she could, but there was never enough to pay the rent. He was filled with shame and grief, and bowed his head, not daring to raise it to Mrs. Gabuna's face.

"God help us, ma'am."

Mrs. Gabuna said nothing, but turned to ascend the stairs, then spoke.

"Don't be embarrassed by my coming to you. I only wanted to

21

make sure you were all well."

He lingered, listening to her feet ascend the steps until she was gone, then took refuge in his corner of the room, but never closed his eyes.

This time when he had seen her standing timidly at the open door, he said: "Mrs. Gabuna, I'm leaving. We will leave you these copper vessels to make up for our late rent."

Umm Hantas's face paled until it was white. She lifted her wide eyes to the master, and he looked down at her with a defeated, terrorized face. The children stopped chewing their bread, frightened. For a moment their eyes met.

"Get up, Umm Hantas," said Awadallah. "We're going to gather up our things and leave here."

The day was still young when they went out. Umm Hantas looked back for a last glimpse of the house in which she had long dwelled. She walked down the alley behind the master, and spoke to some of the women sitting in their doorways.

"Good-bye."

Her neighbors asked her nothing. Perhaps they did not understand the change behind this exodus, perhaps it had not occurred to them or perhaps it was too difficult for them to ask about.

"Good-bye," they said almost inaudibly.

Fula could feel the city receding behind her back, and the littleness of their procession along this country road amid the vast fields, and was seized by fear.

"Where are we going, master?" she whispered.

He did not look at her, but trained his eyes on the horizon. They kept walking, like two poor people under one blanket.

"I couldn't make a living in Tanta, Fula," Master Awadallah told her. "We'll go out into the country. We may find good fortune."

She was silent a little while, distracted, then spoke softly, as if to herself.

"Let's find a Christian village, Awadallah, with a church and a good priest."

A dream like the white wing of a boyish-faced angel brushed the side of his heart, and he sighed.

"Jesus will protect us, Fula."

Fula looked around her and swiftly made a sign of the cross, and Awadallah continued speaking in a low voice.

"The village chiefs and important men in the country don't wear those hats with tassels. Umbrellas give them prestige *and* shade."

Then he bared his forehead to the breeze, and the bitter taste of exhaustion in his mouth mingled with the taste of his glistening tears as he murmured his prayers. ". . . lead us not into temptation, but deliver us from evil . . ."

Ali Effendi closed his big notebook and pushed it aside after entering the mules' feed, then revised the expenditure vouchers from the original and three copies, working unhurriedly, singing softly to himself as his son, Attiyah, sat, his legs swinging down from the chair, laughingly watching his father.

"Abu Asakir!" called Ali Effendi.

A truly odd-looking man entered, diminutive and painfully thin, with a long face and narrow eyes, but with a kind laugh. When he laughed his eyes disappeared completely, but he could still see at least. He could just barely find his way here and there in this village office; he was one of the perverse, sallow, emaciated sweepers, cart-drivers and stable hands, a leftover in this land of handsome people, mild-tempered and courteous among a people whose hostility and wickedness abounded, looking about with their spies around Ali Effendi and in the face of his constant rebuke.

"Abu Asakir, sir, come with me and I'll issue you the feed from the storehouse. And I swear to God, stop eating the nuts meant for the mules."

"That has not happened, Effendi."

"Don't hold God responsible for your faith, Abu Asakir. Eating the mules' nuts is a sin. Do you know why these mules are healthy and strong? Because they eat wisely, and they don't overeat. But you — if you get your meal at home, you'll bring in half a basket of bread, for sure. And the women have to spend their lives grinding grain and making dough and baking bread. And in the office, sir, you fill your room with the mules' nuts and spend all day cracking them."

"That has not happened, Effendi."

"And yet you're sallow, potbellied, you have indigestion. You don't heed the saying of the Prophet of God — 'All disease is from the stomach, and zeal is the best medicine.' You have no zeal, just rancor and your raids on the mules' feed."

Thus Ali walked through the courtyard of the office as far as the storehouse, tall and slim, his fez on the back of his head exposing his thick, glossy black hair, chanting these words and stressing the end of each one, absentminded, his eyes not settling anywhere.

23

He dispensed the feed to Abu Asakir, took his son's hand and went to Niazi Effendi, the head of the office, who raised his head from his documents, startled. Ali Effendi stuttered awkwardly in apology for having interrupted. After some flattering smiles and a pat on the well-bred boy's head, Ali Effendi resumed his singsong words, relating what had happened that workday as Niazi Effendi signed vouchers.

"And so it went today, exalted sir, and so it ended, and so I seek your leave to go home."

"In God's keeping, Ali Effendi."

"Will you do us the honor of having lunch with us today?"

"I would love to, but my wife and the children are in Tanta."

"So we are out of luck. No fortune. No way around it. Good-bye, and give your family our best."

This rite ended the work of the day. Ali Effendi bid Abu Asakir a good afternoon and proceeded through the neighborhoods of Mahallat al-Gayad under the noonday sun, greeting people and asking them how they were. He bought dates and guavas and headed home, his arms loaded with purchases, to his wife, who silently rushed to him, her eyes examining his features, which were frankly feverish and exasperated. She took the groceries from him and he handed her his fez.

"The whole house smells of mulukhiyah," he said. "Mulukhiyah and rabbits?"

"We slaughtered the little black one. The old peasant man caught and skinned him."

Attiyah burst into tears.

"You killed my rabbit!" he sobbed.

"No, sweetheart," his mother said quickly. "Your white rabbit is still there — go in and see for yourself."

After the afternoon prayer, Ali Effendi went out, as was his daily custom, to the center of town, to the main street lined on both sides with willow trees. On this particular afternoon he found Master Awadallah Awadallah, his wife, Fula, and their children, Lawza and Hantas, on the side of the road. When he came near them he knew from their faces that they were Copts, and his supposition was confirmed by the crosses tattooed on their wrists. He did not greet them by saying *salaam aleikum*.

"Good day," he said instead.

"Good day to you," said Master Awadallah hastily, disconcerted.

Ali Effendi looked around and found a big rock; he sat down on

24

it and held Attiyah to his chest, ready for a long, pleasant mid-afternoon conversation.

Master Awadallah, at the head of his little band, had kept journeying along the farm road for a long, long time as the people of the city came out of their vile confinement into the vastness of the country air. They were intoxicated by the open horizons. As he walked, he was not overtaken by fatigue until after some time, when he came upon the first village that appeared, he and his group sat down on its outskirts. He took out his things, and was busily engaged in his craft while the two children played in the dirt. Fula was silent, immersed in anxieties, watching his untiring hands as they deployed his tools. A few customers squatted around Master Awadallah; this was a good omen, but country people were poor, and they were afraid of falling into the snares of city people. Master Awadallah smiled sadly, a smile of despair, and his wife watched him in silence. She saw him lower his price time after time, contenting himself with whatever he could earn. They ate the bread and salted cucumbers the peasants gave him, and slept wherever evening overtook them.

"I am an umbrella maker," Awadallah said when the watchman came at night. "I go around villages trying to make a living."

He offered the guard a cigarette, and he sat down with Awadallah, gratefully smoking the cigarette and chatting for a while before going on alone. So it went, in village after village; slowly, slowly, fear crept into Master Awadallah's bones, and without a word it spread from him to his wife, Fula. The children's silence grew more profound, as did their questioning gazes at their parents. What next? Day followed day, and his living was sufficient. What next? The vastness of the horizons was terrifying. He looked around him, and from the depths of his heart he silently cried out, *O Jesus Christ, Son of God . . .*

As if Fula could hear his heart's prayer, which his lips did not whisper, she too stammered: "Jesus, Son of God."

They resumed their journey until they saw the town of Mahallat al-Gayad in the distance. Master Awadallah marveled at the lovely street, bent over and sat down, resting his back against a tree. He took out his tools and spread them out, and began to apply himself to his craft, until the sun was about to set — not a single customer had shown up, until Ali Effendi came upon him.

"So you are an umbrella maker, my man," said Ali Effendi.

"Yes, sir."

"There are no finer craftsmen than the Copts."

Master Awadallah smiled warily and Fula gathered up her cloak around her.

"There are many Muslims in this trade and they are all excellent," said Awadallah, adding, "There are lots of livings to be made."

"Yes, yes," Ali Effendi assured him. "And you, it seems, live in Tanta."

Awadallah could not fight the pounding of his heart; he was tired and hungry.

"We used to, but we were far behind in paying the rent, and our landlady —"

"What is her name?" Ali asked, interrupting him in his surprise.

"Mrs. Gabuna."

"God shame her!"

Awadallah was alarmed at the misunderstanding he had caused, and said, "She —" but was interrupted by an agitated Ali Effendi.

"But throwing you into the street like that!" He sprang to his feet and announced gallantly, "Come with me, man, and your children, to my house, as an honored guest, until God gives us morning."

Awadallah and Fula exchanged looks of despair that penetrated into the soul of the other, and Awadallah lifted a beseeching face to Ali Effendi.

"By God, please excuse us. We do not want to be a burden to you."

But Ali Effendi's determination swept everything before it and there was no resisting it.

"Gather up your things, man, and get up. A man is nothing in this world of ours unless he honors guests. Gather up your things and get up, and God shame that Gabuna!"

He turned to Fula, who was motionless and silent.

"And you, my lady, get up. All is still well with the world."

Then he took Attiyah and Lawza each by one hand and began to walk with them. There was nothing Master Awadallah could do to stand in the way of Ali Effendi's will: he was tired and hungry, so he walked behind him carrying his bag. Ali Effendi in his splendid white robe strode leisurely ahead, greeting everyone he saw, laughing with them and answering questions, until his triumphal procession ended at his house. He pushed open the door and went in with the children, his two guests behind him, and called out.

"Children! Children!"

His wife came out to him, their perplexed-looking daughters behind her.

"God has honored us with guests," he smiled. "Good people, thrown into the street by their landlady, named Gabuna, without pity."

His wife looked at the guests silently, then whispered, "Welcome."

There was a moment at a standstill, with all of them standing not knowing what to do, so Ali Effendi took the initiative to speak, and give his wife orders.

"You know that little room. Clean it up well, put in fresh mats and fix up a bed and pillows. Find a nice lamp, some water, and a chamberpot for the children. Do I have to list everything you need to do?"

"We'll do it," said his wife meekly.

"Prepare some supper for them in their room," Ali Effendi went on in his commanding tone. "They are very shy people, and if they ate with us they might be too embarrassed to eat much."

"Yes, sir," said his wife.

When the door of the room closed upon them, Awadallah felt that he had fallen into a pit. His body was hard with fear, and Fula was pale and bug-eyed. This was a nightmare. How had one day delivered him to the next day, and the next, to arrive at this strange hour? How could he have been so stupid as to abuse Mrs. Gabuna? She was kind and honest and had done nothing to hurt them.

"I wish we could get out of here," said Fula in a trembling voice.

"How?" whispered Awadallah.

"I'm hungry," Lawza begged them.

Fula broke off some bread in a dish and poured mulukhiyah over it, and felt almost like vomiting at the greasiness of the food. Awadallah was frightened and said to her: "We should eat something too. We have to eat something."

Abd al-Aziz knew Brother Talaat. He had seen him for the first time in class at Tanta High School; it may have been Talaat's first class at that school. The teacher was quarrelsome and severe. He asked a question of Talaat, who diffidently stood up to reply, tremendously tall and broad-shouldered. Nothing was easy for him. Perhaps because Talaat was so large and imposing, the teacher went into a rage and slapped him across the face. Abd al-Aziz was terrified and looked at Talaat's face and the red mark of the teacher's hand on his upper cheek. Abd al-Aziz imagined that the force of the blow had dented Talaat's face and made it perversely flat as he stood, bug-eyed, his jaw slack, but Abd al-Aziz later discovered that Talaat had been born that way, his head as flat as a round loaf of bread on his shoulders. He also discovered that he was afflicted with a deviated septum and always breathed through his mouth. Perhaps this changed the taste of his saliva or dried out in his throat; you always saw him sucking moisture into his mouth audibly. His gums bled incessantly, which made his smile nauseating, but he was a good person and rather simple-minded. He looked about curiously at the expressions on the faces around him, anxious and fawning. Abd al-Aziz had come to know him at Muslim Brotherhood meetings, and learned, to his delight, that he was from Mahallat al-Gayad.

"Do you know Ali Effendi in the village council?" he asked him.

"I know him," Talaat smiled. "Ask him about me. Ask him if he knows Talaat Mashriqi."

"Are you from the Mashriqi family?" asked Abd al-Aziz.

He smiled that same smile and murmured his assent. When Abd al-Aziz next met Uncle Ali Effendi and asked him about Talaat Mashriqi, his uncle was surprised, and curled his lip scornfully.

"That's pretty blatant, trying to associate himself with the Mashriqi family. His father took the name Mashriqi only to ingratiate himself with that family. He is from the small, starving Abu Habbah family. His father is a minor schoolteacher in the government school."

Abd al-Aziz was very surprised at this, but said to himself that there was nothing wrong with a person coming from a poor, unimportant family; a man could make his own way, and Brother Talaat was one of the most active young men in the Brotherhood at school. Everyone had approved him as a scholarship student, so the mission gave him a charitable stipend after the previous recipient received his high school diploma and went on to the university. Talaat had a fat, pale brother at al-Azhar University who came from Cairo with a huge folder of papers, seeming tired and distracted. The Brotherhood of Tanta welcomed him with open arms. While he stood delivering a sermon, he fired them up with an eloquence that made them forget everything else; Talaat watched from a distance, smiling with pleasure. Abd al-Aziz never forgot to see Talaat on his visits to Mahallat al-Gayad, and even after they had both moved on to the university and Abd al-Aziz's

relations with the Brotherhood slackened and then ended altogether, he asked about Talaat in Mahallat al-Gayad and saw that
he was very active and that everyone was talking about him. He
was all over town, night and day, doing the Brotherhood's work.

Abd al-Aziz later learned that Talaat, who always found time
for people despite his many commitments, had met Ali Effendi,
who was on his way back that night from an evening of prayer
with the Sufi Brotherhood at the home of Sheikh Sayid al-Hasari.

"Peace upon you, Ali Effendi, and God's mercy," was Talaat's
greeting to Uncle Ali Effendi.

"And upon you peace, Talaat, sir, and the mercy and blessings of
God, and a very good evening to you."

"I wish you'd call me Brother, not sir — it's closer to the heart."

"You are our brother and our respected sir."

"God help me! Thank you! We'd love to see you sometime at
our mission."

"The mission is in all our hearts, but our group devotes its meetings to reading fortunes and venerating al-Abasiri's cloak."

"God's scripture is more important and more beneficial."

"Every word in it is the breath of God, Brother Talaat."

"Even the hallucinations of dervishes?"

"They are the servants of the holy men of God, and the perfume
of his Prophet!"

"It is the faithful that are the servants of God, it has nothing to
do with kinship, and 'Arabs are no better than non-Arabs unless
they are more pious,' as the Prophet said."

"I am of a family honored to have touched the thresholds brushed
by the perfume of God's Prophet."

"That is paganism."

Ali Effendi answered him with a few lilting verses:

> *"The abodes were told to be abodes of night*
> *Enter into the walls, the walls*
> *It is not love of the abode that stole my heart*
> *But love of Him who dwells within."*

"Read the Koran, Ali Effendi."

Ali Effendi did not like this didactic manner.

"Talaat, sir, I fill my heart with love."

"You are never out of our thoughts, Ali Effendi," said Talaat,
resuming his flattering tone.

"God and I respect you, Brother Talaat," said Ali Effendi in-
dulgently.

"God love you."

"By the way," said Ali, "I wanted to mention a good man to you, a Christian umbrella maker. He used to live in Tanta, but his Christian landlady kicked him out — she just threw him into the street, leaving him and his children homeless. I found them in the street and took them to my house. I would like the mission to take an interest in him."

"Strange!"

"His little boy and girl were pale with hunger."

"Of course we are interested in him. We must act charitably towards non-Muslims, and incline their hearts to Islam. I'll drop in on you at the Council and we'll see what we can do."

"We'll have a nice glass of juice together."

"Good, because I don't smoke, or drink tea or coffee."

Mashriqi Bey, the mayor of Mahallat al-Gayad, woke from his sleep at noon, his eyes swollen and his mood very bad. Fatimah bint Abu Asakir, the new maid, told him that his bath was ready. He put on his wooden bath clogs and clomped along the tiles on the second floor of his large residence, his thin white nightshirt showing clearly his nakedness underneath. He let the cold living room cool the breath of his warm body. He delightedly poured hot water over himself, then lathered his body with soap several times and rinsed himself again with warm water, thinking of the girl Fatimah bint Abu Asakir, and of her beautiful round breasts. She had worked for a rich family in Cairo, so was clean, not chapped and rough like a country maid, washed clean of all that country dust. He fondled his male parts with pleasure, delighted at the thought of how he would take each of her breasts in a plump handful. He would get her into his big brass bed, and they would cavort naked under the blanket. His wife, with all of her prayers and "Praise Gods" could be damned. She had kicked him out of her life to the upper floor years ago and never came up to see him, leaving the maids to look after him. When he was done, he laughed as he dried himself off and went out to the balcony, where his breakfast was waiting on the little table. He sat down and dunked a large, fresh morsel of bread into cream and honey, and watched the girl Fatimah fill his glass from the jug set on the balcony wall. She came and went, her arms young and white, filling his stomach with food and giving him drink until he was satisfied. The girl came to him with a little pot of coffee, lifted up his plate and took

it away. He contemplated the curve of her rump and the lines of
her underwear under her thin housedress, this city sight strange
amidst the crudeness of the country. They had brought her here
to marry her to any fool from Mahallat al-Gayad. Who deserved
this lovely, graceful thing? He drained the last of his coffee and got
up unhurriedly. Now, he knew, she was making his bed, and he
passed from the salon into the bedroom, breathing quickly, the
frenzy of his lust almost making him lightheaded. He closed the
bedroom door behind him and hugged the girl — she straightened
up in a panic, but he pulled her to the bed with the heft of his
body, his hands exploring her soft back under her dress. He pulled
the dress over her head and rolled his head around in her breasts.
He pulled down her panties and opened her thighs forcibly, and
drew his member out of his underpants. It was not hard enough,
but he thrust it despairingly into her vagina, to no avail. With a
sudden burst of force the girl escaped from him and began to run;
he got up, panting, full of contempt for himself, straightened his
clothing and went out. The girl will talk to my wife, the Haja, he
thought, and the Haja will slap her around, insult her, and he himself would stand abjectly before her. He went down the stairs. The
servant, Saadawi, stood waiting to admit him, and on the radio he
could hear the voice of Sheikh Mustafa Ismail chanting, "'So Moses
struck him with his fist, and killed him.'"

"Bullshit!" shouted the mayor irritably. He switched off the radio
crossly, muttering to himself, "What kind of man can be killed
with a fist?"

He sat down in his big armchair and crossed his legs. Saadawi
stood before him, humble and afraid. The mayor gazed at him and
then spoke sarcastically.

"You're standing there like an idol. God damn you. Make me
some coffee."

The boy sped off like an arrow, and the mayor stayed still as he
sat for a few moments, then got up and went to his darkened office
room. It smelled like dirt. He walked in the dark to his wardrobe
and took out a bottle of cognac, filled its cap three times and
drank it down, then replaced the bottle in the wardrobe and went
back to his big armchair. He sat down looking serious, and while
he thought absently of the liquor coursing through his body,
Fatimah came to him with a printed handkerchief.

"Here you are, sir."

He looked up at her; he could read affection in her eyes, and he

31

felt tenderly towards her.

"Go away!" he shouted.

He did not want her to go, but she went away quietly. Saadawi brought in a little table and set the coffee beside the mayor, then disappeared quickly. The mayor began drinking his coffee. From a distance, Saadawi called out warily.

"Mr. Talaat, Abu Hanna and Ali Effendi, scribe of the Village Council!"

"Send them in," said the mayor, without looking up.

Their entrance filled the still air of the room with noise. The mayor motioned them to sit with a slack movement of his hand. He felt small before their commanding stature and broad shoulders.

"The mission makes progress every day thanks to the help of the mayor," said Talaat.

"Thank you," murmured the mayor.

Ali Effendi waved his arm as if he were onstage.

"As God is my witness — and I am a newcomer to this town — no one can deny what the mayor has done for us. This is what Niazi Effendi and I were discussing in the Council. We never get tired of repeating it."

The mayor was stealing glances towards the doorway to see whether Fatimah bint Abu Asakir might come back. Suddenly he realized that Ali Effendi had finished speaking, so he nodded.

"Thank you."

Talaat spoke up hastily.

"Ali Effendi, you are no newcomer here, you're one of us."

"Of course," the mayor agreed.

Ali Effendi resumed his stage declamation.

"And God is my hope — this is what gave me the nerve to come along with Talaat today to see you, after your concern for that Christian, the umbrella maker, whose landlady — who was of his own religion — pitilessly threw him into the street."

So this is why they came, the mayor said to himself. Saadawi should have told me something about that at the beginning. He turned to Talaat, who picked up where Ali had left off.

"The mission has decided to take an interest in the man. Muslims are enjoined to be kind to the People of the Book, and to incline their hearts to Islam. So we have made a comprehensive campaign for all people to have their umbrellas repaired by that man, or to buy new umbrellas from him. We have set a fair price, neither too high nor too low. On top of that, we have a campaign to collect donations of money, food and clothing, which will be reckoned and classified and delivered to him. The important thing is that this matter is now the main thing on our minds — everyone in the whole town is in on this."

Talaat paused to catch his breath, and Ali Effendi looked at him admiringly. The mayor looked around distractedly, and there was a moment of silence. A Coptic umbrella maker, said the mayor to himself; one of the People of the Book, whom they want to incline to Islam; the mission, the Village Council, the whole town; a mouse fallen from the rafters. They will play with him until the blood runs out of his nose, or dress him up like a Boy Scout and march him bare-kneed through the town, shouting *Allahu Akbar.*

Ali Effendi broke the silence.

"The truth is, Mr. Mayor, sir, the man is staying at my home, and that is fine with me — even if he stays forever. I'm just afraid it will embarrass him or bother him. So we were thinking that if he could get some little place to live, it would be better. We thought that the best thing might be Fakiha bint Tarawah's house."

"It's small and charming," said Talaat. "It is also near the mosque and the mission."

"The mosque and the mission?" the mayor asked quickly, not bothering to conceal his sarcasm.

"Talaat means that these are two places where there are people," Ali Effendi explained. "This artisan has to be where the people are."

"That's what I meant," said Talaat.

The woman who had owned the house in question had died leaving no family or heirs; the mayor had compiled an inventory of the estate and sent it to the Islamic Court. The house was judged to be the property of the state treasury, and the executor sold it publicly, with only the mayor present; he pounced on it, as he had many other properties, at a rather low price.

"Saadawi," the mayor said, "tell Mukhtar the watchman to give them the key to Fakiha bint Tarawah's house, and tell Sheikh Hasan the telephone operator to draft a rental agreement in Ali Effendi's name for thirty piasters per month, for three months."

The men thanked the mayor and left. He watched their backs recede with the utmost hatred.

"People cannot abide trouble. Not even one in forty thousand. Horrible."

His depression left him as he gazed through the half-open door, hoping for a glimpse of Fatimah.

Master Awadallah could not sleep at night. He was beset by a sort of waking faint in which nightmares and terrifying dreams opened his eyes in a deathlike state. Then he would close his eyes again, but as soon as light first glowed in the window, he got up, fetched his bag, looked around cautiously and was immediately absorbed in his work. Fula rose, sitting where she had been sleeping, gathering up her black clothes, winding them on her feet and head, sending her husband tender glances from under her eyelids. He was getting skinnier every day, his face was growing paler and his eyes seemed to grow bigger. When Fula looked at him now, she saw his bones under his robe and inside his sleeves, and was filled with anguish. The master sewed the cloth for the shade of the umbrellas, not raising his eyes to Fula, though he knew she was watching him, cradling him, and her heart wept. They had loved one another from the day he had seen her as he sat before the house of her father, the church deacon in Kafr Sulayman Yusuf, the center of Mit Ghamr. He was still just a youth. His father had been crippled by illness.

"My son," he told him, "now you have sharp eyes and nimble fingers, and I am tired. Take the bag. Hang the umbrellas over your arm like a true artisan, and go out to my customers. You will please me if you do that."

He set out across the country, to Kafr Sulayman Yusuf, among other places, where he sat in front of the deacon's house and saw her, and from that day he went out with his bag in Azbat Ghali in Mit Ghamr. She was all he saw; he went around to his customers and came back again, and she was all he could think of. This went on for long years: he did not lift his eyes to hers though he knew she was looking at him, he did not speak to her though he knew that she bore the cares of his heart. When making a living in Mit Ghamr became hard for them, they said good-bye to their friends and moved on to Tanta. Once again living grew hard, and again they left, but what troubled him now was a strange thing that he had never foreseen. He recalled his father's face as he lay on his deathbed, and the face of Mrs. Gabuna, her soft voice filled with grief.

"Jesus Christ, Son of God, deliver us," she whispered.

Ali Effendi knocked at the door of the room and came rampaging in.

"Good morning, sir! Look at you, hard at work before the birds are up! That's a real blessing, as we say. Sheikh Sayid al-Hasari and I said the dawn prayer together and had some coffee. If I had known you were up, I would have had you join us, but there's still coffee, and you and I will be drinking lots of coffee together."

Awadallah did not know what to say in reply to this speech of Ali Effendi's. He mechanically murmured, "Yes, of course, oh, fine," without really knowing what was being said to him, but the two children fidgeted and cried on the reed mat. Fula turned to comfort them, and Ali Effendi asked what was wrong with them.

"Nothing," Fula said, but he came closer, and with his expert eye saw that both their bodies were covered with boils. Fula tried to hide them from him, but he addressed her in a loud voice, as if onstage.

"Don't be afraid. Let me probe them with my hand. I'm very used to children. Our house in town has more children than chickens or ducks, lambs, goats or calves. The courtyard of the house is so full of all these species that you don't know where to step! I was used to children even before I was married, and then afterwards, of course, too. Don't be afraid. Let me see. Aha! I have some very wholesome medicine for that."

He got up and found a tube of ointment, and dressed all the boils while the children kept sobbing, but then they abruptly stopped, and turned around. Awadallah and Fula turned, and so did Ali Effendi; heavy, decisive footsteps sounded from the courtyard of the house — it sounded like a company of soldiers. There was a knock at the door, and Brother Talaat came in, with a small group of young men of the Muslim Brotherhood, all strong, slim and good-looking, with powerful shoulders and necks, each with the dark callous of frequent prayer on his forehead and a Brotherhood book in his hand. Their robes were clean, and the sandals on their feet shone; their presence proclaimed unity and obedience, and they gazed at Awadallah and Fula with wonder and delight. Brother Talaat spoke.

"The house of Fakiha bint Tarawah is ready at last, after the Brotherhood's long days of work, and now they have come to move Brother Awadallah into it.

"I was hoping that Awadallah would be staying with us for good," said Ali Effendi regretfully.

Awadallah did not understand what was going on, and did not know what to say. The young men started picking things up to

35

carry them away, and spontaneously, without thinking or understanding, he began to gather together his work tools and put them
in the bag.

"This mat, this bed, everything in this room, all of it belongs to
Brother Awadallah," said Ali Effendi.

Awadallah did not know what he should say.

"On behalf of the Muslim Brotherhood, thank you, Ali Effendi,"
Talaat announced.

They left the house carrying all the items. Among them was
Awadallah with his bag over his shoulder, and Fula with a bundle
on her head and a child by each hand. Ali Effendi watched the
procession recede.

"Where are they taking Uncle Awadallah, Daddy?" sobbed
Attiyah.

"To a new house, son," Ali Effendi comforted him.

Master Awadallah tried to follow the steps of the handsome
guards, trying to show his loyalty. Fula and the children walked
behind, their sallow, sick faces fixed on the man walking before
them, seeing nothing else in the world at this moment. He was
ready to collapse in anguish. Brother Talaat led the group of
young Brothers as they tramped methodically along, proclaiming
greetings to passersby in hearty military tones and receiving clear
and strong responses. From the doorways of houses, the women
doused the road with water to settle the dust, waiting patiently for
the procession to pass before stepping out, perplexed, to marvel
at it. The men tightened their fists on their animals' reins and
watched the procession with exultant but silent satisfaction. A
powerful, vehement spirit had penetrated their hearts; as Talaat
wished peace upon all of them, he was testing that spirit, and seeing that it was indeed clear and strong, and he marched resolutely.
"Please come in."

Master Awadallah stepped into the house and stood in the courtyard silently. He did not know what to do. Fula stood beside him,
holding hands with the children. The Brothers put down the household effects they were carrying and stood in a semicircle around
the master, and now Talaat addressed Awadallah and Fula both.

"This is your new house, and we beseech God to bless you in it.
Now we'll move along and leave you, but before we leave we
would like to present you with a gift, in the name of the Muslim
Brotherhood of Mahallat al-Gayad. Here it is—God's book. I hope
you will accept it happily."

Talaat held out a printed book, and Awadallah held out his hands and accepted the book as he stood there. Talaat pointed to a marker in the book.

"We hope you'll read this part first."

"I will read it. I will read it," said Awadallah.

Another Brother stepped forward, very eager and excited, and set some books in a niche in the wall.

"These are the memoirs of our greatest spokesman for the Muslim Brotherhood and some books by the great al-Ghazali and some accounting forms."

They all said good-bye and left Awadallah standing where he was, holding the Koran in his hands, then, exhausted, he fell onto the bench behind him. He closed his eyes for a few seconds as the three faces watched him in silence.

"Let's leave, Awadallah," Fula whispered. "Let's get out of here."

"It's too late, Fula," he said. "It's too late."

He opened his eyes and looked at the place where Talaat had pointed out the marker. The script in which the book was printed was unfamiliar to him and read with difficulty.

Didst thou say unto mankind, Take me and my mother as gods beside God? He saith: Be glorified! It was not mine to utter that which I had no right. If I used to say it, then Thou knewest it, Thou knowest what is in my mind, and I know not what is in Thy mind. Lo! Thou, only Thou, art the Knower of hidden things. I spake unto them only that which Thou commandedst me . . .

The master could read no further. He rested his head against the wall behind him, and tears streamed down his face as he whispered: "Jesus Christ, Son of God, may Your name be glorified."

The wording of the prayer was more than he could take . . . more than he could take.

The food at Uncle Ali Effendi's house was always excellent, and Abd al-Aziz ate his fill of fried eggs and beans in oil; now he dipped a big morsel in white honey and cream and munched it with luscious greedy pleasure. The house was clean and covered with morning dew. They were sitting at a table in the little courtyard; Ali's wife and daughters had rolled out reed mats and were sitting at a wide, low tray. On a shelf on the wall was a radio, with Sheikh Mustafa Ismail spreading a festive mood with his melodious chanting of the morning Koran selection. Abd al-Aziz ate with gusto, and Attiyah spoke to Uncle Ali Effendi.

"The table is for men and the tray is for women, right, Papa?"

"Yes, yes, yes," replied Ali Effendi delightedly. Attiyah continued: "We are men, right, Papa?"

Abd al-Aziz laughed, and the girls on the floor laughed.

"Yes, yes, yes," recited Uncle Ali Effendi.

"I'm a man, too, right, Papa?"

Abd al-Aziz collapsed laughing, as did the girls on the floor. Uncle Ali Effendi spoke up theatrically, though his wife sat stony-faced.

"You are a great man, Attiyah!" He added seriously, "Let's drink our tea and get down to business. We have lots of work to do today." He turned to Abd al-Aziz.

"I'll be back from Tanta this afternoon."

"I'll come with you," said Abd al-Aziz.

"Fine."

They walked through the neighborhood, up to Fakiha bint Tarawah's house. Uncle Ali Effendi pushed the door open and they went in, Abd al-Aziz behind him and looking in over his shoulder. The house was crowded with young men from the Brotherhood, and Master Awadallah sat in the midst of them, pale-faced, very thin, his eyes bulging. The Brothers made room for the visitors.

"There is no god but God — peace upon you, Sheikh Awadallah, al-Mahdi!" was Ali's greeting.

"And peace upon you," replied Awadallah, his eyes wandering.

Talaat drew Abd al-Aziz aside to rouse him from his distraction, and greeted him. They shook hands warmly, but Abd al-Aziz was still distracted and preoccupied.

"How are things at the mission?" he asked Talaat.

"Never better," said Talaat enthusiastically. "I'm in charge now, and, God willing, I'll be doing most of the work."

"Oh," said Abd al-Aziz.

The lines of Talaat's face laughed. "Today we're announcing his conversion in the Islamic court."

"I've heard the story," Abd al-Aziz hesitated. "But he looks sick, doesn't he? He's so pale."

"Faith has lit up his face," smiled Talaat.

"Really? Strange."

The procession moved outside. Abd al-Aziz noticed the wife standing in the far corner with her two children, all three faces ashen and staring in terror, and his heart skipped a beat. They went out into the alley, where the ascending sun had still not burned off the morning dew, and the procession, led by the master flanked by Talaat and Ali Effendi, got under way. The rest followed behind, energetically greeting the people, who clamored their greetings back. Some of the crowd, carried away by zeal, shouted greetings to the master, and then cried, "*Allahu akbar!*"

Others embraced him and pounded him on the back, while some of the women kissed his hand and asked him to pray for them. The master obligingly gave them his hand and murmured inaudibly. Abd al-Aziz never took his eyes off him. It was like a market day: every moment they saw people slaughtering calves or sheep. The animals fought and kicked, but the blood spouted out of their throats. Some people had done their sacrificing early, and hung the carcasses up by their doors. Some were still inflating their animals and hitting their bodies with sticks, while all the people around the animals shouted with joy. The procession moved out of the town and proceeded down the street, on its way up to the station. The shouts of the people still filled Abd al-Aziz's ears, and the din of sticks hitting the animals' swollen bodies. They boarded the train, the master flanked by Talaat and Ali Effendi; Abd al-Aziz was at a good distance but did not take his eyes off the man. He noticed that there was a youth from the Brotherhood standing beside him whose face burned with zeal. He looked at him listlessly — the food he had gobbled at breakfast was now a weight within him, as his stomach soured and filled with gas. The boy spoke to him.

"Brother —"

"Abd al-Aziz."

"You are one of the Brothers, of course."

"I used to be."

"Why did you quit?"

"Maybe I wasn't lucky."

"Man seeks God — he doesn't ask God to seek him."

"You are right."

"Have you read this?" He held up the book *Thus We Learn* in his hand.

"Not yet. I've had it for some time, though."

"Do you fill out an accounting form before you go to sleep?"

"To tell you the truth, no."

"That's strange. I can never fall asleep until I've looked back on my day and written down my sins on the form, then asked God to forgive me for them. *Then* I can sleep."

"I haven't slept very well for a long time anyway."

"You have to repent and start over."

Abd al-Aziz was silent a while before asking the young Brother, "Did you help guide this man into Islam?"

"We all did."

"Was it very hard?"

"From the time the man first came to our town, until this morning, we never let up for a moment."

"That's impressive."

"For the important occasion, we're organizing a big religious symposium in town, and we'll invite Brother Said and all the branches in the area."

"Great."

"Yes, Brother, Islam is on the march, thanks to young people who believe in their Lord, and the guidance we give them."

"Oh. But the torn, confused ones, nothing marches on thanks to them?"

"What's that? I don't understand."

"Just a thought, never mind. Now we're in Tanta."

At the station, the procession disembarked amidst throngs of country people with their luggage and children, flowing out into the shabby streets of the old city. Abd al-Aziz seized Ali Effendi's hand, his heart pounding.

"I'm thinking of going back to the village now."

"Brother, you only spent the night at my house."

"I know, but I really want to go back."

"God!"

"I'm sorry, but I'm uncomfortable here."

"Was anything wrong at my house?"

"Good God, no, I'm more at home in your house than I am in my father's."

"So?"

"I just haven't felt very well the last few days."

"As you like."

"Thank you, to you and my aunt."

"God forgive me, as if you have to thank us! Remember me to your other uncles and aunts."

"Of course, God willing. I just want to tell Talaat."

Talaat tugged at his arm.

"I'm sorry you won't be able to stay for our celebration."

"I'm the sorry one, but there's nothing I can do." Then he said, "I want to say hello to this man."

Abd al-Aziz went to the master, whose eyes were wandering so that he seemed to be seeing practically nothing, and took his warm, sweaty hand. Abd al-Aziz contemplated his face and wanted to say something. He embraced him but the words stuck in his throat. He shook his hand cordially, then let go of it slowly so that it would not drop. He turned towards the whole crowd and passed through the mass of bodies, seeing nothing, not hurrying, letting himself be carried by the currents of moving people, saying to himself, "This has to stop. This has to stop." Still wandering, he screamed to himself, "I have to intervene and stop it myself!" He looked at his watch: three hours had passed since he had left the people. The thing must be completely over by now. He closed his eyes and shook his head.

"How horrible it is to realize something too late, after everything's ruined! How horrible! I'm sorry!"

The late Abd al-Hakim Qasim is one of modern Egypt's least-known great writers, thanks to two ironic circumstances: his political imprisonment and exile, and subsequent desire to avoid controversy altogether. Rather than address political issues in his fiction, he focused on the people and events of village life of Egypt and the folksy, Sufi Islam practiced there. His books tended to be published abroad, in Beirut and Baghdad, rather than in Cairo.

Qasim was born in 1935 in al-Mandara, Lower Egypt, and joined leftist organizations in the 1950s — "I was a Communist — once upon a time, and I was very young," he remarked in 1989, but this brief political affiliation was fate. The Nasser regime arrested him on December 24, 1960, and in 1962 a military court sentenced him to five years in prison. He was released on May 14, 1962, after intervention on behalf of leftists during Nikita Khruschev's official visit to Egypt that spring. Qasim began writing short stories in prison.

After his release, he completed his law degree at the University of Alexandria in 1965 and began publishing stories in magazines. He supported himself and his wife with a minor job in the Treasury, avoiding literary circles. Offered a scholarship for graduate study in Germany, Qasim left Egypt for West Berlin in January 1974. This voluntary exile became compulsory after he openly criticized Egypt's Camp David agreement with Israel.

Abd al-Hakim Qasim

Al-Mahdi, written in Berlin, was first published in Beirut, Lebanon, in 1984. It is typical of Qasim's skill: more like a novel in miniature than a short story or novella, it is a brisk and visual tale, full of events and people, but not crowded. The title is a proper name, one often given to converts to Islam. Coming from the verb hada, to lead or guide, it means "one guided [into the faith]."

In different hands, the tragic story might seethe with villains, especially given Qasim's dislike for religious extremists. However, the cast of al-Mahdi have real blood in their veins, from the weak mayor to the fervent Muslims of the Brotherhood and the lonely teenager, later in the story, who joins the Brotherhood to stay close to God — he thinks — when actually it is to be close to the real object of his passion, another boy.

This short novel bears a certain resemblance to Qasim's best-known novel, The Seven Days of Man (1969), which is probably the best portrait of Egyptian village life ever written. When Qasim published al-Mahdi, though, he paired it with one of his strangest and most modernistic novellas, Good News from the Afterlife, which depicts a man's death and the simultaneous rotting of his body and judgement of his soul. That story is largely told through the elaborate dream of a young boy who falls asleep on the grave. Qasim was nothing if not versatile, and subtle; al-Mahdi ends with a death, and the next novella opens virtually at the gates of the Hereafter. The two novellas are to be published together, in 1995, by Temple University Press.

Qasim finally returned to Egypt in 1985 and died of cancer in Cairo in December 1990.

— Peter Theroux

Five Poems
Yang Lian

— Translated from Chinese by Brian Holton

BEFORE DAYBREAK

iron wings of butterflies   pass like spokeshaves
tranquil stamens are always deadly poison
sluice gates start lifting   in the eyes of cataract sufferers
the world is a vague translation

back to the window   a man creates his own nightmares
with words made of darkness he feeds the beasts locked in his body
the carpenter's hand carries a bloody axe
to seek out that nest of bedbugs between a woman's thighs

boneless details   make description still more perfect
when the sense of smell, wrapped in skin, falls sound asleep
cries   are like salt dead in boiling water
no one can squeeze through this narrow gate   except flat ghosts

MOUNTAIN VALLEY

as we come to darkness   on the valley floor we see light
rocks   deep as the sky
suddenly snap like a dangerous staircase
timid fingers bent toward the violent stars weep
turn us into cripples
or deceive our eyes

Yang Lian

when light becomes a creature   we are dead
these tiny squirming bodies
drill holes into us   shining
moonlight falling as though spreadeagled
a city lying on a bed overgrown with illusion
reading a dark book   its cover the ocean
its back   the sound of wild animals' hooves on mud
pitfalls   when you think of it, are always underfoot

once distance has vanished   we touch a bright red rivulet
wrinkled with stones   exhibiting every terror that ever was

THE GARDEN ON A WINTER'S DAY, 1

trees frozen red in the snow   as if wearing a worn-out windcheater
snow crunches underfoot
the hurried night always wears brand-new soles

goats fear loneliness   for every ear
cries become bitter weeping

the path   a cow, just dropped a calf
scarred head to tail by the whip, panting paralyzed in bloody mud

streetlamps come on earlier still   lovers dim as stones
stand, faces blurred, by a metal bier
the vole is an exhausted nurse   stealthily
slinking into the garden's wounds to dream
flowers   are preserving their pink flesh below ground
as after children die   straightaway, fresh tender ghosts

underdeveloped stars   lock us up with iron railings

Yang Lian

THE GARDEN ON A WINTER'S DAY, 3

some people, addicted to corpses   love to stroll in gardens in winter
people who salute ruins   can appreciate
a plot to drown a kitten in a ditch
pressing its head down as if crushing a walnut
it's definitely children   children running into the garden

children know better than anyone how to trample flowers underfoot

even our dying day is unreal   a piece of a charred pole
poking slantwise from the ground like the crocodile's long snout
the sky is so gloomy it seems like daylight sleep
fishbones vomited by the ocean   stab us too
in dreams live fish, scraped clean of scales, are stabbed one by one
alive beneath the travelling knife

all flesh is reduced to a place with no power to look back

touch   all that is touched is non-existent
and cancer swells impalpably in the depths
a black pregnant woman   enwrapping a raped springtime
a treetrunk sliced by sight
swans' necks become pale underwater snares
once we have divided the world with our fractured compound eyes
we are all blind   both spectres set the white snow off
exposed in the dry ice-hard wind
endure the pain of bones budding

until   the garden is shamed into color
lashed all its life by an unidentifiable season

Yang Lian

THE FOUNDATIONS OF TERROR

with carnivorous greed terror digs upwards
the breath it buried below ground   simultaneously buried in the sky
a child smothered by a teat of stone
skeleton split open   like scattered stars
pallidly glittering after a storm
in a paralyzed body   only hatred can be reborn

live again   take the ugly organs
and expose them again to the saturation bombing of spring
blueprints   soak into the bloodstains
develop the first aerial photo of our ruins
we are destroyed   and you appear

you are all destroyed   and he appears

they are all destroyed   we squat at the foot of the wall, digging
with the precision of a timepiece a thousand gloamings create the next
child   when parents are dug out of the childbed of the sky
all are born to commemorate their own disappearance

live   living stones still must carry on
collapsing inside   warrior in a secret battle
thighs embracing his horse
time and again galloping the length of the rooftops of green grass
he hears behind him   mother earth healing like the surface of the sea
that smothered child already a thousand years old
long ago turned blue   walking in the dense fog that shrouds birthdays

with our bodies   dying

we build a village which covers the world from below

———————————

I first came across the poetry of Yang Lian some two or three years ago when, at the invitation of John Cayley of Wellsweep Press, I made English versions of four of his poems for an anthology of material from the Chinese literary magazine Today (now published in English as Under-Sky Underground, Wellsweep, 1994). I was immediately struck by the strength of this work, its bleak surrealism, its savage humor and its technical elegance. There was nothing "misty" about this stuff, nothing like the fluffy kitsch which too often passes for modern poetry in official circles in Beijing. Interesting, I thought, and moved on.

Some months later, my literature class was interrupted by a message that an urgent phone call had arrived. When I picked up the telephone a humorous and earthy Beijing voice told me that he, Yang Lian, was at London's Heathrow Airport en route to Australia, and that he had been shown my translations of his work at a conference in Berlin. Would I like to translate his collected shorter poems?

There's only one answer to a request like that: within a few weeks his manuscript had arrived, and we began the business of agreeing on an English style, arguing about the final title, discussing the details of exactly what was meant by this or that line. Throughout the extended palaver of getting acceptable English poems from the Chinese originals, Yang proved an exacting but unfailingly helpful collaborator, so that we now have poems which go as far as we can to reproduce in English the strength and the anger of the originals.

Though its basic form is the vers libre familiar in twentieth-century Western poetry, that form is imbued with a sensibility which is deeply Chinese, and which relies for many of its effects on an understanding of the long and book-haunted world of the Chinese tradition. Yang is both conservator and originator; he is deeply read in his own tradition but tireless in his innovation (he is currently experimenting with an alliterative form, something which has never to our knowledge been attempted in Chinese before).

This is exacting poetry. "The ruthlessness of the poetry lies in this," the author says: "it's just unsayable . . . and with each step forward you see an even greater wilderness before you." Savage in its anger, it makes demands on the reader no less exacting than the demands the poet makes on himself: it is a poetry in which the interplay of darkness and light create a landscape in which the struggle for wisdom is enacted.

47

Yang Lian

"Darkness is just a word; light is another; they are in fact a single event seen from two differing perspectives," writes the poet. So death looms large here. We must "learn from the shape of death," for it is the shape of death which gives shape to and defines our lives. Nothing less is being played for here — invoke Rilke, Kafka, Nietzsche, Yeats, the magisterial sorrow of the outcast Qu Yuan, the high and austere world of the Book of Changes: this is poetry to be heard to the shaman's drum, poetry that unites present and past in an attempt to bring a new world into being, poetry which excavates from the tradition a new and modern consciousness for a new and changing China.

— Brian Holton

In the Woods of Nevoso
Claudio Magris

— Translated from Italian by Lawrence Venuti

1.

IN THE BEGINNING was the voice of Signor Samec, deep and some-what rasping, with the faintly perceptible hiss of his Slovenian s's. "And then I told him," he started over again, grazing his neighbor with a pinkie that a slight arthritis — perhaps from the damp of many years in the woods — had bent into a hook, "pardon me, your Excellency, but with your permission . . ." In the beginning, or nearly, since in the forest everything had already begun and in fact was always beginning to end, crumbling into the earth and sinking into the rusty red strata of myriad leaves, the falls of many years, no longer distinguishable. When entering the forest for the first time, even as a child, you somehow felt that this wasn't the first time, and anyhow its proper history didn't originate in memories associated with it, but a long time ago, time preserved and meas-ured in the circles of tree trunks, yet still farther back. And in this awareness lay no exaltation or melancholy, only the silent feeling that it was so, and that's all.

Signor Samec almost never managed to finish his story (which the others believed they had already heard to the end on many oc-casions), because Rudi started to play *Za Kim*, for whoever, and recall his possibly noble or simply imperial ancestors, seeing that his grandfather — or perhaps his father or great-grandfather — had been found as an infant crying by a bush in Schönbrunn Park, in Vienna, apparently the illicit fruit of many high-ranking sins. Or else, still at that table in the Sviščaki clearing before Planinski Dom, the Alpine lodge, someone's attention wandered from Signor Samec to notice the continual embellishments and additions to the cottage of Signor Voliotis, who had long since celebrated his silver wedding anniversary with his wife, children and grandchil-dren, and this someone remarked that the management of the porno cinema which Signor Voliotis had assumed some years ago in Trieste, where he lived, must be doing a better trade than the timber company to which he was more dedicated for his family's sake. Yet the person who, above all, doomed Signor Samec's story to incompleteness was his wife, Anna, an unfathomable beauty with her snub nose and slanted eyes, tender and rapacious, set in a face marked by the passage of time. She nodded to him to stand and escort her back to their cottage.

The Excellency to whom Signor Samec referred was a government official from Fiume, whose favor he gained by accompanying him on a bear hunt and dissuading him, with discretion, from an imprudence that might have been fatal and for which he paid dearly — but here the story was confused, because the impatient listeners interrupted at precisely this point — a gamekeeper or forester, whose jaw was torn to pieces by a bear's bite (in some versions male, in others female), forced for the rest of his days to nourish himself by sucking food and drink through a straw. Nonetheless, this misfortune did not interfere with the small benefits — a license here, a commission there — that the official's gratitude procured for Signor Samec's large hardware shop at Ilirska Bistrica, known then as Villa del Nevoso (literally "the town near the snow-capped mountain").

To say "then" is to say "always," since it was Ilirska Bistrica then too, seeing that a name doesn't disappear, despite what a redrawing of border lines may lead you to think. No, a name lives whenever someone tells what happened to a person, place or bear that was called — and therefore is still called — by that particular name. The forest is the memorial of names: Volk Samotar, the lone, elusive wolf that terrorized the woods of Snežnik, near Nevoso, between 1921 and 1923; the mason Josek Ronko, remembered for living in a small wooden cabin at Prevale after 1903, as if he were appointed the feudatory of some castle; or the marksman Fajstric, who in 1983 was required to protect Prince Hermann von Schönburg-Waldenburg, lord of Nevoso, on his first bear hunt, but who, when faced by the wounded bear, fled up a tree, obliging the prince to get him out of the scrape.

Most of all, the memory of the forest bespeaks the vanity of possessing it. Its deep breathing teaches us to experience life as an impartial indifference, at once welcoming and inexhaustible, a sentiment I felt whenever I entered those woods, the first and every other time, and when I later saw children also feel and learn it forever, so that after a while everyone experienced this feeling as something that always existed even if they couldn't recall when it started, like breathing. The forest — at first Austrian, then Italian, then Yugoslavian, finally Slovenian — mocked those changes in name and border; it didn't belong to anyone; if anything, they belonged to it, at least for that short period when you could belong to someone or something, since the forest too was mortal even if it existed from time immemorial. Like the roe buck that suddenly appears in the field at dawn, before the gun barrels or before no one, and his life — including that of his species, so much longer than a still venerable empire or a brief Federal Republic — lasts only for an instant. When you lift your eyes towards Ursa Major, or the morning star, fading in August over a red fir tree in the clearing at Pomočnjaki, there is nothing but the instant of the buck's appearance and his leap into that clearing.

Ilirska Bistrica, the energetic and anonymous industrial town at the foot of Nevoso, is the capital of the wooded massif that rises sharply toward the northeast and, beyond the summit, descends again, on one side toward Mašun, on the other toward Leskova Dolina, a depression filled with hazel trees, and Kozarišče, in the direction of Postumia, extending and sloping east as far as the Slovenian border. A lung of woods, consisting mostly of beech, fir and larch trees, rarely found elsewhere preserved so intact in the wild, tended with civility and wisdom by a forest administration that has no great desire to alter and force natural rhythms but respects the tempo of the trees, every so often opening a road yet ensuring that others are so harmoniously integrated as to be camouflaged, leaving several areas peaceful for years while working in others, guarding the wood — except perhaps for some indulgence shown to hunters, particularly Milanesi — and protecting it from construction, exploitation, abuse.

The 27,600 hectares of Nevoso contain no hotels, but some houses, several cottages and cabins, the remains of a couple of Italian barracks, a lodge on the summit and another in the clearing at Sviščaki, the Planinski Dom comprising three rooms fitted with bunkbeds, finally the royal palace and the center of Snežnik. If the maps — the most splendid were hand-drawn by Professor Drago Karolin, the ninety-odd-year-old tutelary deity of Nevoso, and reproduced on postcards — indicate Mater Dei or S. S. Kozma and Damjan, this is due to a stone incised with the saints' names or, at the most, a recent innovation, a tiny niche dedicated to the

Madonna, which replaces the carved stone previously set there. The highway engineer in Snežnik (to which the Italian army donated some excellent streets after 1929, still sound and fit for traffic, like the road leading to Orlovica, Monte Aquila) remembers the forest director Josef von Obereigner, in the service of Prince von Schönburg-Waldenburg, who in the last century marked out and tended lanes and paths and endowed them with names and physiognomies. Today Drago Karolin's postcard maps are the plan of that universe, wherein the smallest detail is worthy of attention and identification, as if the cartographer wished to tear it from the amorphous mingling of the wood.

The architecture of Nevoso consists of platforms built on trees, swaying seats and sturdy cabins, their wooded planks fresh, solid and drenched from years of humidity, posts constructed to await animals and, according to the circumstances, to slaughter them, as do the legitimate owners of those platforms, or only to observe, as do the abusive visitors whose odor, in the opinion of hunters who pay $15,000 to kill a bear, pollutes the wood, frightening the animals and driving them away from the posts and from death.

But Ilirska Bistrica is only a stopover hurriedly crossed during the journey — Nevoso is midway between Trieste and Fiume — a place to get petrol or to fix a tire, inevitably punctured on roads rocky and bristling with all manner of pointed things. The chief town in the district is actually Sviščaki, a clearing that is slightly wider than the others at 1,242 meters; traditionally it is the point of departure for the small excursion to the summit. Several cottages encircle the clearing that gravitates around Planinski Dom, the lodge of the Slovenian Alpine Association; camouflaged by the trees, they loom a short distance away, arranged haphazardly, set close to one another, the recent additions to a new Sviščaki.

History — even many years after my first encounter with Nevoso, when two children had traversed the globe but continued to know every glade and every old path engulfed by the forest, plus every appearance of that bear who was a bit darker and larger than the others, and whom everyone had seen, even when chancing to arrive at the lodge by car, except for us four, notwithstanding the nights and dawns spent waiting motionless in the clearings — history was measured by summers passed at Planinski Dom and by the succession of custodian-hoteliers at the lodge, committed to memory like the dynasties of a kingdom.

Every change of dynasty, moreover, was painful and created

embarrassment, because in the beginning the new managers were among the strangers, and it was humiliating to be taken for passing tourists or ignorant greenhorns, treated like foreigners in a place that was rather their home and native country. Up there I know who I am, as the great Julius Kugy said of his Julian Alps, and the same applied to me and Monte Nevoso, but the others also had to know this, or at least the official authorities of the lodge which was our residence. Thus, when an Ivanka succeeded a Meri or the Valenčič couple the Pugel couple, I forced myself to write a letter of recommendation, over Professor Karolin's signature and in Slovenian, which praised the qualities of our entire family with special reference to our love for Snežnik and our adaptability to hardships. Professor Karolin added, through his own initiative, the honor of having as a guest a scholar and writer whose books were translated into various languages and even mentioned in the *Delo* of Lubiana. With this letter we presented ourselves to the new managers, who were amazed by the request to welcome beneath their sloping roof the only family who was likely to remain up there for a long while, and who therefore permitted them to earn a little money that hadn't yet been changed to thaler.

Snežnik, similar to Fujiyama, rises above Sviščaki, over a sea of woods. The house facing Planinski Dom, on the other side of the clearing, was reserved almost every year by vacationers who worked in the timber industries at Ilirska Bistrica, and it was managed by Milivoj, a Serbian with a long moustache and Mongolian eyes who was said to have come by this position because of his heroism in the partisan war. Even when people didn't yet (or once again) think that being Slovenian, Croatian, Serbian or Yugoslavian was a contradiction to be resolved by bloodshed, when, if anything, they seemed proud of the red star that not only effected the just restoration of Snežnik to Slavia, but improperly enriched the latter with Italian lands — even then, Milivoj invited suspicion and vague allusions to acts of cruelty. Of course, some evenings, when he was drunk, he started to shoot into the air, and Jadranka, the custodian of Planinski Dom, proudly drew a contrast with her husband (actually she said "our") who quietly went to sleep when he got drunk. Anyway, Milivoj died before the collapse of the Federal Republic induced, by fusillades not directed into the air, the proliferation of these disguised debates about cultural differences, which were not limited merely to comportment during intoxication. The Bosnian foresters, moreover, meek, diligent workers who did not shoot into the air or anywhere else, left the area while the lynxes continued to prosper.

A postcard, sold at Planinski Dom, resumes the history of the lodge from 1907 to 1972, but it is silent on D'Annunzio's lodge, which can be found beside the present building and which, although bombed by the partisans, still showed some small traces of his existence until a few years ago. Apparently, the poet never set foot there. For Immagnifico, Nevoso was a word, it was the music and light of that word, its luminosity. In fact, in 1924, on the eve of the union of Fiume with Italy, requesting in his triumphal speech "a sign of recognition" for his own merits, he suggested, indifferently, the title of Prince of Monte Nevoso or Prince of the Adriatic. But before he made this request for an imaginative word, the poet who perhaps more than any other grasped the fascination of technology, Medusa and Muse of modernity, expressed the desire for a private airport at Gardone. He had to content himself with a melodious trisyllable.

2.

In the beginning was no bear, just the story of a bear. The company at Sviščaki didn't pay attention to Signor Samec because they long knew, long before they knew Signor Samec himself, the story about the hunter with the shattered jaw forced to feed through the straw. The rumors refer to bears, hunters and the most diverse places. According to Drago Karolin's authoritative version, reported in the little green volume *Snežnik* published in 1977, the misfortune would have occurred on 18 July 1900 to the hunter Andrej Žnidaršič, who was accompanying the Duke Heinrich von Mecklenburg, guest of Prince Hermann von Schönburg-Waldenburg. The director Bercè, who from Kozarišče manages and protects the forest preserve of Snežnik, denies this episode, which rather happened elsewhere, as he puts it, and offers a different account of the duke's hunt, which was equally perilous and well resolved for the nobleman, killer of a cub, only because the rage of the bear that attacked him was overcome by maternal love, compelling her to bring the other cub to safety. This version, however, which is certainly worthy of attention, includes neither shattered jaws nor straws.

Such details recur in other reports and in other places. The most illustrious archetype is undoubtedly the story of Julius Kugy, which dates back to 1871 and is set in Val Trenta. The wounded man is his faithful companion on climbing and hunting excursions, Antonio Tozbar (also called Spik), who lost his tongue and speech as well — an episode known not only because of Kugy's fame, but also because of the authority of Giovanni Gabrelli, renowned jurist and lawyer, who repeated it for years during trips to Carso and the valley of Vipacco, until even his most tolerant friends forced him to stop it. A variant of this topos is the story of the man who, when attacked by the bear or hastening to aid the victim of an attack, brandishes an axe and in the excitement wounds himself more or less seriously by bringing the axe down on his own thigh and cutting his leg or inflicting less threatening damage.

Every two or three summers this story surfaced and was related and amplified. On one occasion the place was Stare Ogence, on another Sladke Vode. The bear was always a female bear defending her brood, even if there were more amiable episodes, like the one about the bear that fell with her cub into a cistern at Koritnice and was helped by the foresters who tossed her a tree trunk whereon she clambered out.

Still, the recurrent motif of the man who wounds himself in a struggle with the bear can be traced back to an origin, to an event that happened near Mater Dei and was provoked by a Magyar count on holiday at Abbazia: he desired a bear cub and sent someone to capture it. Yet the suspicion arises that, before any real or invented occurrence, there must have been a story, an imagination that conceives it by thinking of a bear, the word that founds and creates the reality. In the beginning was the word; the heavens and earth come later, along with the forests and the bears. The forest possesses no word; it is the primordial confusion that draws back into its womb all things and forms, it is Artemis who cannot be watched and cannot be described, life that dissolves lives and does not comprehend the language that articulates the incessant metamorphosis. The story seizes a form, distinguishes it, tears it from the flux and from oblivion, fixes it. Those legends and fantasies about the bear impose a meaning and an order on the dark beast that stirs in the thicket. They are civilization's revenge on the shadow of the woods.

3.

Where does the forest begin? The doors are invisible, and yet you clearly notice when they open and close, when you are in and out of the woods, quite apart from being surrounded more or less by trees. One entrance, unquestionably subjective, is the clearing at Pomočnjaki (which means very humid). It is situated by the side of a road — a *gozdna cesta* in Slovenian, a wooded route with no guarantee of unobstructed passage — which connects the plain of Padežnica, where snowfalls are frequent, the two houses of Mirine and the clearings at Grčovec, full of knotty trees indicated by name, and at Travni Dolci, dense with grass, before rejoining the principal road, so to speak, which climbs toward the summit. One morning, in the clearing at Pomočnjaki, with the steam ascending from the meadow, the scarcely risen sun created a perfect cathedral cast in light, for a few seconds, a form that thinned out as it moved higher, culminating in a point. The door, a great Gothic door, was a luminous dust, a thick resplendent curtain, which hid the woods that lay behind it. The figure next to me, close at that moment and over the years, had risen from the grass at the edge of the woods (where we both had stood waiting for things to emerge from the dark, foreshadowed by the unmistakable scent of dawn, or for the morning star to fade precisely at the top of the red fir tree before us, almost immediately invisible in that twinkling) and slowly headed toward and beyond that door of light, entering and vanishing in the impenetrable brightness, stolen from sight.

At that moment, you could believe that every disappearance, even in crossing the final threshold (that roe buck in the clearing would certainly have crossed it quickly, given the fusillades that started echoing in the mountains), meant only a passage through a similar curtain, and beyond lay no reason for the obscure, distressing fear that year after year deprives things of sense. Yet unlike the clearing where the figure reappeared in the golden grass, now gradually seen to be dotted with daisies and bellflowers, white artemisia and purplish red thrift, the woods restored nothing. What vanished had vanished forever, devoured and dissolved in the damp mold, without the pitiful lie and illusion of burial, like the stag in the clearing at Dolčice or the badger at the side of the road through Trije Kaliči, the deepest and most disquieting hollow beneath the peak of the mountain. The golden grass turned brown, gold burnished by time simply elapsing, decomposing, vanishing, just as you finally spit out the bit of fir bark you've chewed for hours while waiting for an animal to arrive — lovely, fresh and bitter bark that clings to your teeth and produces saliva, until it is spit out and mixed with the damp mold.

There, however, beyond the door of the dissolved cathedral, the forest began, opened, so ready to exclude anyone who travelled through it, to make him feel foreign and external to the dense woods surrounding him. Padežnica, Pomočnjaki, Grčovec, Travni Dolci, Dolčice, Trije Kaliči, Črni Dol, Črna Draga . . . these clearings constituted a shared history. As the years passed, they seemed to take on the lineaments of a face and the color of thoughts and feelings; they certainly formed an amorous landscape, because at dawn it was easier to love the closest face that emerged distinct from the darkness. In shadow you were no one, and so, stripped of every personal defect, loving was easy, because nothing interposed between love and life, which so often confronts love with obstacles, plots and traps, like those the hunters set for game. The strong animal scent of dawn doesn't contain any mud you have to shake off, like the doe that abruptly landed in a puddle at Pomočnjaki, scrambled to her feet and dashed away, happy with the mud on her back, as good and clean as clear water, which she didn't shrug off, fine as her skin.

The doe in Pomočnjaki, the roe buck in Travni Dolci which hastened to the love call, imitated with skill worthy of major undertakings, and vanished disappointed baying foreseeable comments, the wolf in Trije Kaliči, big and tawny, and very close, slowly turning around, the two stags bent over the little spring in Sant'Andrea, the frightened and sleepy dormouse on the path in Planinec, the attentive and wakeful boors in Pales, the hawks, the wildcat, the dormouse that worked throughout the night over the platform mounted on the tree, while for the nth time you hoped to see a bear . . . But the bears — year after year everyone else saw them, even the people who wandered around the forest making a racket and scattering garbage. Only we knew the dens where the beasts went when they were lethargic or gave birth, but we never saw them, and the summers followed one another measured by this suspense, by this search and, above all, by their failure.

Not even Boris managed to get us to the right place at the right time. Boris the gamekeeper, who saw many, many bears, once four together, and at Pales, when he scattered corn and used some carcasses as bait, he had a guaranteed appointment with a bear, who once came to uproot the stake where a dead cow was tied and dragged it into the woods. But when Boris brought us with him, the bear didn't come, not even tempted by a rotting horse. Year after year without the bear; at the most some fresh tracks or recent excrement, which on returning was announced triumphantly, while the others — children too, who without admitting it made the missing bear the focus of summer and perhaps of other things as well — congratulated themselves, laughing, for that excremental crowning of the season they awaited every year.

4.

At Gomance, beneath a thick, tangled fir tree that hides the earth, there must still be a German helmet, perforated by a bullet. Only right to leave it there, after finding it by chance; it may be the sole (even if substitute) grave of the man who wore it and probably perished, since the forest, unlike the fields, contains no recognizable burial places to give a bit of order to the world. The woods of Nevoso were a nerve center of the partisan war; small swift companies operated there, and it was the site of important command posts, especially bases for the couriers who maintained clandestine links with the remote divisions of Tito's IX Corpus. Snežnik was a theater of the Yugoslavian resistance, which would have demonstrated extraordinary capabilities for political organization, military efficiency and courage. Yet these qualities soon vanished when the valiant and cruel rebels in the woods became a managerial class that was generally inferior and parasitic, and that long survived itself through artificial means, shielded by Marshal Tito's genius and clever mystifications.

Partisan hospitals were hidden at Beli Vrh and Požar. The Germans set up their command at Ilirska Bistrica, and, a few kilometers away, at Zabiče, they formed a squad of *chetnik* allies led by the Duke Dobroslav Jevdievič. The Italian barracks at Morele and on Monte Aquila had been abandoned in '43 and destroyed. Some Italian soldiers joined the Titoist partisans, soon realizing that the just and proud rebirth of a nation oppressed by fascists was in turn transforming itself into a fierce nationalism which proved equally oppressive compared with the Italians.

The partisans were soundly beaten, their guns oiled with the fat of dormice. And the foresters executed by the Germans at Klanska Polica knew how to face death. The most important encounter occurred at Mašun, where the Tomsič brigade arduously blocked the enemy's path before withdrawing to Leskova Dolina and burning the castle in the small village. The war in the woods also wove the threads of a politics conceived in global terms and designed not only to free a country, but to create a new social order. The partisan conference at Mašun in September of '43 was attended by the military commanders, but also by Edvard Kardelj, the Slovenian capo who may have been Tito's only heir, capable of saving the Federal Republic from its atrocious and shameful collapse. Kardelj devised the self-scrutinizing administration that for several years seemed to be — and therefore was — a real socialist alternative, a model for a broad segment of the unaligned world during the Cold War and the instrument of an effective internal liberalization, unknown to Communist countries, distinct from the international policies developed by Tito with a great leader's gifts and the aid of Baron Munchhausen. Kardelj, moreover, played a significant role in the invention of Golj Otok, the bare island in the upper Adriatic where the Titoist regime created a terrible gulag to imprison and torture its political adversaries, especially — after the break with Stalin — Stalinists, including Italian Communists who had been willingly transferred to Yugoslavia to contribute to the socialist project.

Thus, during the war years, these pacific woods, secluded from history, subject at the most to incursions made by the Turks in 1528 and by the Islamicist Wallachs in 1758, became the site where an intricate web of hopes and lies was spun, projects for freedom and plans for totalitarian violence, the spirit of sacrifice and of rapacious domination. A small nameless pyramid remembers the unknown partisans buried in the forest, which knows no illustrious tombs or gravestones.

Kardelj, Tito, Nevoso and naturally the bear stand out in an anonymous painting that the owner, the Party, never took back and which now lies in an attic in Postumia. It represents the woods, a fire and a felled bear around which stand several hunters, among them Tito resting his hands on his knees and Kardelj with the purple cheeks of a sausage-eater, gesturing, evidently imitating the threatening claws of the freshly killed animal. Unfortunately, Kavcic is there as well, a leader who fell into disgrace immediately after the completion of the painting, who couldn't find the place that should have been his by right and had to be removed from circulation. The bear, lying on the ground, is well nourished and doesn't look dead, but rather blissfully asleep; you can imagine the sound of him snoring. He is the only thing that gives pleasure, despite so many *coups de théâtre*. One eye seems half-opened, casting a mocking sidelong glance at the leaders of the hunt and of the political scene; it is the proper way to look at history, askance and sly.

And so the forest too is touched by history, with its constant change of decor and theater. When the people who felt they were Yugoslavian fought in these valleys, they were proud of their own worthy revolt from fascist oppression, possible only because of Yugoslavian unity, and they even consented to the injustice committed in its name toward the Italians — not in Nevoso, which was always Slovenian and usurped with the annexation to Italy after 1918, but in the Italian lands of Istria, visible from the summit of Snežnik or Orlovica, annexed to Yugoslovia after 1945 during the persecution inflicted on their people. Until recently Josip Križaj, the ace Slovenian airplane pilot who also fought in the Spanish war and was downed in 1948 through some mysterious incident in these woods, near Monte Cifre in the Jarmovec area where a monument remembers him — he too was a Yugoslavian hero. For some time the rumor circulated that the Serbians were the ones who shot him down. In the castle museum at Kozarišče the portrait of Princess Anna, sister of Prince Hermann von Schönburg, is expected to be restored; the portrait, together with many others from various castles, had been removed to adorn one of Tito's villas at Brdo. Now, like the others, it will return to its ancestral feudal seat. History is like moving furniture, a storage and removal of objects from attic to parlor and vice versa.

5.

The castle of Nevoso, at Kozarišče, mentioned by old Janez Valvasor in his monumental seventeenth-century work in honor of Carniola, was neither destroyed nor burned during the Second World War, unlike so many other castles in Slovenia. Credit is due to the steward, Leon Sauta, a Czech who administered it on behalf of the proprietor, Prince Schönburg-Waldenburg. When the victors of the moment arrived, taking possession and wishing to feed it to the flames, he told them they were now the new masters of the castle, which therefore was and would remain their property, and hence any attempt to level it was senseless and self-destructive.

He said the same thing to the Italians, the Germans and the partisans, and that simple, impeccable argument convinced occupiers as well as liberators, time and time again, demonstrating that logic and grammatical analysis, if a bit more trust were put in them, could spare many ruins. The world would be a little safer if you learned to care for and respect it as you do your own property, to consider common property — and therefore your own as well — the things lying about you, trees and houses, roads, the colors of a season. Leon Sauta has many things to teach many people and, today, especially those ex-Yugoslavians who are destroying themselves, mad drunk to raze their cities to the ground and to slit one another's throats, oblivious of the fact — in the most imbecilic of fratricidal wars, the tragic failure of the great Titoist attempt to create a state — that the life they're destroying is their own. But the civility of these woods, as of Slovenia in general, is far from that pre-civic barbarity.

6.

The chronicles speak, with obsessive insistence, of frontiers and borders. A handwritten compendium of them is preserved in the castle at Kozarišče. It is in German; the author, Franz Schollmayer, compiled it in 1923 to recapitulate the vicissitudes of those lands and, above all, of the princes Schönburg-Waldenburg, in whose service he was employed. Conflicts recur between the lords of Nevoso — or the Schneeburgs, as they are called by the author and previous chroniclers — and the city of Laars, with the resulting jurisdictional complications, but there are also conflicts between the foresters of Nevoso and those of Čabar, on the other side of Klanska Polica. That line is an insistent and fatal demarcation. Possibly a matter of contention between Gepids and Celts, it was the Roman frontier against the Scordisci, much later a contested stretch of border between the Austrian empire and the kingdom of Hungary settled definitely by a mixed Austro-Hungarian commission only in 1913, then the border between Italy and Yugoslavia and finally between Slovenia and Croatia — until recently, therefore, between two republics of the same federation and today between two states that are not at war but inclined to look on each other with suspicion. "He must be a Croat," said Milka, the manager of the Planinski Dom, when he related that his daughter was divorced from her husband.

Wars between empires and between poachers, family quarrels, neighborhood stonings, turning points in history and the quotidian minimalism of cottages in the forest — these fanaticisms lamented by the chronicles, in Slovenia and Croatia, are the symbol of the centuries-old tribute of violence that is often exacted by a border, an idol demanding of bloody sacrifices. The border is necessity, fever, curse. Without it, there can be no identity or form, no existence. The border creates life itself and furnishes it with claws, like the hawk that can live and care for its brood only by pouncing on the blackbird.

The forest is both an exaltation and cancellation of borders. A plurality of different and antithetical worlds, yet caught in the great unity that embraces and dissolves them. Even the light in the forest has sharp edges that create diverse landscapes and, in the same instant, varying times. The black light in the densest thicket, or the underwater green beneath a vault of branches interlacing over a path. In the golden clearings, meanwhile, it is still broad daylight, a faint transparency. A few meters beyond it is already evening, heavy shadow.

But the forest, ever since Actaeon was torn to pieces by dogs, is absence of distinction, Dionysiac destruction, return to the primeval magma. The myth expresses the fear of the wood, and it is the fear of getting lost, erased. Long summers, familiarity with the glades, the thickets and the paths was not enough really to enter the unknown, which remained untouchable even when you walked through it during the fall, in the crystalline, windy air that muffled the faintest noise, even the creak of a branch. Old Drago Karolin, yes, he was in the woods, never left it, not even when he went down to the city; the clearings of Nevoso enveloped his entire life. Walking beside him for hours wasn't enough to be in the woods like him. Despite advanced age, he scoured Snežnik, putting directions at crossroads, repainting old faded signs, drawing maps that recorded the most narrow paths, fathering and polishing roots with bizarre shapes, angrily treading on his hat when he mistook the road, conversing with his guests in a courtly, archaic German, authoritatively hushing his wife, the gay Signora Ida, and dedicating noble paintings and verses to Nevoso.

For Karolin, the forest was open, a garden or house to be tended and kept in order; the lynxes and the age-old moldy fir trees around the spring Andreas Quelle, or Andrejev Izvir, were like the kitchen cat or a chest that needed cleaning. To others the forest yielded

little, ironically repelled them in their awkward urban strangeness, vainly impassioned; perhaps this is why the bear didn't appear. Being at home in the woods probably requires the ability
to write those stereotypical, rhymed verses of Karolin's: "down
there, in the distance, rustle the leaves . . ."

7.

A Slovene raised in old Hapsburgian Austria, the professor spoke
to me in a ceremonious, obsolete German, favoring the use of in-
direct forms: "I told my wife," he said, for example, as we warily
crossed a clearing frequented by boars, "'Beseech our most esteemed friend if by chance his revered consort prefers hers with
or without grappa.'"

On one occasion we went to visit him since we were aware that,
at ninety-two, he was bedridden for a few weeks due to circulatory
problems, which caused him some difficulty with his speech. He
was sweating and feverish, exhausted, but his eyes were always
bright and alive, tender in that face sculpted by decades into an
expression of severe authority. Next to the bed sat several parcels
and boxes in which his wife — in conformity to wishes that he expressed arduously but always in the tone of instructions admitting of no appeal — undertook the orderly assemblage of his things
so as to proceed later with their elimination: books, bizarre roots,
the stuffed head of a roe buck or a marten, paintings, drawings and
photographs of the mountain, letters, documents and relics. The
old man was unloading his existence, emptying it of the beloved
objects he collected with enthusiastic pedantry. He wanted to
make order in his life and to renounce what had adorned it, just as
the Hapsburg emperors, according to the baroque ritual, would not
be received in the Crypt of the Capuchins until they divested
themselves of the titles and insignia of their glory.

Before we left, he presented us with a postcard of Nevoso, on the
back of which were printed — obviously in Slovenian — some of his
verses, a nineteenth-century quatrain on the wind in the woods
and distant peaks. Lifting himself up on the pillow with his wife's
support and relying on two enormous magnifying glasses, he translated the quatrain into German for us in one great, trembling
stroke.

When we said farewell to him, the sheet with the four verses in
German seemed to us a testament, a definitive seal. But even

someone past ninety can reserve pleasant surprises and give the lie to banal prognoses. A few months later a letter arrived, naturally in German. The large, uncertain characters on the envelope at once revealed him as the author, but they gave no hint of the firm even if subdued exactness recorded in the old man's handwriting, trembling but rigorous in logical and syntactical sequence, in punctuation and orthography, in spacing and paragraphing. "Most esteemed friend, the last time, when you came to visit me, I gave you several of my verses, which I translated into German. My wife, who stood at my side observing me as I wrote, maintains that I had written *das Berg* rather than *der Berg* (the mountain). Should this be so, I entreat you to correct this deprecable error and to pardon me. I have suffered various circulatory problems, with some momentary amnesia, and if I have committed an error of this kind, I certainly did it because of my condition. Now I am better, I have risen from bed and taken short walks at the edge of the woods."

The professor found it inadmissible to go without correcting the mistake and resolving, for himself and others, every doubt in the matter. He must have spent a couple of months brooding, trying to remember whether he really used the erroneous *das*, the neuter article, in place of the masculine, or whether this was only a false impression of his wife, whom in those two months he must have harassed somewhat on just this question. Passion issues from vitality, but also stimulates it, and so, thanks to the professor's worry over a grammatical error and his strong desire to correct it, he regained his strength, left his bed, rediscovered a bit of his woods, the world, life.

Linguistic correctness is the premise of moral clarity and honesty. Many dirty tricks and violent prevarications occur when grammar and syntax are muddled and the subject is put in the accusative or the object complement in the nominative, switching the cards and exchanging the roles of the victims and culprits, altering the order of things and attributing events to causes or agents that differ from the actual ones, abolishing distinctions and hierarchies in a fraudulent heap of concepts and sentiments, deforming truth.

Language is a grate over the subterranean discharges of the irrational, from which derives its utterly precarious life. This is why a single comma in the wrong place can bring about disasters, cause fires that destroy the forests of the Earth. But Professor Karolin demonstrated that respect for language and truth can be strengthening: it enables you to stand a little firmer on your own legs and stroll out to enjoy the world with a sensual vitality that is both unconstrained and free from the confusion of deceptions and self-delusions. Who knows how many things, how many sweet pleasures and joys are owed, unwittingly, to the red pencils of schoolteachers. . . .

8.

The faithful Schollmayer's chronicle, which opens with an invocation to Clio, recapitulates the entire history of Snežnik, but is dedicated to "Nevoso in possession of the princely family Schönburg." In the course of centuries and vicissitudes, the castle and mountain have passed from one family to another, but they are certainly most identified with the line of Schönburg-Waldenburg, who acquired them in 1853 and held them until nationalization in 1945. These latter-day feudal lords have left a good record. Although the first proprietor, his Highness Anton Viktor, who owned some thirty castles, never set foot there, Prince Georg not only educated the forester's sons, but instituted a rudimentary social security system and founded the first school of forestry in Slovenia, while Hermann repopulated the forest with animals after the farmworkers slaughtered them in the uprisings of '48.

Prince Hermann is the lord of Nevoso by antonomasia. He was German and lived near Dresden, but spent many months in the castle at Kozarišče, where you can still see, intact, his various salons — Oriental, Venetian, Egyptian — and a library rich in literary and juridical works as well as a bound copy of the hunting magazine, *Jagdzeitung*, and a seventeenth-century *Storia Universale* in twenty volumes. His portraits display a gaunt, melancholy face, a bourgeois interiority that recalls Chekhov or Schnitzler more than any aristocratic vigor. Vinko Sterle, hunter and descendent of a mythic hunting family in the prince's service, the rhapsode of hunts from times past, has handed down accounts of the lord's kindness toward his subordinates, as well as his severity toward a nephew who wanted to shoot a deer in the back but was prevented by an emphatic gesture from the hunter Matja Martinčič, who knocked down his gun barrel.

The legendary chief huntsman of Nevoso was Franc Sterle, Vinko's grandfather, whose office gave him the right to sleep in his master's cabin during hunts. Once, the night before bagging a wood grouse, as they undressed, Franc, who was wearing his best and newest thick flannel drawers, observed that the prince's underwear was patched in ten places with different mending, so he told His Highness that he could permit himself better linen. "Ah Franc," roared His Highness, "you are just like my housekeepers, who don't want to sew or wash and would rather throw away a shirt than mend it."

The prince felled his first bear on 16 May 1893, a beast of 220 kilos which today stands, stuffed, in the entrance hall of the castle. He did not climb to a safe position among the branches of a tree, but met the bear face to face, because — according to Vinko — he was required to undergo this test of courage in order to win morally the right to be lord of the woods. Notwithstanding his introverted gaze, his feudal heritage probably impressed on him the atavistic superstition according to which blood is a necessary baptism, killing is a way of loving and death is a communion between killer and victim. But on one occasion he must have opened his eyes to the wretched deceit in this glorification, which seeks to ennoble suffering in life and death. Now an old man, he was hunting deer with Lojze Sterle, Vinko's uncle, another teacher in Nevoso whom he had encouraged to study languages. The prince shot, struck and penetrated the thicket where the animal lay. Lojze wanted to reach him, but the prince shouted to stay where he was. Lojze waited for some time until, curious and worried, he made his way into the bushes. The old prince was crouched down, holding the dead deer by the horns and weeping.

Perhaps this wasn't only pity. At that moment he must have seen the vanity of what he was doing, and of everything — as if, shooting and entering that thicket, he had entered reality from the stage door and seen the stereotype from behind the scenes. Those horns would become an umpteenth trophy, stupidly nailed to the wall, and all those hunting trophies stacked side by side on the walls and stairs — glass-eyed birds, ungainly bears making clown-like grimaces, rugs ending in a wolf's head that looked like a threadbare ball of yarn — formed a common and inevitable display, the destiny of every life, which enchants for a moment, but which a little powder and a well-oiled gun are enough to remove, like a cloth animal, and reduce to straw, springs and buttons.

The prince continued to shoot. But a bit of the void he encountered in the thicket next to the slain deer insinuated itself into the inexhaustible hunting stories that Vinko Sterle told with such passion. As when Franc, in the vicinity of Gašperjev Hrib, pursued and wounded a wolf, killing it with his rifle butt in a hand-to-hand struggle only to realize that it was a she-wolf with four cubs who remained there gazing at one another; or Matija's relentless pursuit of a feared lone wolf, in 1923, which he tracked by himself for hours through the snow, in the moonlight, obsessed and as weary as the beast, pushing ahead almost without noticing where he put his feet, until he shot something he spotted behind a bush and struck the wolf who, exhausted, was sleeping and didn't even awake to die.

These stories reveal the strangeness of the forest, which withdraws inaccessible and does not allow itself to be grasped, but strews the paths with false tracks and errors, blunders and equivocations, like the accidents in which Sunday hunters take turns shooting one another. Even if tractors and cement conquer it day in and day out, rendering it no longer threatening but threatened, the forest would somehow escape, would bring the realization that, despite the butterflies so drunk with love that they allow themselves to be taken delicately in your fingers on the road to Peklo, or Rima, despite the red bitch that once pursued a marten for half a day with her barks and shrill yelps fading in the woods, still every summer something is missing, like the bear you never managed to see or Signor Samec's voice growing faint before the end of his story and getting caught somewhere in the trees, interrupted and inconclusive: pardon me, your Excellency, I told him, but with your permission . . .

There are those, many in this country and in England, who want to see thought or thinking removed from fiction altogether (much as there are English departments that profess to have removed the subjective element from the teaching of literature). Claudio Magris, for his sins, is one of those authors who think their way through a novel or novella, and let the reader make the best of it. His novella, A Different Sea, for instance, begins with a Greek tag (Ἀρετὴ τιμὴν φέρει) almost at once glossed in German after the English version — virtue brings honor — in the first sentence. This may not tell you where you're going, but it must tell you where you are and with whom: what kind of literary artist. How different it would be if he hit us with Greek halfway through. A profoundly literary writer who sees literature and commentary as in no way alien to each other, Magris has translated Ibsen, Kleist and Schnitzler, and he writes creatively as if literature were made from literature, which it is; Malraux made the point about the visual arts in such books as The Voices of Silence and The Metamorphoses of the Gods. It is good to remember this in a time that has fiction cast as unpretentious sociology and the sentence, that magical core of literary art, as a wrapper: paper or plastic?

Magris reminds us, in both his short and his long work, that fiction is an enterprise of pensive finesse, hardly a commercial enterprise at all, although with his Danube a European bestseller, he is in a good position to appraise the vicissitudes of the belletristic book. In America he will always run into the tradition of Jack London and Theodore Dreiser: the book that's written within the expectations of the reading public. You can't have it both ways: a country of decreasing literacy cannot sustain a popular tradition of articulate writing. Only in America do elites feel guilty, because undemocratic, and I suppose that soon those who insist on English as the language of the country's literature will feel guilty about that too.

Into this mess comes Claudio Magris, a university teacher, an unusual phenomenon inasmuch as few European writers support themselves by teaching. Perhaps isolated, like Enrico, the young intellectual hero of A Different Sea who lights out for the Patagonian pampas with his favorite Greek texts. It doesn't sound like Hemingway or Faulkner, but it does remind me of Ernst Jünger, the German botanist-soldier-dandy who, almost one hundred, goes on perpetuating a suave holism that Magris is also privy to. American taste, so-called, needs to brace itself for serious and solid European writing: not the capering froth of Julian Barnes and James Fenton, but the terminal moraine left by Thomas Mann and perhaps Hesse, or, in Magris's own country, Pavese and Manganelli, still sustained by Anna Maria Ortese. For too long Calvino, the lightweight, has been the synecdoche for Italian writing: dote on him, skip the rest. This has been a pity, and we now try to put things to rights. Let's hear it now for cosmopolitan transcendence, for Italian that's written.

— Paul West

Poems and Rengas
Araki Yasusada

— Translated from Japanese by Tosa Motokiyu,
Ojiu Norinaga and Okura Kyojin

TELESCOPE WITH URN

The image of the galaxies spreads out like a cloud of sperm.

Expanding said the observatory guide, and at such and such velocity.

It is like the idea of the flowers, opening within the idea of the
flowers.

I like to think of that, said the monk, arranging them with his
papery fingers.

Tiny were you, and squatted over a sky-colored bowl to make water.

What a big girl! cried we, tossing you in the general direction of
the stars.

Intently, then, in the dream, I folded up the great telescope on
Mount Horai.

In the form of this crane, it is small enough for the urn.

DREAM AND CHARCOAL

And then she said: I have gone toward the light and become beautiful.

And then she said: I have taken a couple of wings and attached them
to the various back-parts on my body.

And then she said: all the guests are coming back to where they were
and then talking.

To which she said: without the grasp-handle, how would you
recognize my nakedness?

To which she replied: without nothing is when all things die.

Which is when she had a wild battle with the twigs.

Which is when the charcoal was passed from her body to mine.

Which was how she rose into the heavens, blinding the pedestrians.

Which was how our union was transposed into a dark scribble.

Which became the daughter calling, calling my name to wake me.

GEISHA AND IRIS

(Bought the liver with rusty coins.)

(Walked in a hill's direction.)

(Chanced to find an iris.)

(Unnaturally large for sure.)

(Plucked it with a sexual longing.)

(This was at the edge of the radius-sweep.)

(Though flowers beyond are also large.)

(Two prefectures from here.)

(As the stick and mud home was as I'd left it.)

(Random chickens most happy.)

70

(A small garden doing well.)

(Gazed at the photo of the sultry geisha.)

(On newspaper liver was wrapped in.)

(While eating liver with radish.)

(Beneath the iris which was towering.)

UNTITLED HAIKU

Slate bed — I dream of genitals at an angle

*

Cool night — the rag tipped with moon

*

Chrysanthemum's scent — no hail under the long rock

*

Obediently bowing — the white flowers

*

Sake's transparent — I pat the pig

*

The wild grasses — so here I am

*

I dream of my daughter — the silk-worm farm

71

Araki Yasusada

HORSEHIDE AND SUNSPOT
July 17, 1962 Hiroshima Municipal Stadium

Chalk-lines, in sun, extend themselves infinitely.

Cleat-tracks and *[illegible]* engrave the paths ephemerally.

(Also, horsehide and pinewood are soundless and.)

Thus now Carp and Sparrows tense their tiny bodies and leap hither.

On the diamond where a temple once stood.

As seventy thousand voices are fused by a sphere and.

A corolla of screams ringing absence is viscerally real.

And so, like a sunspot, is baseball.

[*Hiroshima Carp and Yamaguchi Sparrows are major league baseball teams of Japan. The poem is written on the back of a scorecard. Kusano Shimpei was a major avant-garde figure in Japanese poetry and an acquaintance of Yasusada, Ozaki Kusatao and Akutagawa Fusei.*]

AUTUMN GRASSES RENGA

You see, he says courting her, the universe stretches forever without reason, or else stops somewhere without reason.

Beyond the flowering hedge are rows and rows of taro and radish.

Bending the spray of plum to her nose, she remembers her parents with a forced detachment.

At harvest, the unconscious motions of the workers are repeated again and again.

They have paused before the fallen nest woven of rice shoots.

She presses her ear to the wall, hearing the cries of the bride, as if they were not her own.

While pushing the perambulator through the darkened temple grounds, a trace of light remains near the top of the trees.

"The shortest way to the outhouse," hisses the monk, "is through that long patch of graves."

And so from the tea-kettle of birds comes the sound of wind-swept pines.

Nor will he ever forget the grove of lean saplings beneath the autumn moon.

"Whenever his left eye wanders outward," she confesses, "it causes me an uncontrollable irritation."

Wherefrom they argue over money near the dry and crumbled silkworms.

"One could say romantic things," he says, "but I resolutely refuse to do so."

Thus they part, taking different paths through stalks of dried sunflowers.

Now, to the sound of spring rain, he records his findings on a certain kind of mollusk.

He wants to write to them, but is afflicted with indecision.

Of course, he knows his daughter's acne is causing her much shame.

Some people are found still standing, burned to a dark crust.

In the photo, his wife's cosmetics and hair ornaments seem ordinary, recalling advertisements.

Slender autumn grasses are growing along the crest of an ancient earthen wall.

— by Yasusada, Ozaki Kusatao and Akutagawa Fusei

Araki Yasusada

SUITOR RENGA

You are the most beautiful girl in Hiroshima, and I am the suitor.

Around the stone the irises are moist and lascivious.

Although the suitor written above does not exist.

Nor are there traces of suitors left in Hiroshima to speak of thus.

Even when flower-bearing (even when a passerby cries, "Oh, there goes a suitor") the latter is an *[illegible]*.

You are the most beautiful girl in Nagasaki and.

You are shy and wear a large pin in your hair.

Now we have come full circle and.

Don't lean too close, your eyes seem to be saying.

"The radius delimits the unnatural size of the flowers."

You are running like a sprinter with a bluish bubble on your back.

Now we have arrived in the area of the white blossoms.

You are a little girl with blistered face, pumping your legs at a great speed beside the burning form of your Mother and.

Now we have arrived in the area of the white blossoms.

"And now darling, says the tourist, have we come to the long slate-bed of Kamakura suitors?"

A suitor emerges joyous from the meeting, for he has conquered shyness by assuming *[illegible]* mannerisms.

— by Yasusada, Ozaki Kusatao and Akutagawa Fusei

Araki Yasusada

SENTENCES FOR JACK SPICER RENGA

Walking, we insisted the *Manyoshu* was a blur, and why we said it
on that path is also a blur.

(seven beats, rapidly, ko-tsuzumi)

The tile has a pattern and a dancer walking there.

(rrrr went a bell, and the dancer went rrrr.)

The lover was like a rose, beneath the light of the bar, leaning.

Going out and into the shadows that are massed against the sound of
a bell.

(one strike, densho)

You wouldn't believe what the others said:

(five seconds, random, shakuhachi)

They said things like "Death," "Yukio Mishima" or "Have a nice
day."

(five seconds, random, hickirichi)

The lover lay down on the stone and I pulled off my shirt or vice-
versa.

(ten seconds, random, da-daiko, uckinarashi, mokug-yo)

There were flowers, flattened, in the closed book.

Alias, I said, I quote you.

(one strike, densho)

Alias, the book is near your ear, in the photograph that is about you.

(one strike, densho)

Araki Yasusada

(His seems to be a "heady" sort of writing, in love with the trace of thought itself)

So the writing is barely legible on the ancient screen.

(seven beats, rapidly, ko-tsuzumi)

So I call back his arm, drifting into the massed shadows of the rose.

(one strike, densho)

Now the dancer is tracing a pattern over the pattern, feet clicking against the tile.

— by Yasusada and Akutagawa Fusei

[*Ink-brushed notes added at bottom of page in Fusei's calligraphy:*] No messages, no intention to share emotion. No lyrical intensity — percussive soundings within patterns of harmonic or dissonant chords; utterance as autonomous fact *and* its saturation in context (*this* tension). Gaps as intrinsic to such grammar — less as caesura than as sign. Spicer's ghost as a concave form I glimpsed, hovering, a few feet above poem.

[*Yasusada's cursive note added in pencil:*] Ask Mr. Davidson: What does he think that word truly means — "lyrical." And ask him also, what is the meaning of those broom-like forms attached to the front of his skirt?

UTTERANCES AND HEPATICA

And then he said, there is a language and I make it.

And then he replied, don't take the ancient engravings so solemnly.

And then he said, I want to crawl away and hide in the thought to which I am leading.

To which she inquired, why are you so certain about the utterances of the Tokyo people?

And then she read, "Kikuyu is a very sad case. She made a bad marriage, and she came here afterwards."

76

And then she screamed, if a man had a tough hairy hide, his world would be different indeed.

Which is when he threw her bath utensils randomly to the tile.

Which is when he imagined her body as the portal of a valley.

Which is when she touched herself in sorrow amidst hepatica.

Which shall be the queen of all flowers.

So this was written in the egg-laying season of the moths.

So in such a time their body is swollen beyond all proportion to their wings.

Which was when someone lifted her solemnly toward the clouds.

Which was when the radius of the area was reproduced a large number of times.

Which was on a day the suitor was bearing a large bouquet of hepatica.

Which shall be the queen of all flowers.

————————————

The notebooks of the Hiroshima poet Araki Yasusada were dis-covered by his son in 1980, eight years following the poet's death. The manuscripts comprise fourteen spiral notebooks whose pages are filled with poems, drafts, English class assignments, diary entries, recordings of zen dokusan encounters and other matter. In addition, the notebooks are interleaved with hundreds of inser-tions, including drawings, received correspondence and carbon copies of the poet's letters.

Although Yasusada was active in important avant-garde groups such as Ogiwara Seisensui's Layered Clouds and the experimental renga circle Oars, and was an acquaintance of several well-known writers and artists like Taneda Santoka, Ozaki Hosai, Kusano

Araki Yasusada

Shimpei and Shiryu Morita, his work, along with that of his renga collaborators Ozaki Kusatao and Akutagawa Fusei, is virtually unknown. But the writing found in Yasusada's manuscripts is fascinating for its biographical disclosure, formal diversity and linguistic élan. Much of the experimental impetus, interestingly, comes from Yasusada's encounter in the mid-1960s with the poetry of the American Jack Spicer and the French critic Roland Barthes: Yasusada had fluency in English and French, and there are numerous quotes from, or references to, both of these literary figures in the later work. The notebooks reveal, in fact, that Yasusada was undertaking a work parallel to Spicer's letters and "translations" in After Lorca, to be entitled After Spicer.

Yasusada was born in 1907 in the city of Kyoto, where he lived until 1921, when his family moved to Hiroshima. He attended Hiroshima University sporadically between 1925 and 1928, with the intent of receiving a degree in Western literature. Due, however, to his father's illness with cancer, he was forced, in the interests of the family, to undertake full-time employment with the postal service and withdraw from his formal studies.

In 1930 he married his only wife, Nomura, with whom he had two daughters and a son. In 1936, Yasusada was conscripted into the Japanese Imperial Army and worked as a clerk in the Hiroshima division of the Military Postal Service. His wife and youngest daughter, Chieko, died instantly in the blast on August 6. His daughter Akiko survived, yet perished three years later from radiation sickness. His son, Yasunari, only nine months old at the time, was with relatives outside the city.

Yasusada died in 1972 after a long struggle with cancer. Akutagawa Fusei died of similar cause in 1971. The fate of Ozaki Kusatao is unknown to us. The selections here are part of a much larger collection that we are in the process of editing and translating.

     — Tosa Motokiyu, Ojiu Norinaga, Okura Kyojin

Three Poems
Coral Bracho

— Translated from Spanish by Forrest Gander

OF THEIR ORNATE EYES OF CRYSTALLINE SAND

From the expirations of these marble fish,
from the sleek silk
of their songs,
from their ornate eyes
of crystalline sand,
the calm of temples and gardens

(in their acanthus shadows, in the shale
they touch and tenderize)

They have opened their beds
have dredged their channels
under the fledgling leaves of the almond trees.

They speak of their tactile
sparkling,
of tranquil games taken to the limit,
to the languid edge of sunsets.
Of their frigid lips.

Jewelled eyes.

Of the spume they blow, the fragrance they give off

(In the atriums: candles, amaranths)
over the least altar in the arena.

Coral Bracho

(From the temple:
the perfumed bales,
the scales,
the deer. They speak of their sheer reflections.)

At night
the delicate marble of their silence,
the prized tattoos, the pristine outlines

(they have drowned the light
at the shore; on the sand)

above the limpid image,
above the standing gift
of meadowland.

YOUR LIFE REFRACTS ME LIKE AN ENIGMA

Like a translucent mirror
among shadows, the deep backwater lies open; the inverse
to this thirst which
I drink, which I touch like a sphere, inextricable,
beneath the liquid flash. Voice

— From between the dance and the vesperal ardor
The most delicate song   Between the green of stupor, of pleasure — What it is
     that incinerates in the high amplitudes
vividly combines. What makes it quiver
The wind

and the superlative fleece in the strings of the Aeolian harp.
The crystalline eucalyptus. Sap
in which the calm
and the disposition of water is
enciphered

What I drink in, what I apprehend like a reflection of that
     impregnable contact; the clarity
of its rootedness in the night, of its vault.

Full, profound consonance above the forests like a roar.
In the fluid hollow of the snail; against the leaded crystal
— They make music

the ebony flagstone
before the fire that reflects the dragging the inflamed ululate
in the circular
niches of song, the peril — The talisman sensed under those formal springs,
    within that light —

Like a flame within
birch forests, gentle multitudes. The atemporal
between their lit bodies. The sound
they plant (— The children trace its liquid howl
in the burning like a vegetal spectre)
Between the temporal vessels   The spring:

What quivers there.
— The blaze drains the night, in their submerged roots — Its fluid

roundness,
its presence — In what I drink, what I touch

UNTITLED

Your voice (in your body rivers stir
a calm foliage; grave and cadenced waters).

— From this door, the pleasures, their thresholds;
from this ring, they are transfigured —

In your forests of liquid sand,
of dense, pale jade (deep water cleaved;
this door carved on the barks of dawn). I enclose
your fountain — Water
which holds to the light (in your body the rivers fuse, solidify
in the nitrous ceiba trees. Flame — door of igneous glimmer —
you circle and sweat me out: all about this glass, under those spongy valleys,
between this blanket, this flesh

Coral Bracho's poems read, in Spanish, as though they were poured onto the page. They are fluid, lapping long-lined toward the gutters. Her images evoke an oneiric, sensual realm of dispelled logics. Her diction spills out along ceaselessly shifting beds of sound. Listen to this in Spanish:

> Dicen del tacto
> de sus destellos,
> de los juegos tranquilos que delizan al borde,
> a la orilla lenta de los ocasos.
> De sus labios de hielo.

Bracho's poems make sense first as music, and music propels them. Sad birds in the luminous ceiba. Oiseau Triste, Debussy. Then it is as though the very syntax has begun to run, has been heated to a magma by the sensual fingers holding the pen, by the pulsing resistance, the friction of accumulating words, of echoes bandied back and forth between lines like flames between mirrors. Bracho's syntax slips and recombines and flows lubriciously around its conventionally obstruent limitations.

When I was living in Dolores Hidalgo, in Mexico, I found El ser que va a morir, which had won the Premio Nacional de Poesía (Aguascalientes) in 1981, in the local bookstand. It was Bracho's second book, and the poems made me think of Mei-mei Berssenbrugge's work: the long lines, the meditative tone, the radical syntactical strategies. Though Berssenbrugge's work leans toward the philosophical and Bracho's toward the sensual, both poets allow for an unusually high degree of abstraction, repudiating the dominant dictum of modernist poetics ("Go in fear of abstractions," wrote Pound).

A book collecting her two earlier volumes, Bajo El Destello Líquido, was published by Fondo de Cultura Económica in 1988 (with a cover collage by the poet Alberto Blanco). Bracho sent me a copy when she was a visiting professor at the University of Maryland; she was having a difficult pregnancy at the time. Asked for a statement about her aesthetics for an anthology I was editing (Mouth to Mouth: Poems by 12 Contemporary Mexican Women, Milkweed, 1993), Bracho responded, "My feeling is that any such statement would implicitly be an evaluation that I think is not up to me to make. Besides that, I think it would also interfere between the reader and the texts and set a limited pattern of approach."

For me, the pleasures of her poems derive from their open-endedness, from their music, their delicious vocabulary and from the tension between an insistently telic rhythm and a dehiscent narrative. As readers, we sense that our arrival is imminent, but the destination keeps dissolving.

— Forrest Gander

Five Beirut Poems
Faiz Ahmed Faiz

— Translated from Urdu by Andrew McCord

AFTER HAFIZ

My advisor tells me pain is love's vocation
And for prudent men there is better work than that.

— Hafiz

Brown sugar in mouth, there's better than that.
The delicate tongue, there's better than that.

Grace of spring in season of leaf-fall —
Jasmine petals, there's better than that.

In sharp sultry weather nightingales
Come to the garden — there's better than that.

Hard and heart-breaking, heartening and hot —
The thought of my country, there's better than that.

Body a taper, robe like a lighthouse,
Beauty of flesh, there's better than that.

Who in love is not in pain?
Prudent man, what's better than that?

Faiz Ahmed Faiz

QAWWALI

Patience reaped and lit again,
Sighs rise like smoke again,
Every straw in the thatching
A gift to the cold, cold wind again.
Morning of grieving,
A river of tears again,
Lamentations of evening
Start on all sides again.
In every quarter of this tract
Weeping sounds to God again.

From somewhere time masses
Its savage battalion.
Thunder and crack of the whip
Come over the field again.
The pens that write the story
Are cut from our thin necks.
The auction is on of our wits
While tongues wag, lips
Pull against the stitches,
And mouths begin to bleed.
In every quarter of this tract
Weeping sounds to God again.

In the cold, cold wind,
I am tortured by the fire again.
Wherever I go, whatever I do
You've mastered my heart again.
Pretenders go round got
Up like your messengers,
In the temple the fetish
Lays claim to your godliness,
And Lord preserve you God
From the creed of your lords.
In every quarter of this tract
Weeping sounds to God again.

Faiz Ahmed Faiz

TWO POEMS FOR PALESTINE

I.   The Dead Who Went Abroad for Work

"Country I come from, wherever I went

I took in my heart the scars of your debasement,
I took love of your honor burning like a lamp.

Your affection, your aching memory, went with me.
The smell of orange trees blossoming went with me.

A retinue of unseen compatriots was with me.
How many hands did I shake heartily?

On unwelcoming thoroughfares of a distant province,
Along unrecognizable streets in a strange city,

Over any bit of earth where my blood unfurled
Flew the flag of the Palestinian land.

Your enemy laid waste to one Palestine.
The blood of my wounds populated a dozen."

II.   Lullaby

Child, don't cry.
Mother now
Has cried herself to sleep.

Child, don't cry.
It's just a minute now
That Father's pain
Took leave of him.

Child, don't cry.
Brother,
Chasing a butterfly,
Has left you behind.

Child, don't cry.
Sister's with her darling
In another country.

Child, don't cry.
In the courtyard
The body was washed by the sun
Then buried by the moon.

Child, don't cry.
Mother, Father, Sister, Brother,
Sun and Moon
Will not make you cry again.

Smile now
And sometime maybe
They will come back
To play in disguise.

GHAZAL

It does not happen that torture teaches dedication.
A fetish does not show the way to God.

Longings come to nothing on the body's killing floor.
My executioner will not sell his reckoning cheaply back.

In the world of the heart forewarnings are useless.
Here there are no compacts between friends.

Every night, every hour seems like the end.
In the morning, the day of judgement does not happen.

Feel how the sky oscillates in heaven.
What you say is done with has yet to happen.

Faiz Ahmed Faiz

BEIRUT

On the killing field there is no mosque or tavern.
Where to trust grief at the world's ways?
Make the call to prayer at the slaughtereds' graves.
See who tears a shroud and comes forward.

Faiz Ahmed Faiz (1911–1984) was an enormously popular poet and probably the most important literary figure in India and Pakistan since Rabindranath Tagore. Salman Rushdie refers to him as an exemplar and it seems sometimes that every would-be writer in the Hindi- and Urdu-speaking parts of northern India and Pakistan has an essay on Faiz to pull out at the drop of a hat. Faiz was steeped in Persian, Arabic and classical Urdu poetry, and many of his poems are ghazals, a rhymed, strictly metered classical form. Nevertheless, he is criticized for diluting his tradition, particularly in his later work. This complaint, though, comes mostly from academics and it is often commingled with envy and a point of view that would deny the possibilities of modernism. The poems here come from Faiz's last individual collection, which was published in 1981. They cover a period of voluntary exile from Pakistan that began after General Zia-ul Haq seized power and imposed martial law in 1977. Faiz makes his way to Tashkent, Samarqand, Moscow, London, the United States and Paris before coming to rest in Beirut. In the poems he takes up inherited forms and structures of imagery to build a response to the world he confronts and also to old age. His allusions become suggestive in entirely new ways, political but not always politically parseable. The old forms console. Their reassertion is quite distinct from recent formalism in English poetry. In Faiz form makes an argument for making things despite disintegration, failed hopes, defeated movements. Oddly, he takes a less despairing literary stance in a more desperate worldly situation.
— Andrew McCord

From Secrets
Nuruddin Farah

1.

ONE CORPSE, three secrets!

2.

My name Kalaman conjures up memories of a childhood infatuation with a girl four and a half years older than I, memories on the heels of which arrive other recollections. Like an easy answer to a seemingly difficult riddle, my name evokes surprising responses in many people, especially when they hear it for the first time. Some, at the risk of sounding ludicrous, have been known to wonder aloud, "But what sort of a name is it?" Give them a clue, as I am prone to, nudge them in the right direction and you will observe that slowly, like a mysterious door opening, their faces will widen with grins as self-conscious as a sparrow dipping its head in the river's mist. My interlocutors often ask, "Now why on earth did we not think of that?"

There was a brief period when I thought of altering my name altogether. I had been infatuated at the time with Sholoongo, whose animal powers were mightier than mine. I resented my squeamish behavior not only because of our gender difference, but also because my mother held the girl's guts in ominous awe. My grandfather appeared at times to go out of his way to encourage my cultivating her friendship, arguing that it was salutary for me to meet a woman who was my equal. Then he would change the subject and engage my interest in the stars and, between irrelevant asides, would point the Milky Way out to me and explain the myth behind it, indicate the twenty-odd stations along the path of the moon and how each of these affected the weather and a person's destiny.

Sholoongo was so domineering I could never say my own name in her presence without stammering. My mouth would open a little like a bird feeding, and my tongue would push itself up against my palate, only I would fail miserably either in making it to the K-sound, or be incapable of getting to the L before finally seizing up altogether. Unable to unjam my tongue, I would become aware of a feeling of despair and inner rage.

Months went by before I asked Nonno why I could not stand up to Sholoongo's mysterious power, or just couldn't shrug off her spells, like water off a crow's back.

He said, "I gather that Sholoongo was delivered of her mother when the stars were bivouacking at a most inauspicious station. She was born a *Duugaantii*, that is to say, a baby to be buried. And that was what her mother tried to do: she carried the infant out into the bush and abandoned her there. But Sholoongo survived, she lived to haunt the villagers' conscience, especially her mother. I cannot vouch for its truth, but in the version I heard a lioness adopts her and raises her together with her cubs, feeds her, then abandons her at a crossroads, where some travellers find her, travellers who bring her back to the nearest settlement, which happens to be her mother's hamlet. The stuff of which some people's misfortune is made is myth galore!"

"And then what happened?"

"Rather than own up to any of this, the girl's mother commits suicide, a most heinous crime, which is punished by the villagers. The woman's corpse is left to rot and the villagers remark that even vultures will not dare to go anywhere near the dead body."

"My God!"

"The girl's father turns up," Nonno went on, "a seaman on leave, and the villagers do not dare tell him the whole truth. Only that he has to slaughter several goats as part of a sacrificial ceremony for *his* safe return. But no one mentions that his daughter is *Duugaantii* or that his wife has taken her own life."

"He slaughters the goats?"

"And having done so, brings away his daughter and marries another woman, who supplies him with a son, Timir. Suddenly his young wife goes insane, no reasons are known, and people point a superstitious finger at Sholoongo, whose father consults a savant who prescribes ostrich eggs as a cure."

"How do you know all this?" I asked.

He had a mischievous glitter in his eyes as he said, "I've managed to glean all this from the ears of a legion of untold secrets."

I took a sip of chilled water with a dash of tamarind in it, the same concoction being the wondrous secret drink with which Nonno wet my lips at birth. My larynx loosened up, so did my pharynx, my voice organs bounced into action, with the Adam's apple jerking into life, functioning with the ease of a recently greased engine. And I sang the songs Sholoongo had taught me.

"Do you have any idea why she makes you stammer?"

I explained in the hesitant language of a child of eight-plus that I believed that I had occasional seizures. Then I compared my stammer to hiccups with which it shared at least one feature: that I responded positively to chilled water with a dash of tamarind juice.

As though impressed, Nonno said, "Well done!"

One day, following hard on the heels of an exchange between me and Sholoongo about my name, she and I had a no-holds-barred quarrel. Nonno's name, of necessity, occurred in our conversation, and Sholoongo, who could be very mean, inflicted an obloquy on my ancestry, describing my grandfather in the vilest language by referring to him as "a closet literate." Although I didn't know what the phrase meant, I felt affronted, left her in a huff and travelled to Afgoi, where Nonno had his estate, with the express intention of asking him what the phrase "closet literate" meant. In the event I got carried away and we spoke about why he had named me Kalaman.

We sat in the shade of a mango tree, Nonno and I, eating our fruit salad out of the same wooden bowl with our fingers. He had pre-pared the macédoine himself from the produce of his own orchard. We shared our talk in measured quantities, and paid regal atten-tion to each other. He was a very large man, with an overbearing personality, a most agreeable character whose charisma charmed many a woman in the very spot where some are deemed to be hard. Although young, I observed that a lot of women were not averse to being teased all the way to his bedroom, laughing, with half the knots of their *guntiino*-robes undone. I loved him all the more for his occasional self-abandon, which was as guileless as a child's, and adored him for the wicked grin blemishing his features.

Part of me suspected that I was committing a flagrant disloyalty by insisting that Nonno tell me why he had named me Kalaman, the other part was weighed down with a curious feeling of dismay at my inability to ask him why Sholoongo had called him a "closet literate." Silent, his mouth thronged with unmade sounds, a harvest of nearly three score years of memories of which he had been a faithful depository. At last, he said, "Because it is a cul-de-sac of a name, that's why."

I said I did not understand his meaning.

We fell under the spell of a silence that had something of a hissing quality to it, a sound not too dissimilar to that of a snake moving over wet grass. I stared for goodness knows how long at a small bird, with a nervous twitch, a shrill whistle, creamy white abdomen and a grayish chest, a bird which held me spellbound until it flew away, vanishing in the hollow of the hillock beyond. I couldn't decide if I had seen the bird before, or what its glorious name might be, when his voice interfered with my thoughts.

"Commonplace names need propping up," he said, and paused, maybe because he too was having difficulty identifying the bird, which we had both seen. He went on, "Commonplace names need to be spoken in conjunction with a father's name, or a grandfather's, or to have a custom-made nickname added at their tailends. Otherwise they do not feel right, as if there is something incomplete about them." He fell quiet, and stirred in his chair restlessly, adding, "I had the foresight to call you Kalaman because I knew it would stand on its own, independent of your father's name or mine."

Borrowing a few of his complicated words, which I had half-understood, and propping these up with a few of my own, I wondered what had prompted him to give me such a name. Was there something he was hiding and of which he was ashamed? I didn't mean to be disrespectful, but maybe I was. Some of these things are too difficult to judge, especially if you are only nine and the girl with whom you are infatuated prods you with pointed questions. Mind you, Sholoongo wasn't alone in maintaining that Nonno was withholding a secret, because another woman, a friend of my mother's, alluded to the fact that whereas both Nonno and my father "hung down a ton," I didn't.

"Unless . . . !" I said, and trailed off.

Maintaining a stately silence, Nonno refused to rise to my challenge. Earlier, I had rehearsed the scene in the bus on the way to him and in my script he had asked, "Unless what?" and I had prepared a tentative response. However, my grandfather, faithful to his agenda of priorities, had his own ideas anyway. You could tell from the way he spoke that he did.

"Curse the day!" he said. This was one of his favorite phrases, he had a plethora of them, shibboleths pointing to his nervous or joyous state.

"You see, Nonno," I said, "I am eight-plus, a big enough boy to know that there are adult secrets which you may not share with a child of my age. I understand."

I could tell from the restlessness which swept over his features that he would change the subject. "Speaking of trust," he said, speaking in haste as though I might interrupt him, "your mother's worries are contagious, and I for one cannot help being contaminated with them. But tell me, has she taken you into her feminine trust?"

I made a disparaging remark about my mother.

"That's not a nice thing to say about your own loving mother," he replied.

I returned to the script as I had rehearsed it on the bus. Surprising even myself, I told him that I doubted very much if Sholoongo had anything but respect for my mother. Why, she had suggested that I drop my father's name and in its place take my mother's.

He lit a cigarette and pulled on it long and voraciously, inhaling a chestful of smoke and exhaling only pencil-thin jets through his nostrils. He wheezed and coughed a series of convulsions like a cat choking on a fish bone. "The girl is making a fool out of you, can't you see?" he said. I argued I didn't believe that Sholoongo meant ill.

And in the silence which followed, Nonno and I listened to a small flock of starlings communicating with one another in liquid squacks, their whistles fruity. To exonerate my calf-love of blame, I explained that since Nonno's, my father's and my name were all dead ends, would it harm anyone if I added my mother's name to this jamboree? Not only was this fair to the woman who carried me for nine months, but in more than one sense it was also a daring thing to do in a country where nobody contemplated such a step. I put this across as though it were my own idea, not Sholoongo's.

He was firm. "I wouldn't advise you to," he said.

"Why not?"

"Because you would be attracting the kind of dastardly comment you would do well to avoid. I'm sure I needn't remind you that

children of unknown male parentage are referred to as the mis-
fortunates, or are burdened with nicknames bearing associations
with their mother. The one exception to this general Somali lore
is the prefix *bah* which is added to a mother's name in order to
identify a woman's offspring or the house-name siblings in a
polygamous situation. This won't apply to you; after all, you are
an only child of a monogamous union."

The adult in me took me over with unprecedented punctilious-
ness as I retorted that our society was unfair to women — this was
a view I had often heard him advance. "Fancy the unfairness of it
all," I went on. "Imagine the outrageousness of it, not to be allowed
to take my own mother's name, if I wish to."

He nodded his head, but said nothing. Nonno was given to drawing pleasure from my changes of mood and to appreciating my
habit of abandoning my child's nature and assuming that of an
adult, not only in the register of my language, choice of vocabulary, but in my bodily gestures, too.

"That'll make your mother most unhappy," he said.

This wasn't the first impetuous confrontation I had had on the
nature of fatherhood with an adult. I was barely seven when I insisted that I had made a woman pregnant, and no one could persuade me that I hadn't. At four I remember seeing a drawing of the
sun which my father had done in very bright colors and ascribing
to him immense powers beyond a mortal's. And as such I believed
that girls were given shape in their mother's wombs, and that boys
emerged out of their father's penises.

Nonno was saying, "If you do not wish to displease your mother
then you must abandon the idea of drawing anomalous attention
to your beginnings."

My mind was elsewhere. I concentrated on the erratic movements of a flycatcher perched on the dead branch of a nearby tree,
a flycatcher hesitating whether to pursue its insect prey, which
was restless and frightened, a victim in flight.

With neither of us speaking, Nonno and I sat eating our fruit
salad in the afternoon's lacework of bright sunshine and criss-cross
shadows, and I watched birds flying solo, in pairs or in flocks,
whereas my grandfather's stare was fixed almost all this time on a
singular bird which moved its head in the repeated figure of seven.

"What's so special about Sholoongo?" he asked.

I started to say something, but stopped just in time.

I dared not betray Sholoongo, my secret-sharer whose daredevilry never ceased to amaze me, who would sneak into my bed in the dark after her half-brother had started to snore in his bed in the same room. I dared not speak of how thrilled I was when I thought of the diabolical nature of what we were up to, so excited that I was able to meet her rivalries with an equal bravado — other boys' braggadocio underlined for me their overtly explicit male self-awareness, although with her, our secretiveness redeemed us. I doubt that I enjoyed the sexual aspect of our relationship, for my sex hadn't *broken*, nor had my voice.

It all started one night when I dared the lark in her, having slipped into her bed for what seemed to be an innocuous cuddle when her abundance sought me out and touched my groin and I was all erection. I held my sex between my thumb and forefinger, and asked whether she could find some cavity for it to dip its head in. She retorted, "Why, you're no bigger than a navel-button, whereas your father hangs down like a leather strop."

I confess my male ego was hurt on the two occasions when women whom I had desired were so indiscreet as to emphasize my smallness. Insulted, I was annoyed and called them whores.

Maybe to hide his discomfort, Nonno prevaricated, then equivocated, and finally spoke like an elder addressing a few words of advice to a youngster. At last, he said, "Apart from the obviousness of their being a blessing or a curse, one's offspring are there to reform the progenitor's arrogant ways. And you've done wonderfully!"

Then he spoke at length as though he were at an elders' council meeting, rhetorical, quoting proverbs, paraphrasing poems, supporting his arguments with a rehashed myth here, a legend there. He was a great orator, quite impressive. But I paid little heed to what he was saying in the dubitable belief that he was talking to himself, not to me. And I let him.

"But she is fun," I said, "she is great fun."

The expression on his face darkened at first, and then I saw his features widen with a grin, a ghost of a grin really, which you might say had a specific task to perform, after it transformed itself into, perhaps, a frown, who knows!

"You take care!" he said. Now I was certain he was hinting that I had better leave.

And then we heard a huge blast coming from the direction of the river, a little to the right of his woods. We had barely given ourselves time to think what it might be when Nonno's housekeeper arrived to announce that a crocodile had swum away with one of the laborers. More men arrived, and one of them guessed that the gunshot we had heard came from Fidow's matchlock, Fidow being Nonno's general factotum. Together with several of his farmhands brandishing spears and all manner of clubs and axes, Nonno left armed with a gun, hoping either to recover the man from the crocodile's jaws or to kill it. The crocodile was known to be a nuisance, a greedy beast, which, having tasted human blood and made off in the recent past with two little girls and their mother, had returned to swim away with the head of that very household, in broad daylight at that.

As he joined the lively excitement generated by the threat posed by the avaricious crocodile, Nonno said to me, "I suggest you take home with you the pot of honey, and that you take care."

Alone I felt light in the head and in my heart, too, and rather too eager to be reunited with Sholoongo whom I would feed on the honey collected by Fidow. The question was, would she take *me* in?

3.

A glint of yet another piece of daredevilry now glittered in Sholoongo's left eye as she pulled me away from where a woman neighbor was engaging her half brother Timir in meaningless banter about the son of another neighbor, whose parents had married him off before his fourteenth year to his first cousin and playmate. Barni, the neighbor, was in her mid-thirties, childless and thrice divorced, had her own place in a rooming house a couple of gates away. She had no profession as such, and, like many women in urban Somalia had no obvious means of support. Everyone knew that this woman was rather keen on establishing closer ties with Sholoongo and Timir because of her interest in their father, Madoobe, whose fascinating style had charmed off her underpants. Once a sailor, Madoobe made his living out of taming wild horses and exporting them to the Middle East. What's more, he was reputed to have been the first Somali ever to employ an ostrich as a guard to mind his horses and zebras, a feat which turned him into something of a celebrity.

"Listen to her," Sholoongo said, glancing in Barni's direction in derision. "Bla, bla, bla, my God, she never stops, and doesn't take my father's no for an answer."

I quoted my mother's wisdom that love is subservient. No one could explain what Barni saw in Madoobe, whose moods were determined by the rise and fall of his fortunes, whose disappearances were shrouded in mystery, away one month, back the next, never condescending to being questioned about what he had done in the intervening period. I knew that Madoobe was asleep at this very hour and Barni hung around, patient like a groupie waiting for an instant's sight of an idol.

But now that we were out of Barni and Timir's hearing, I could tell that Sholoongo was up to some mischief. For she held right under my nose a piece of paper on which she had drawn what I took to be a pair of prominent lips, with a thumb protruding out of a corner. Not knowing what to make of it, I looked at her grin, which appeared to belong to the face of a pirate who had made a sortie into a treasure trove.

"What do you think?" she asked.

I grunted out a few words, because I didn't know how to express myself well. Basically I saw a figure seated in yogic communication, only the sadhu had a leg missing. I had barely formulated my thoughts when I realized that I was actually holding the drawing upside down, and so I said, "What did Timir think? Have you shown it to him?"

"My half brother sees the hand of a vet busily pulling out a calf's forelegs in an attempt to deliver it from its mother," she responded.

Not saying anything, I concentrated all I had by way of a gaze on her chin, which sported a singularly long hair, so lovely to fondle. And then upon her insistence I explained I would rather I demonstrated what I saw, now that I had the drawing the right way up. I extended a middle finger which I held up, with nearly all the other fingers remaining folded away; then I pouted my lips, as if I were sucking a half-bent forefinger. Finally I rubbed my index finger against my lower lip.

She said, "Fingers, mouths and lips, corks!"

I felt very hot blood running into my cheeks and towards my eyes, and for a moment I couldn't see anything or hear my own heartbeat. Sholoongo had inelegant ways of reaching for my crotch or suddenly placing her hands on my groin. To her, I was a cork, she a bottle containing a jinni; in her idiom, she the hole in a flute and I the finger. A little later my ears were drained of the tepid blood of lust and I could hear Barni saying to Timir, "When you have no luck to ride!" And in my memory I tasted my fortune in my saliva, a river of blood, thimblefuls of the finest quality, Sholoongo's, finger-licking savory.

When next I picked up the thread of Barni's conversation with Timir, the woman neighbor was speculating that probably Madoobe had "a heart as hard as the callouses on a camel's tongue" and the young boy nodded his head not because he agreed with her but because he wished to get away from her.

Myself, I was ready to pursue Sholoongo to the ends of the earth, Sholoongo who I had hoped would be in the generous mood of taking me into her. "A thumb in a mouth closing in on the nail!"

Ouch, you're hurting me!

4.

I sensed from the first instant that my mother set eyes on Sholoongo that she would disapprove of her. "She is as dangerous as live wire," she said as soon as the girl was out of her earshot. And her advice? "I would treat her with caution, and as if she were static, wouldn't touch her with my bare hands." In those days, I was interested in the origin of things, how rivers came into being and why they ran and where. I was also keen on knowing where babies began and how, where the dead ended up, and whether, once interred, the buried awoke in the dark of their tombs and were immediately reborn, and if so in what form, child or another grownup, or did they stay curled up, like baby snakes which had been knocked senseless on the head? I was a self-questioner, and my head teemed with the drone of unpacified anxieties buzzing inside me like angry bees. And remember I wanted to change my name. If every given name had its tensions and every newly acquired one its birth pangs, why, so did every new friendship, and mine and Sholoongo's was surely no exception?

It upset my mother to hear me speak fondly of anybody except my immediate family. As far as I knew, I was not an unhappy child, but my mother had reasons to suspect that I should be. She was a worrypot, bubbly and bursting with aqueous energy; she was a flood of words, an avalanche of emotions, the corners of her eyes mere assembly points for her tearful expostulations. Asleep, my mother's cheeks would be stained: could it be that she wept as she dreamt? Often there was vapor circling just close enough to her eyes, which appeared moist like early-morning fog.

My mother suspected others of wanting to undermine her influence over me, her only son. She took pride in her intuitive powers, which she claimed to alert her, in good time, to the inwrought patterns with which Sholoongo's long-term designs on my destiny had been worked. "Come, come," Nonno would try to allay her unfounded fears, "the boy is not yet ten for goodness sake, and Sholoongo is only fourteen."

My mother didn't find Timir vulgar or threatening. To her, he was the saintly figure in a household of fiends. Only her instincts never warned her of his unhealthy influence over me. "In my dreams," my mother once said, "Sholoongo is long-nailed, and is endowed with a stout head, protruding teeth, with legs that are abnormally short, with rounded ears which resemble a ratel's. She is busy for ever digging, without a moment's break."

Any further attempts to persuade her that Sholoongo had no long-term designs on me would subsequently prove to be highly unlikely. Pale with fright, my mother would repeat her nightly nightmare: of a honey badger chewing its way into her viscera. For his part, my father would speak a gentle rebuke, suggesting that she relax. Nonno would equally counsel self-restraint, reminding her that she might be accused of untoward prejudices. "It wasn't the poor girl's fault that she was abandoned to a suckling wolf," he would argue. "Besides, what evidence do you have that she alters her human nature to that of an animal?"

My saliva thickening as though it were dough fermenting, I would explain to my mother that it had been at her own insistence that I was introduced to Sholoongo, her brother and her father, too, "a threesome of originals who had erupted out of nowhere, clowns of a tragic reenactment of a sexual farce," my father's words. My mother would listen very intently to every bend in my every phrase, register my pauses and watch the curves in my words: she might have been listening for some evidence that I had been bewitched.

And she commented, "I lie in the haunted darkness of my sleep, separated as I am from your father by my nightly visions of horror. Hardly have I fallen asleep when I have a night filled with ominous dreams in which ratels chew their way into my viscera, elephants go amok, their huge ears raised in fury, nightly visions in which a hippopotamus crushes through the flimsy fences of my sleep. Where there are graves, they are dug up; the corpses are buried anew not in the ground but up in the trees, in nests intended for birds the size of owls, and the mounds of newly dug-up earth have the appearance of anthills, with openings woven with spiderwebs. I am sorry but my fear is most intimate and I can't rid myself of it. I wish I could."

I sought Nonno's opinion about the possible explanation as to why my mother had such a gut dread of the girl, how come she fed my mother's unconscious with a fodder of frightful dreams? In his reply, Nonno drew my attention to "the idea" of ratels, which, he said, "were partial to the pupae of wild honey, nocturnal animals with the habit of making deep burrows in the earth." He elaborated that there was a subterranean link between a ratel's feeding on carrion and my mother's suspicion that Sholoongo was endowed with the power of transforming her human nature into the animal of her choosing.

As for Timir, her half brother! He arrived, his skin as flaky as the arid desert whence he had come, some provincial capital in the interior of the country, whose residents were as immune to thirst as camels. I had been infatuated with his sister, and hadn't many friends in those days. Because my father liked Timir, my mother acquiesced to the suggestion that the boy give me valedictory encouragement to strike up a friendship with him, to whom I would teach the city ways, and from whom I would learn the culture of the nomads.

How could I ever forget the detailed attention paid to all the arrangements to ensure that my meeting with him would be crowned with immediate success! It might have been a marriage, my father assuming responsibility for its being consummated. There was a period of supervised courtship lasting almost a month, with my father present in his role as an overseer, a counsellor. Meantime, our two families were in each other's houses like the hands of thieves in one another's pockets. And Nonno agreed to lend Madoobe half of the required funds to finance his horse-taming business.

The truth about the boy was sadly more complex. He helped me precious little. If anything, he was more interested in his sex eruptions than he was in the burgeoning fabric of my ideas. At least she and I shared a keenness of spirit, a genuine interest in the beginnings of things. She: who could unravel mysteries; who taught me the basics about what I took to be something akin to the Sufi tradition; who offered the clearest feminist interpretation of the Carraweelo myth yet; Carraweelo, the queen to whose reign is traced the period when the male order of society in the Somalia of old replaced the country's matriarchal tradition, because women were accused of betraying the male vision of things, and of being unable to rule in a just manner.

The benefits I gained from being associated with Timir were no doubt invaluable. His kind interventions helped prevent Sholoongo from interfering with my mother's unconscious. Now that my parents were at their most relaxed, it was Nonno who advised to be cautious, "because volcanoes never become extinct, although they may not be active. Be careful of volcanoes that explode and turn into lakes of lava."

Timir would have *eruptions*, as he called them, and you never saw anyone looking as pleased with himself as he did on the moment of his final coming. He took the sex business as seriously as his father did that of smoking his water pipe, rituals ensuring their unflagging vitality. Timir beat his five when dejected, gave himself a dry quickie when under the weather. He admitted to having done it with other boys before, that he had made love to elder women and prostitutes. But there was nothing as enjoyable as coming in your hand with a little help from the leaves of a *gob*-tree. Only once did I join him in chewing a palmful of leaves, and *although we* exploded together, my eruption wasn't as satiating as when I had an escapade with his sister. Mind you, I often wondered if he and Sholoongo had had it off.

To find out I spent a night at their place.

5.

Tense, I stayed awake for much of the night, feeling drowsy just before dawn. I am a light sleeper and remember stirring in my half-sleep and sitting bolt upright when someone walked past my bed. Dawn hadn't quite broken, nor had I heard the muezzin waking up the faithful Muslims to their duty. Madoobe, their old man, went out of the room, his movements quiet as the night. I presumed he rounded the hut to make water; then no sound issued from him for a long, long time.

Unable to contain the upsurge of my curiosity, I got out of bed and out of the room, and searched anxiously for any change in the general makeup of my surroundings. I was stiff with attentiveness, noticeably uncomfortable, and was able to relax only when I saw

Madoobe standing ebony dark in the near distance. He was stark naked.

In his hand he had an object resembling a wand with which he was rubbing his back, up and down, up and down. In a bid to see better, I moved closer, half-crawling on my haunches. I frightened one of the cows, which, assuming my posture to be perilous, dug its hoofs into the ground with menacing repetitiveness, its horns at the ready, ears rigid from excessive fear, like an angry elephant's. I ceased moving, and remained in a half-bent position for some time before getting up to show my two-legged nature to the heifer. The cow then lost interest in me, and turned its back on me. And where was Madoobe? What was he up to?

He dipped the wand in a metal pail which I presumed to be full of water, and as before rubbed the stick between his shoulder blades. He repeated the same process several times and then finally walked away from the pail, still undressed. Now his nakedness was as prominent as an erection. In a moment he was standing behind a heifer, saying something, his voice even. The nearer I got to him and the cow, the clearer his voice was, only I couldn't decipher his words, maybe because he was speaking to the cow in a coded tongue, comparable to children's private babble. Was he appeasing the cow's beastly instincts by talking to her in a secret language?

A little later and after a lengthy invocation, he inserted his erection in the heifer, still talking, but also breathing hard. I might have been listening to a man and a woman making love, for the cow was *muttering* something too. When at last he came, Madoobe returned to where he had left the metal pail, to wash. He kept uttering a louder salvo in a secret tongue.

A few days later I broached the subject with inordinate caution. I didn't expect a windfall confession, and was surprised to be told that I had misunderstood the symbolic nature of a ritual involving Madoobe and what I took to be a heifer. After all the cow wasn't a cow.

"No?"

"It was a cow," Sholoongo said, "whom my father has decided to domesticate, that's to say, take as his wife."

A couple of days later, Madoobe brought home a young bride. When I pressed them to explain what was happening, Sholoongo took refuge in prevarications. Dissatisfied with the explanations given, I wouldn't let go of the topic. Perhaps to dissuade me from pursuing the matter any further, she told me an African folktale her father had learned from a Nigerian fellow seaman, a traditional tale in which a hunter stumbles on a skull while chasing game. As is expected, he exclaims aloud more to himself than to anyone else, "I wonder how this skull got here?" To his surprise, the skull replies, "Beware of divulging secrets, because that is what got me where I am."

Put out by the confusion brought about by a talking skull, the hunter returns to his village to share his news with the other villagers. His story reaches the king, who insists on being shown the speaking skull. Only there is a snag: the skull does not respond to the king's queries nor to the hunter's appeals or provocation. Enraged, the king orders the hunter's head cut off. Finally, when they are by themselves, the skull asks of the hunter how come he is there, dead. The hunter's head replies, "Talking has brought me here."

Then Sholoongo made me pledge that I would hold her father in deference, apparently because he possessed numerous magical properties.

It is just possible that Nuruddin Farah holds "a key to open any door of the Republic," in which case, it is a very dangerous door. Exile, polyglot and metaphysician, Farah stories the incredible lore and the terrible facts of his original home, Baidoa, in what is now Somalia. He transmits letters, indictments, remedies, memories. He renders the news less remote though nonetheless brutal.

By virtue of idiom and fluency, Nuruddin Farah is a stylist. The writer treads confidently along the intricate webs of tribal gossip and mental absorption. He is a writer of ideas in the high, novelistic sense of the word. His ideas have scope and relevance. In Farah's narratives, a lone woman's thoughts or an old man's or a boy's are the only architecture capable of withstanding the force of oppressive government matched by oppressive faith. Palaver between characters becomes a dialogue which leads to discussion; discussion leads to individual acts which have consequences which can upend the vertical arrangements of the village and the city, and the state, and breed, naturally, discontent. No legacy is left unexamined. Not the postcolonial life nor the life that preceded it nor the one before that. In Farah's world the ideologue is always suspect. "Good writing is subversive, bad writing is not," says the journalist Medina in Sardines.

He has published a trilogy of novels, collectively titled Variations on the Theme of an African Dictatorship: Sweet and Sour Milk (1979), Sardines (1981) and Close Sesame (1983), all of which have been newly reprinted in this country by Graywolf Press. He published the novel Maps in 1986 (released in the United States by Pantheon). He has written other novels, stories, plays and scripts. He has been the recipient of a DAAD Fellowship from Germany, the Tucholsky Literary Award from Sweden and the English-Speaking Union Literary Award. He is one of the central interpreters of exile. Nuruddin Farah's exile is no literary convention, and his books steadily, defiantly monitor the borders without bowing to the exception made of his own successful status as an intellectual.

Farah's books are the articulations of one who has grown accustomed to deciphering the service within the Service, one for whom language is a rudimentary tool, yet the only tool of intervention. "People are always sabotaging your expectations," he said in the course of our first conversation. Something he picked up in his wandering.

— C. D. Wright

From Island to Island
Harold Schimmel

— Translated from Hebrew by Peter Cole

From island to island
on ship's deck, between
islands the same sea

whose depth is not
what it seems at
night with bleached boards

beneath your back your
head on wood of
a sweater from Mykonos

island lambs of sea
foam's salt bequeathed it
color like straw from

wild wheat in late
Iyyar the heat's mist
by day a screen

between you and a
path up toward the
unfamiliar you cross it

and cross again its
like wherever you land
you'll find yourself utterly

Harold Schimmel

there the time from
place to place like
glue that binds you

reach your hand between
thin strips of wood
into a crate where

leaves (still green) keep
a cluster of grapes
fingers alone make it

back to mouth, sweet
hens tied leg to
leg cattle bound by

their legs and you
wrapped in a sleeping
bag you wanted what

did you want entirely
on water just as
entirely under summer sky

the course of a
star falling into the
Archer's range and there

fixed, the mast lamp
moves to the wood's
sway as the wood

moves with the ship
and you see this
light among the sky's

what was it you
wanted is now entirely
yours or maybe you

didn't want more than
this than "this that
there is" in that

it's there truly for
all that the heart's
a bird fluttering some

for what in a
breast-bone cage which
also breathes and expands

according to a script
of land thought a
script of pastness he

who was who makes
you you the engine's
sound a song just

now you're alone without
a head by your
head without knowledge of

what will be don't
scare yourself in any
event it all proceeds

by plan by what
must be (you'd like
to think) important for

you is the phosphor
alive beneath the water
creatures returning light just

like for you the
light's important the wait
till morning always hard

Harold Schimmel

not that night itself
isn't "something" but the
thing itself is morning

light from that we
start you tire yourself
with passing thoughts with

hope of sleep correct
(a question) what did
you want (excuse my

coming back and back
to this) but now
and really what did

you want for the
future accept the time
allotted to do what

with already you've filled
several days and you
have nothing for which

to be sorry (or
so you think) this
is negation's way and

you don't seem like
that shape up I'll
leave you now and

you me for the
time being this once
friends for the journey

———————————

The Pez-candy pink, green, yellow and blue of Strabo's recon-structed map of the Mediterranean basin stretch across the cover of Harold Schimmel's fourth collection of Hebrew poems, Sepher Midrash Tadshei (The Book of the Midrash on "Bring Forth Grass," Genesis 2:11), and in many ways serve as guide to the kaleidoscopic landscape of Schimmel's opera, easily among the most innovative and eccentric in contemporary Hebrew poetry. "The most beauti-ful," the better critics add, a little tired of the standard fare.

Ar'a — Schimmel's ongoing epic of the earthly and the land (cf. Daniel 4:20), of which the new book forms part XII — works the full range of Strabo's world and then some. It also cuts across time as calmly as it moves between cultures, centuries and individual histories. So the reader hang-glides, as it were, from contemporary Jerusalem to Kabbalistic or Troubadour Provence to Boston circa 1955 to idyllic Manhattan to pre-state Palestine and the updated timescapes of the pre-Islamic odes or qasida.

Schimmel is a birdlike arranger, a draughtsman-poet for whom memory is as physical as seeing, and seeing as complex and lux-urious as a meal in all its stages. Like Callimachus, another of his Alexandrian models, he avoids the "carriage roads" in his epic, preferring the risks of the "narrow course." Also Alexandrian is the manner in which his poems highlight the poetry's construction without virtuoso display. The nonessential and awkward are taken in — the new book opens: "It's possible to eat/a slice of radish/on a piece of/French bread and be/happy (here) the walls/are set for song" — alongside Piero della Francesca's The Resurrection and an adaptation of Hölderlin and Alceus that comments now obliquely, now directly, on the religious landscape of Israel during the inti-fada. As in "From Island to Island," the syntax is collapsed through-out, the poems' words pressed up against one another in a dance-floor grammar of sensation, at times reminiscent of the unvocalized, unpunctuated and often unspaced manuscripts of early and me-dieval Hebrew, whose difficulty Schimmel speaks of with affection, and at times more like Portuguese sardines still shimmering in their net.

A multilingual approach to the poem comes naturally to Schim-mel, who was born and raised in the States and then spent sev-eral years in Italy before moving to polyglot Jerusalem, his home for the past thirty-two years. In addition to his books of poems, Schimmel has written extensively on twentieth-century Hebrew poetry and has translated many of Israel's important poets into

Harold Schimmel

English, including Yehuda Amichai (Penguin, 1971), Avot Yeshurun (Jewish Publication Society, 1980) and Uri Zvi Greenberg (forthcoming). Schimmel's own poems have also been translated by Guy Davenport and Gabriel Levin. English essays by Schimmel on the Objectivists have appeared in Sagetreib and in the National Poetry Foundation's Man and Poet series.

"Check thoroughly the skin/of your hands and streams of your veins," he writes in a poem about poetic figures and their fathers, "to understand the anxiety of influence."

— Peter Cole

Variations for My Brother Alfonso
Carlos Germán Belli

— Translated from Spanish by Rose Passalacqua

1 (almost a sonnet)

Where, for your coming change, will you find
earth, light powder, a safe, warm place
in which your tortured feet with tender steps
could balance the blood of your body's weight?

Oh, when will there be a wind to impel your flight,
arriving at your side like a living breath
and dancing you from pole to pole,
flying over the building, the valley, the sky?

For you are fixed like a hard, hard oyster,
with no one to call to you or stroke,
my brother, your newly feathered wings.

Why does the light not cross the threshold
of your bones, that your feet may yet run
for the first time over this very sea?

2

The roads that go through his neighborhood
have not touched the borders of his feet.

The ardent village girl next door
goes by, leaving him to trail behind the world.

His body does not know the openness of space
because the wind has never come to help him.

111

3a

Once upon a time
the sea horse
swayed
between a frozen current
and a warm one —
oh, my brother,
always so far away! —
without once trespassing
on the territory of lime,
without change,
between reflections of the necks
of doves.

But the vegetable green
and the birds
with their wings
will descend to fortify
some day
the inner workings of his feet,
when at his path,
with sensorial pedals,
the hour of revolt arrives.

3b

Like unto the mountain springs
that gush at once
from hardest rock,
through the azure ozone of the wind,
the hour of revolt will grant you skill
to speak,
to write
and float above the clouds,
catching the eye like a dying wisp of ash.

4 (phonemes)

Flush with the ground
baby legg-o lacocalea
little boy legg-o weegeelee

Ya man legg-o locololo
using walking sticks tic tic

In-a the morning legg-o lacocalea
in-a the evening legg-o locololo
in-a the morning electorec
rec recc recccc
in-a the evening electoroc
roc rocc rocccc

Carlos Germán Belli, a contemporary Peruvian poet, has been publishing since the late 1950s (this series of poems is in fact from his first book, Poemas, of 1958), but, while he is highly thought of by several Latin American writers (Mario Vargas Llosa is his most championed champion), he is almost entirely unknown in North America. The fate of poetry on this continent in general partly explains his obscurity here, but I would also point to the belligerent difficulty of his language – its strong attachment to the Spanish Golden Age, its bizarre experimentations, its use of long-dead and just-born vocabulary – and the fact that Belli has no overt revolutionary (in the narrowly political scene) ambitions.

What most attracts me to Belli's poetry is the figure of the amanuensis ("the poor amanuensis of Peru" as he calls him in one poem), a weary clerk who spends his days copying the words of others, filling out forms, watching his life drain away in the tedium. This vocation leads the clerk to the conclusion that he is incapable of original verse and therefore must copy (or half-learnedly copy) the lines of Góngora, Quevedo and company to gain legitimacy. The clerk also has a brother named Alfonso, who has been confined to a wheelchair since childhood and who depends for everything upon his bitter brother. Alfonso becomes a recurring theme in all of Belli's poetry, and the clerk sees their fates as coengendering

113

and coterminous. *Alfonso drools and stutters; he cannot get a date, and he cannot go to the bathroom unassisted; even as a fetus, the clerk tells us, Alfonso was doomed to remain forever in the bottom of the barrel, to be trampled upon by those who are luckier, stronger and richer. The clerk frequently uses the same images, even the same vocabulary, to describe his own lot.*

"Variations" tells an abbreviated version of the story of Alfonso: his brother's vain hopes for him, the plain cruelty of his situation, intimations of his fate and the breakdown of his few capabilities in "phonemes," which gives the pathetic punch line of an unsphinxed riddle. Whatever end we imagine for Alfonso's mostly miserable life, following the chronicle of it in Belli's poetry is for me one of the most compelling alleyways in contemporary poetry. I imagine that when Belli gets the news that this poem has come into print in English, after adjusting the wheelchair at the dinner table, he will with some pride say to his brother, "Our poem will make us famous."

— Rose Passalacqua

From Lac
Jean Echenoz

— Translated from French by Mark Polizzotti

WHEN IT RAINS TOO HARD on the Champs-Elysées, men who have nothing better to do seek out a dry corner and wait for it to pass. Their shelters are bus stops or shopping galleries, cinema lobbies, awnings. Several deluxe automobile firms have long been established on the Champs-Elysées, and in the showrooms their latest prototypes are parked, resting on new tires like wild beasts sculpted in repose: exorbitantly expensive models that these men with enough time to prowl around them, having sought refuge there, can never afford.

Beneath the hoods, like opals in their cases, shimmer engine blocks, twelve V-shaped cylinders, hydraulic thrusters and dual vertical downdraft carburetors. The men prowl in silence, afraid to touch. If they are in twos or threes, they whisperingly compare the options behind the laminated windshields; having opened an audacious door, they don't dare close it. But these showrooms also house elegant young fellows, devoted heart and soul to the head office, whose main function is to joke with the dazzling hostesses batting exhilarating eyelashes, then casually to shut any protruding door. The shutting sound produces a perfect chord, major and lubricated, the way the keys of a new tenor saxophone sound in the void; those prowling around the prototypes admire the sound but feel no liking for the young fellows.

From the Mercedes entrance it appears the rain has calmed, as outside people reappear by the dozens: hundreds of silhouettes, with thousands more that can be divined all around — among them the outline of Franck Chopin, still dressed in a light-colored suit hidden beneath his dark blue raincoat. Above him, in the heavy but clearing sky, two fat zinc clouds weigh like wineskins, from which several little pure-cotton fugitives seem to have escaped.

Chopin walked down the Champs-Elysées, heading from home with a small box in one of his raincoat pockets: a tiny cage of braided wire that housed a live fly. After the traffic circle, the avenue's arboricultural zone unrolled like a green carpet, bordered by wide sidewalks that were prolonged by public squares. On a bench in the first square, a girl sitting in a boy's lap laughed up-roariously at we'll never know what; on the following benches, rows of temps downed silent yogurts. Indistinguishable among the silhouettes, Vito Piranese was surely not far away. He had been watching Chopin for a week: every evening at the same hour the telephone spluttered in his home, and Vito gave the tall blonde a detailed report of Chopin's day; each time there was no deviation from the predicted schedule. It was the last day of his surveillance and Vito was relieved — although it was always the same thing, you get attached to the client. Chopin continued walking toward Place de la Concorde. The sky finished wringing itself out.

From the sidewalk, the travelers from Wisconsin or Schleswig-Holstein had ventured out to the middle of the avenue: caught between opposing traffic flows, they photographed each other in the axis of the Arc de Triomphe, which limply waved its protec-tive nets and giant flag in the distance. Near the Elysée Palace something like a brief official parade unfurled, raising a trail of whistles and sirens, sudden as the downpour had been, sweeping the blacktop clean by momentarily whisking the pedestrians back onto its banks. Chopin looked at everything: the women and cars that caused him so much worry, the official parade.

Like the others, Chopin would also glance at the tenth young woman after the traffic circle walking up the avenue in his direc-tion, the one protected from the fading storm by a multicolored acrylic scarf whose designs recapped an adventure of Tarzan's — but lo and behold that having met, their glances held and did not move away, became a single glance that enveloped them, warmed them, lasted. Chopin was moved: love at first sight, breath comes short and blood pressure goes haywire, ouch my heart is breaking, ay ay ay I am shattered. She passed by, more dazzling than the most ex-plosive hostess from Maserati.

Since all of that had actually happened at the speed of light, the gaze in question known to be highly charged and very piercing, Chopin remained speechless for a moment, without the slightest capacity for rational thought, and when he turned around she had vanished. So it would be in other circumstances that he'd meet Suzy Clair.

Three days later, a party at Bloch's, a fair number of people.

Alongside the pale faces from the laboratory and their spouses were a few women, some not too bad but most not so good. The vast majority were unknown to Chopin, among them three who worked in advertising, two radiologists from Douai, a humanities professor at the Beaux-Arts and two or three Cameroonian students. On the green sofa, Chopin was consoling Bloch for having not been elected, yet another year, to the admissions committee — when he saw her again, standing near the champagne fountain, alone and dressed in something that was also green, with very padded shoulders and zipped diagonally.

"Still, it happens all the time with the union," Bloch sighed while torturing the filter off a Craven. "You remember the effect Fluchaire's motion had." But Chopin had risen, walked toward Suzy Clair without any particular plans, mind empty and heart tripled, mechanically repeating to himself that it happens all the time.

Although it could have been an icebreaker, no, they did not mention their glance on the Champs-Elysées: they started from zero. Wondered, just to see, how many mutual friends brought them together at Bloch's: zero. Exchanged names, a few notions of their lives, some idea of their possessions. Chopin stared excessively at Suzy Clair, leaving her eyes an instant for her shoulders and skipping via her chest toward her left ring finger, devoid of ring even though her possessions notably included, as she was just informing him, a husband who worked in Foreign Affairs and answered to the name of Oswald. Right. "With me," said Chopin, "it's flies."

As she smiled, he told her about some of the flies he was studying — the brown ones, reddish-brown ones, red ones, orange ones and violet ones; about the vitreous ones and the ferruginous ones with yellow knees and green or bright blue eyes; and about the more comical aspects of their behavior. And as she deigned to smile some more at his tie, which bore a minuscule embroidered elephant, nothing was simpler for Chopin than to evoke the habits of elephants, those who crossed the Alps or tromped on foot down Rue Saint-Denis; those whose tusks they used to carve in Dieppe when he was a teenager.

Suzy Clair's childhood, back when she was still Suzy Moreno, was spent in Blois. At present, Blois was no more than a small, overexposed, black-and-white memory, even though at a very young age Suzy had become the princess of the high rises: nothing

117

was decided without her say-so in the parking garages and sub-basements of housing developments, standing near the river or leaning over the pinball.

All this, of course, would not be told in one sitting, but via episodes with no particular chronology, in the course of three meetings that week. First Sunday at the movies, sitting motionless beside each other in the dark, brushed by sweeping colors and feverish violins. Then Thursday, at his place; immediately they embraced and admired each other, shivering in little wrinkles as if on the surface of water. But the following Sunday, in the Shakespeare garden of the Pré Catalan, Suzy stared at her nails and said that maybe they shouldn't see each other anymore. Right. "Well," said Chopin, "I don't believe that."

Not far away, like navy blue specters, stooped gardeners tended the bedside of the alley of Scottish moor that was supposed to evoke Macbeth. "So tell me," Chopin said gently, "what is it? Your husband?" She shrugged her shoulders and shook her head no. A pause, of which a blackbird took advantage to attempt an audition. Lowering his head, Chopin gave the young woman a once-over, checking himself in passing in the little diamonds of mirror attached to her ears. He lightly kicked at balls of briar, upset witches' shadows, while Suzy Clair told him what had become of Oswald.

Oswald, when Suzy had first met him, had to his name only a black motorcycle, onto whose rear seat she had immediately climbed; then they had ridden through the city, almost through the night. The cold air brought tears to Oswald's eyes, which rolled along his temples and were lost between Suzy's lips as she pressed against him. Several drinks in an after-hours bar failed to dispel their salt taste, and several months later a son, Jim, was born. After three quick intramural changes of address, Oswald swapped the cycle for a station wagon; then they left the capital for its suburbs.

That was six years earlier, when Jim wasn't yet six months old. They'd found themselves in a new building, in the heart of a new town southwest of Paris. Foreign Affairs forced Oswald to be away fairly often, most of the time for two or three days in Geneva. Each time he stayed in the same hotel with interchangeable rooms and called Suzy as soon as he arrived; the next day he wrote her a postcard, leaning on open binders overflowing with statistics, diagrams and grids.

In the winter, his postcard written, Oswald stared through the hotel window at the curb defined by a snow blower, watching the trolleys in outdated hues that rolled with a sound of felt. Everything seemed muffled, phonically insulated, as if the little school-age figures in bright parkas who covered the dirty white sidewalk had declared a plug war on the world's ears. The text on the back of the postcards was always short, private, generally affective (I'm kissing you in the same spot as Tuesday) or informative (the chambermaid could be Sophie's double), and the front depicted Lake Geneva in every season, or else the hotel facade with a pinprick in place of his window. These cards almost always arrived after Oswald's return home.

Over the harsh winter in which — double victory — Jim began walking and pronouncing the adverb No, Oswald had to travel to the banks of the lake more often. During one of his absences, it got so cold that the leaders and gutters exploded, the ice propping up the cornices with marbled caryatids fringed with stalactites; this time, no telephone call or postcard arrived from Geneva. On his return, Oswald announced that the trip had been his last, that he would no longer have to go to Switzerland. He had brought back for his bride two little compasses, fashioned into cufflinks, that really told direction under curved glass. While Suzy looked for a blouse so as to fix them immediately to her wrists, Oswald, staring out the window, suggested they move. Now that the cycle of meetings in Geneva was over, he would have to show up more often at the ministry; it might be a bit simpler to go back to Paris, and besides I've kind of had enough of this town, what do you think?

Very soon they heard of an apartment whose square footage and exposure would do just fine, in the north of Paris, on the metro line separating the bad part of the Seventeenth arrondissement from the good. Streetside, their windows would overlook the wide trench in which trains came and went from the Gare Saint-Lazare, and the ones in back would open onto two small factories — one producing mirrors and the other making they'd never know what, but whose chimney permanently emitted a compact spindle of very white smoke.

Several days later, therefore, their plants and furniture found themselves sitting on the sidewalk, giving each other doubtful looks, nervous about this departure for the unknown. Then they were hoisted with the boxes of books and clothes into a forest green truck, on which a light green leopard, painted on its flanks, connoted speed. To transport the more precious possessions — six paintings, twelve pieces of jewelry, an especially sensitive crystal service and the cat — an upstairs neighbor named Jacqueline Monteil lent her car, an elementary Fiat that she seldom used. Suzy would act as scout, with Jim in the back of the Fiat lassoed into his baby seat. Oswald would join them once his file folders were packed in the station wagon.

All kinds of folders: with straps, elastics or strings, rings or hooks, spiral-bound or clasped; a hole in the covers of some of them let you pull them out with one finger. Alphabetical and blue or tan, they had covered three walls of Oswald Clair's study up to the ceiling, sometimes towering in double-thick cliffs. Oswald had just stacked them, from A to D, in the front of the car, and hands on hips he was now wondering if it would be the R's or just the W's that would keep the hatchback from closing. Suzy made him a sign with her lips as she started up; Jim waved a fist squeezed onto a one-legged doll. Oswald raised a preoccupied hand, with the smile of a distracted myope.

Suzy Clair, then, thought she was crossing the suburbs for the last time, skirting Créteil-Soleil before joining the beltway. Cords of Vincennes wood paraded by to her right; to her left were hectoliters of Seine, then Marne. Jim had fallen asleep almost immediately. When Suzy twisted in her seat to check her son in the rearview mirror, the seat belt cutting a bit between her breasts, she remembered being in the back of the cream-and-maroon Aronde, on Sundays, when her fidgety parents went to take some air around Blois; she calculated that Jim would be four or five before he started asking if they were there yet every five minutes. An Austerlitz sun shone on Rue de Rome when Suzy parked the Fiat beside the grillwork fence bordering the railway trough. The truck was already waiting at the foot of the new home; the green leopard men came and went, each one under his object, banding together to carry the heavy pieces.

Having very little known family, Oswald boasted no furniture inheritance, and from Suzy's side came just a large willow chest from an uncle's butcher shop, promoted to the rank of bedside table: having known only the acid universe of sawdust, cold and cutting slabs, with no prospects other than to contain bloodstained rags and knives its whole object-life long, this trunk was suddenly facing a warm and miraculous retirement, stuffed with comfortable winter clothing, furs and cashmere, angora, and now it was being carried on men's backs toward the heights of Rue de Rome. Except for this, then, Oswald and Suzy had bought all their furniture together, most of it conceived in the first third of the century. The copy of a Marcel Breuer chair, Eugene Schoen bookcase or René Prou desk; a reissued Edouard-Wilfrid Burquet lamp: such was the Clairs' taste.

Suzy set Jim down in the largest room in the middle of the apartment, on a rolling device encircled by blankets, in the company of stuffed toys and rubber objects; from there, the little boy could easily watch the movers at work. Then she wandered through the apartment. When the large biceps came to ask her gently where do you want this, ma'am, she smiled at them and raised her eyebrows, her shoulders. And when they were almost finished she left the child with them for a moment, leaning in a placid arc over the walker while she went out to get them some beer. She wandered through the neighborhood awhile before finding an Arab market on call, where a very young girl tended the cash register; Suzy felt like kissing her, then returned home by another path. She walked quickly, straight ahead, glancing in every direction while hugging the six-pack in her arms.

Once the green leopards had been refreshed and dispersed toward their truck, hopping onto the seats and starting up as they whistled through their teeth, Suzy put two chairs around a table, installed Jim there with some Magic Markers and began pacing around the apartment again. While injecting a cookie into his nose, Jim immediately began engraving the table's wax polish with the wrong end of the green marker. Suzy came by from time to time to borrow the red one, to sketch a project, jot down an idea for a room or the floor plan of the kitchen. Finally, it was only when the child manifested some impatience, scattering the pieces of an overly abstract puzzle, that she noticed she hadn't removed her coat. At that point, she began periodically checking the clock.

She had turned up the heat when they arrived, but the ambient air remained freshly moved-into, and the beginnings of warmth sounded hollow amid the covers, boxes and transient furniture. Suzy undid her coat, then Jim's jacket, which had been buttoned up to his ears. She plugged in the radio, turned it on, stayed for two seconds on two or three stations, switched it off. When evening came, she lit two lamps — a banal one and the Wagenfeld — then remembered the telephone the way one remembers a forgotten animal: the instrument was huddled against the darkest corner of one of the rooms, linked by its cord to the wall as, by its leash to a pole, an abandoned dog in summer.

Night had fallen, all lamps were lit; Jim had been fed and put to bed in a rough draft of his room. By now, Suzy was nowhere but on the telephone. She called in all directions: constantly at their old apartment, where no one answered; Jacqueline Monteil, who hadn't a clue; as well as her brother Joe, her friend Blanche and even a guy named Horst who'd more or less been her agent or her lover when Suzy had posed for the camera before meeting Oswald. She hesitated, then called the ministry, but no one was there at this hour: just an orderly who didn't, and didn't want to, know anything. She remembered one of Oswald's colleagues whose wife had gotten incredibly drunk at the dinner celebrating the closing of the Vienna conference. She called them, but the colleague didn't know anything either; she could sense him alone in his room, dressed in his bathrobe, his wife at detox cure. It grew late and Suzy stopped telephoning, let the instrument take a breather. Perhaps Oswald was trying to call her.

When brother Joe arrived an hour later, Suzy was turning the yellow pages of a phone book without looking at them. To Joe befell, all night long, the vain task of calling the hospitals and police stations. As usual, Suzy slept poorly. The next day she called the ministry and asked to speak to Oswald's secretary or assistant, his aide, a colleague, I don't know, somebody like that. She was transferred to someone who transferred her to someone else, went through half a dozen extensions, two or three of which were still busy. In the final account, it seemed it was impossible to find anything like what she wanted in the entire network; but the police came of their own accord once Suzy had called the ministry.

The police didn't seem very determined. They came to see Suzy, Suzy went to see them. In the days following they came back, she went back, it dragged on; no one found anything. Oswald had vanished without a trace, like a common pebble that falls into the ocean at night, with no one there to witness its imperceptible drop into the lapping of dark waters, its negligible splash in the turmoil. It was as if nothing had happened. And from that point on nothing would happen, except for a call from a garage mechanic in Villejuif one week after the move. The man explained that someone had left him a station wagon the week before, in front of the garage, with nothing in it except the keys and registration in an envelope in the glove compartment, plus money for a week's worth of storage and the number of a Mrs. Clair, Paris Seventeenth, and what should he do with the car? Absolutely nothing more after that, and now six years had gone by.

Having left the Shakespeare garden, they crossed the Bois de Boulogne. Chopin's Karmann Ghia rolled through the green shadows, the radio played Nat King Cole and Suzy continued to talk about Oswald. So he was, just like Chopin, part of an organization in which people described phenomena, induced hypotheses and discovered laws, except that Chopin dealt in the mores of flies and Clair in bloc politics. A man of tact and science, Chopin stayed attentive to everything Suzy had said about her husband, methodically, as if she were speaking about a new type of Siphonaptera; scrupulously he steeled himself against his consciousness, so as not to wonder overly why he should give a shit about this clown.

On Rue de Rome, the kid wasn't there — weekend in Blois — and Suzy offered to make tea. "After this, I won't say any more about it," she said. But she returned from the bedroom with a large flat box, which she opened: little identity photos floated on the surface of a bed of pictures.

Private pictures, marriage at the town hall of the Fourth arrondissement — Suzy showed her father in the photograph, a dry little man with eyes glazed by forty-five years in the skin trade. Professional pictures, during a lecture or conference abroad: for example, at the Eisenstadt colloquium Oswald was in the upper right, between Professor Ilon Swarcz and the military attaché Asher Padeh; in the first row smiled the delegates Veber and Ghiglion. These pictures were somewhat jumbled, as Suzy often followed her husband when the colloquia were held in warm climates: in the margin of their days in Bogotá, there they were squeezed behind a restaurant table, under the lens of a roving camera, Suzy blinking at a tropical flashbulb that was rudely reflected in Oswald's eyeglasses.

Whatever the photo, Oswald Clair never seemed very happy to be caught within its parameters; one always felt him twisting out of the frame, snared by what lay outside the visual field. At the very bottom of the flat box, a bilingual identity card established by the Canadian authorities for a trip to Vancouver offered a few details about his person (5 feet 9 inches, 139 pounds; distinguishing marks, scars, tattoos, deformities: none), with the simultaneous print of his ten fingers (if any prints are missing, speculated a blue note, indicate the reason; if because of an amputation, it blushed, please give the date).

Soon afterward they went into Suzy's room, where they spoke no more of Oswald; then Suzy went back to the kitchen to finally make that tea. Still in the bedroom, Chopin listened to her bustling about in the distance, pizzicato of utensils and gargle of boiling water, while looking at the images on the walls: a seaport by Horace Vernet, a paragraph by Saul Steinberg tacked above the desk. And on the opposite wall, external daylight on sepia carpet, forty-three maharajas posed in 1925 for the Kapurthala jubilee. Color photography was just coming into use then: if not for several pale, primitive pinks and greens, a possible yellow, a so-called brown, one would almost have thought the photo was in black and white, as it hung over a large bed covered with a lemon-and-strawberry coverlet that was now all rumpled, wilted under the heat of bodies embracing.

The sun on the morning after next was exemplary: blocking onsets of depression, the anticyclone was working like a charm. Chopin had just chosen a patternless tie, lightly barred by a very fine blue line on gray. Once knotted, ready to go out, he made a detour via the kitchen, then via his hatchery.

The flies lived in a plexiglass case equipped with a thermostat, a thermometer and a hygrometer. Inside the case, a glass cube contained pupae resting on a bed of sawdust, and inside another cube made of fine netting, the flights of hatched insects crossed paths. As two of them had in fact taken a fancy to each other, Chopin enjoyed studying a brief coitus under a magnifying glass before tossing the couple a crumb of pork rind.

He was master of his time, accountable to no one for his work at the museum, expected to produce barely two or three articles per year. No schedule, because there was no woman in his life, because he was forever undecided — Carole always being too much of what Marianne would never be enough. In the elevator, a hand more decisive than Chopin's had inscribed *Nacera I love you* in large, feverish red letters near the numbered buttons, where their addressee could hardly miss them; they weren't signed, but Nacera would no doubt have a pretty good idea. Chopin pressed the lower button. Ground floor: the elevator gate, three steps, the glass door, the mailbox-edged foyer and the main entrance.

The mail: usually a brochure or a bill, less often a handwritten letter. And nearly every day two or three flyers, addressed to him personally when Chopin had carelessly let himself get stuck in some file, caught in the web of a list. Most tenants blindly discarded these tracts in the large common bin, others gave them merely a glance. Out of habit and principle, all the while worrying the paper between his fingers like fabric, Chopin read them all.

Apart from a postcard and the catalogue of a specialized book dealer in Zurich, the day's ads concerned a singles' club and a plumber, while a third, emanating from a travel agency, proposed an Adriatic cruise under sunny skies, from Otranto to Venice with a stop in Rimini. *Rimini revealed,* said the pamphlet. "Jesus!" thought Chopin.

A little girl had just pushed open the building door with great effort, run across the foyer and bounded into the elevator, her steps replicating the supple echoes of a young monkey in a baobab, but Chopin heard none of this: he was still staring at the flyer. He folded it in four and slipped it into his jacket pocket, stuffed the mail into his other pocket, and, returning to the elevator, Nacera I love you, rode back up to his apartment.

He unfolded the flyer on his desk, his lamp lit even though the sky rushed whole through the panes. He went to the bathroom to fetch alcohol and cotton, then looked in a drawer for an X-Acto blade and two glass slides that he cleaned with the alcohol, with care, sitting at his desk. Then, leaning over the flyer, he enlarged the word *Rimini* with his magnifying glass, heading for the dot over the median *i*.

Calculating the best angle for detaching this dot from its support, Chopin slid the cutting edge of his blade along the typographical sign, which came unglued, unstuck and tumbled down from Rimini toward one of the glass slides; Chopin caught it under the other slide and fastened the two together with tape. Then he stood up and went to get the enlarger, stored in its box on the floor of the entryway closet at the foot of the vacuum cleaner, between empty suitcases and stacks of journals, among twenty-six unoccupied shoes. Having had nothing to put under its lens for some time, the enlarger was extremely dusty. Chopin wiped it off and settled down to work.

Once the microdot was developed, enlarged and viewed through a slide projector, its contents consisted of a series of letters that made no immediate sense, organized in groups of four, embellished

125

with little black boxes here and there. Chopin read the arrange-
ment several times, searching his memory for two or three elementary grids; he found the key fairly quickly. The text was not
too cruelly coded: he entered it by a double substitution technique,
using the Vigenère Tableau. "You haven't lost your touch," said
the microdot. "We're glad." It was signed Colonel Seck and followed
by a suggested meeting, in one hour at Square Louis XVI.

Letting the square's gate close by itself, Chopin thus headed one
hour later toward the expiatory chapel that stood in its center. At
the building's threshold, a limping guard dressed in a cultural blue
uniform handed him a brand-new brochure describing this off-
putting monument, a cube-temple with a small dome introduced
by a doric peristyle. Chopin perused it like anyone else as he
walked down the stairs, at the foot of which, standing before the
dark marble altar, a navy blue–clad sexagenarian with very white
teeth seemed to be meditating. "It's been a long time," said Colonel
Seck.

"Three years," Chopin specified. "We've never met here before,
have we?"

"The monument is out of the way," said Colonel Seck. "No one
around. It's so depressing, and people aren't *that* desperate. Would
you have a bit of time these days?"

"It all depends," said Chopin.

"Perfect," the colonel translated. "I might be in need of your
services one of these days. Don't stray too far."

"But I thought," went Chopin hopelessly.

"I know," the colonel admitted, "I know."

They resurfaced toward ground level; the chapel guard was waiting at the top of the stairs. Ignoring Chopin, he made a beeline for
Seck, swaying humble shoulders, his pupil tilting upward beneath
his visor. "Colonel," he said, "do you remember Roquette?"

"My word," said Seck, "the name doesn't immediately ring a
bell."

"Roquette, Colonel. Blida, the night of the third, the rebels' surprise attack, and then Roquette, Colonel, a ruddy sort. Saxophon-
ist in the Fourth Engineering, don't you remember? He's looking for something, he's got problems. He'd like to start over, like
me."

"Fine, I'll see what I can do," said Seck. "Tell him to write me a
note, just send it there."

He extracted a minuscule card from his jacket, briefly wincing as if he were pulling an extraneous chest hair. The guard moved a bit closer, his iris confidential. "What should we do, Colonel?" he whispered through his nostrils. "What should we do with you for this country?"

"We'll be in touch, Fernandez," Seck murmured, impatiently handing him the calling card. "We'll keep you posted. Be a good fellow now, and fall out."

Grabbing Chopin by the sleeve and yanking him toward the square's exit, he explained all the concerns associated with watching over the retirement of these men who were too old and damaged to keep fighting: "Of course, it's not my job to look after them myself. There's a special department for that, perfectly capable case workers. But things go faster when they come through me and they know it."

He was silent all the way to the gate, which he pulled, holding it open, stopping at the square's threshold to speak again, the way one might tell one's guest the main thing when seeing him out, on the landing while waiting for the elevator: "You'll get your full instructions in a few days. If there's a problem, I can always be reached by the phone booth on Rue Lafayette, you know, at the corner of Rue Bleue."

For a moment he tilted his forehead toward his long, black, very shiny shoes, imagining himself on his own pedestal; then he snapped his fingers in the void. A green taxi instantly stopped beside him. He plunged inside and shut the door before giving his destination. The green car and the colonel left the perceptible world via the western length of Boulevard Haussmann; Chopin began walking in the opposite direction. A very pretty redhead crossed the boulevard with a backpack, oh, no, it's a baby, what do you know, then an empty café offered its services on Rue Lavoisier. The proprietor seemed like a caseless judge behind his bar. Chopin chose a seat by the large window.

"Coffee," he pronounced tersely. "And a glass of water."

These words echoed in the deserted establishment, then silence returned, pierced through at regular intervals by the synthetic voice of a pinball machine that reiterated its presence by emitting the same formula every five minutes. Welcome, Doctor Bong.

Chopin pondered the surface of his coffee, absorbed as if in a movie screen, projecting on it a clip from his first meeting with Colonel Seck — his recruitment, in other words. He had been going through a bit of a Sahel back then, and the colonel's offer seemed not altogether inappropriate, richly hued, gilt-edged and finely dappled with a hint of blackmail. It would provide a convenient oasis; he accepted. He had immediately been trained in the use of microdots and blank carbon, dead drops, the art of losing tails and all the rest of that crap. Remember, I'm only doing this for a little while, he'd specified at one point; it's just for a year or two, don't forget. You're absolutely right, the colonel had exclaimed, a year or two, that's exactly what one should tell oneself. Besides, just between you and me, the best of us all said the same thing at first. Welcome, Doctor Bong.

Chopin downed this excellent memory in one gulp, then relaxed in his seat. Patting his pockets, he found the morning's mail, which he opened with the handle of his coffee spoon. The bookseller from Zurich sent him a recension of out-of-print entomological works of which he owned several copies — they would end up knowing everything there is to know about those flies, after which there would be nothing more to say about them. Perhaps they had already reached that point, moreover, which would explain why Chopin had all the time in the world, glued like those flies to the large window. Only the postcard remained, one of its sides depicting a calm ocean. *I'll be waiting for you Wednesday evening at my place*, said the other side. *Suzy.*

So on Wednesday evening he showed up at her place; it was the first time he'd come after dark. Suzy had nothing to drink but a drop of sorghum liquor, brought back from China by a friend and sticky as old candy. They nonetheless had two or three shots of the stuff, and Thursday morning, before opening the first eyelid, they were already moving against each other, examining and exploring each other in every detail, plains and valleys, ravines and hills, interchanges and one-way paths — all this might have gone on forever, but the alarm clock had just rung.

They spent one more short moment kissing, then Suzy got up. Chopin watched her reach down toward a kind of Japanese robe: her very white back shot through with beauty marks sketched the negative of a summer's night, a constellation on her shoulder with the North Star in the curve of her hip. Then she left the room to go see to Jim, whose twelve-tone intergalactic siren had been bearing witness to his awakening for some time already.

As the bed was growing cold, Chopin got up in turn, dressed while gazing out the courtyard window. The mirror factory hadn't yet opened its doors, but the other one was already vomiting its thick, tireless, immaculate spurt, as if perpetually called upon to announce the election of a new pontiff, an *habemus papam ad libitum*. Two cars were parked at the back of the courtyard; their gleaming hoods reflected the building facades, which reached into the sky. Behind the closed door echoed the clatter of breakfast cups.

He had just tucked in his shirt when Suzy reentered the room, dressed up to her mirror earrings, her very red lips giving off a quick smile. Indicating to Chopin that coffee was made, she searched in a drawer for her Geneva cufflinks, which she fixed to her wrists then quickly showed him, smiling once more: when Suzy was in a hurry the magnetized needles, already jittery, quivered as strongly as if they were approaching the North Pole. She went as she'd come, leaving the door ajar, rushing toward the deep heart of the jungle with her compass and mirror. Chopin adjusted the knot of his tie before leaving the bedroom.

Dressed in an apple green sweatsuit over whose thigh paraded the yellow words *Carolina Moon*, the young Jim Clair was sitting alone in the kitchen before an amalgam of cereals and a cartridge of chocolate cookies. He returned Chopin's greeting, pointed to the coffee pot and dove back into a *Super Giant Uncle Scrooge*. The telephone rang in the main room; they heard Suzy pick up. Chopin drank a little coffee while looking around him: on an armchair, a cat sat absolutely still, as if dead.

Suzy stayed on the phone for quite a while. Her forward-leaning bust was suddenly framed in the doorway, held back by the spiral of the telephone cord, one hand covering the receiver: "Jim, it's eight o'clock," she whispered forcefully, "kindly get ready." "Yeah, yeah," said Jim. "I'm coming, Franck," she added. "Yes," smiled Chopin.

"So," Jim said unexpectedly, "you like my mom?"

Chopin's spoon twirled in the cup under its own steam; he tried to trap it while pondering the question.

"Children should be seen and not heard," he limited himself to suggesting.

"The rules have changed," young Jim reminded him.

Once Chopin had left for Avenue des Ternes, Suzy brought her son to school, the density of children on the sidewalks increasing as they got closer. Jim said *Hey* to some of them, in a distant tone. A few briefly consulted him in whispers, in one or two words, about some swimming pool or homework business, while throwing circumspect glances Suzy's way; Jim settled matters. His mother, too, greeted the other mothers: the young and beautiful ones with triumphant smiles; but she also smiled at the defeated.

She made a large detour via Place Malesherbes up to the Parc Monceau on her way home. While walking, she rummaged in her bag among her keys and papers, her Kleenexes, a datebook containing a photo of Jim at age five, a blue woollen sock from the same Jim at age two used for holding change, a homeopathic vial, two Band-Aids, a hairpin, a stainless steel clip and a tube of lipstick. From this bag she pulled out a pair of ultra-light headphones, which a stem like a spider's leg clamped to her ears, then chose one of the cassettes lying at the bottom of the bag, a quintet in C-major that she listened to only as far as the scherzo. Among these tapes there was also a Berlitz Russian course, the voice of her astrologer charting her horoscope for the next two years, *Their Satanic Majesties Request* and *Let It Bleed* and the soundtracks from three or four films. She picked one of the soundtracks at random, listened to a few lines of repartee ("Cognac? Before dinner? Why not?"); then andante sostenuto she returned to the quintet in C.

Once in front of the Parc Monceau, Suzy didn't feel like crossing the gates' ornaments toward the lawns' orderliness. She now headed home. Elderly workers emerging from the mirror factory carried long cheval glasses without looking into them, no longer interested in the reflection of their persons, their labors or any of the things that went with them. Below Rue de Rome, the Dieppe local intersected with an express bound for Brest.

She straightened up the house a bit — the kitchen, then the bedrooms and by capillarity everywhere else — vaguely checking to see if Chopin might have forgotten some object, or even left one there on purpose; but no, nothing. At around eleven, she sat at the table in her bedroom and began work, which these days consisted of writing a catalogue of accessories for wealthy ladies — easy and well-remunerated work, which the typewriter wrote almost by itself, each *ding* at the end of a line announcing the birth of a chubby little banknote. Short and close together, two rings at the door straddled the dings of the typewriter bell. Having lowered the radio's variety shows, Suzy got up to answer them.

The visitor was a well-built young man sporting a crew cut, a signet ring on each pinky, a chain around his neck. Drenched in very fragrant aftershave, he smiled, exhaling health as if he'd just stepped from the shower, eye half-closed on a soap bubble that had gotten in. "Come in, Frédéric," Suzy smiled with moderation; then she turned back toward the main room, letting her visitor close the door himself. "Caramba!" he silently exclaimed as he followed her. "That's got to be the best pair of legs in the greater Paris area." Crossing the latter after having sat, Suzy motioned toward a chair and the visitor took a seat, averting his gaze.

"I think I might have something," said this young Frédéric. "I think I told you, I have a friend who can get in there, I mean, who maybe could explain the thing to you himself, in a few days."

"When?" Suzy wanted to know.

As Hitchcock and Godard do in film, Jean Echenoz uses so-called "popular" genres — detective and adventure fiction in Cherokee *(1983) and* Double Jeopardy *(1986), or, in the case of* Lac *(1990), the spy thriller — both as an homage to these "lesser" literary forms that have shaped his generation and as a fresh lens through which to view the more traditional, "weightier" stuff of which art and life are made. Specifically,* Lac, *a tale of spies and flies, interweaves the fates of Chopin, entomologist and recalcitrant secret agent; Oswald, a young foreign affairs employee who vanishes en route to his new home; and Suzy, Oswald's wife, who becomes enmeshed in a tangle of deceit and counterdeceit (in part through her own relations with Chopin) — classic thriller material on the whole, very much what one would expect to find in the innumerable séries noires that line train-station book racks and Echenoz's shelves.*

In Echenoz's world, however, these genres are no mere convention, but a direct access to the specific anomie of modern times. As one French critic noted, Echenoz's particular shrewdness consists in having recognized that we now live not in some holistic moral center, but in "the mind's suburbs," where dwell "fugitive agglomerations of autonomous individuals whose thoughts, dreams, fantasies and behavior obey a tired and worn-out logic, a morality akin to permanent channel-surfing, their passions always unfinished." Beckett prowled these suburbs, of course, and some of his astringency appears to have been handed down to Echenoz, his adoptive fellow countryman and, in France, listmate on the Editions de Minuit roster, alongside such other Echenoz godfathers as Butor and Robbe-Grillet.

What saves all this from being arid unto death — what made me want to translate Echenoz's books as of my first reading — is the comically wry precision of his gaze. I have encountered few writers who can so economically pinpoint a moment, fleeting object or minor player, bringing it in the flash of a subordinate clause into as much life as most protagonists enjoy their whole hero-existence long. Like the great film directors (again), Echenoz understands that a simple gesture, or the placement of an object in a room, is worth all the deep psychologizing that one can throw at a reader. We are the grimaces we make, the cars we poorly drive, the music we don't appreciate. The rhomboid Bock in Cherokee is defined from the outset by his "wide creamy tie [and] chocolate-colored polyester shirt, which made him look like something halfway between a pimp and breakfast." And in Double Jeopardy, Paul's hobbling ineffectualness shines through in his hesitant taste for a model of shoe "decorated on either side with a kind of lapel, like a collar, which gave the laces the appearance of a Texan string tie, knotted, as if around a neck, at the base of the ankle."

Hitchcock once suggested that the best way to convey a particular sentiment is to let the face drain of expression; so Echenoz, in bleaching his landscape of all but these seemingly commonplace details, clears the ground for a starker, but by the same token less encumbered, glimpse of our human, all-too-human motivations. The glimpse is not always pretty, but it is in an incongruous way often funny, and usually — like it or not — true.

— Mark Polizzotti

Five Poems
Bei Dao

— Translated from Chinese by David Hinton

MORNING

those fish entrails as if lights
blink again

waking, there's salt in my mouth
just like the first taste of joy

I go out for a walk
houses learning to listen

a few trees turn around
and someone's become a hero

you must use hand gestures to greet
birds and the hunters of birds

SEEING DOUBLE

who knocks on doors in moonlight
watching flowers bloom on stone
musicians wander the corridors
it makes your heart pound
not knowing if it's morning or night
flowing water and goldfish
adjust the direction of time

a wounded sunflower
points the way
the blind stand around in
light beyond understanding
clutching anger
assassin and moon
walk toward a foreign place

BACKGROUND

the background needs revising
you can return to your hometown

a few words time shook
lift into flight, sink back
divulging no news whatsoever
a string of failures is the shortcut
through silent grandstands in heavy snow
pressing toward the huge bell of old age

and high tide at the family gathering
is a matter of alcohol content
the woman closest to you
always wears the worried look of history
gazes into snowdrifts, goes empty

darkness in which voles believe absolutely

THIS DAY

wind knows well what love is
the summer day flashing palace color
a lone fisherman surveys
the world's wound
a struck bell swells
people strolling in the afternoon
please join the year's implications

someone bows to a piano
and someone's carrying a ladder past
sleepiness has been postponed a few minutes
only a few minutes
the sun researching shadow
I drink water from a bright mirror
looking at the enemy within

the tenor singing
like an oil tanker in a rage
I open a tin can at three in the morning
and let some fish ablaze loose

REALM

where did tonight begin
travelers on a wall drinking toasts
mingling wit with lights

who practices relentlessly
to perform their own life
the bald pianist
whose house a bright sun graces

imitating silence
my hand scrawls across the desk

people chase dogs into history
then excavate
and make them gatekeepers
an old couple turns and hurries away
looking back with a savage gaze

February summons country carpenters
to prop up the sky anew
and springtime beyond the road
allows our obsession with the long view

Bei Dao

Bei Dao is by now well known as the most prominent literary voice in China's political opposition. His work has been not a matter of overt political statement, but the rescue of subjectivity from a government that depends on its suppression. To do this, Bei Dao has employed increasingly surreal procedures, procedures he speaks of as opening a space in official discourse, in the program dictating how people live and think and feel.

Although this program is not so blunt an instrument in the West, it is nonetheless real. Exiled after Tiananmen, Bei Dao has become an increasingly international poet, addressing the various guises this program takes in the world today. Major collections of his work have appeared in many languages, and he is often reported to be on the short list for the Nobel Prize. His work recalls China's ancient masters: clear resonant images set in sharp juxtapositions. But his are decidedly modern clarities, adrift on the terrible mystery of today's world-historical forces. His poems are constructed from splinters of a civilization frittering itself away in a ruins of the spirit; and at the same time, in the private space they create, the poems open forms of distance from those ruins.

— David Hinton

Six Poems
Joachim Sartorius

— Translated from German by Sibylle Schlesier,
Nathaniel Tarn and Rosmarie Waldrop

ALEXANDRIE, BOULEVARD DE RAMLEH, 1903

As penciled on the old postcard
déposé No. 10, Ramleh is the name of a spa,
a major street in the city's foreign quarter,
and a station with trains to the coast.
On the card, the boulevard describes a slight curve
through reddish dust toward the station,
as if it must always be possible
to escape the summer torpor
toward the sea, toward Ramleh, toward Athens.
The whole rotten boredom of this quarter
which Carlo Mieli, manufacturer of the colored card,
could not imagine, is present:
an apathy without smell,
like a waxed silk rose.
What about the Orient? Mr. Mieli has thought of it.
To the right of the foreign apartment buildings,
the white awnings and balconies,
the figurines on the street, too small
to be without expression,
he has inserted a rotunda.
In this circle, you see the Nubian woman, veiled,
the man with fez, the promiscuous boy.
They pose under tattered banana leaves
with, henceforward, immobile faces
that dissolve, under a lens, into brown dots
that may be anything, i.e. nothing,
or just heat spilling from these bodies
the color and hardness of olives.

Yet your attention always comes back
to the bleak boulevard, to a stick figure
in European clothes, in front of the station,
turning, finally, into a dark alley,
Cavafy perhaps, at forty,
though everything speaks against it, and everything
for discovering how close the sea.

HOARFROSTWATCH

Alone on the crust of the earth, earth-gray,
motley cartridge cases on oak-gray paths
crossed by a ray of sun:
And suddenly night. Resin
drops from the walnut tree.
What a year!
"Rounder than the O in Giotto,"
hence lazier, more idle, sadder.
Than what? not the senseless
waving of flags, the seesaw
of time, the opening of the gate.
Not the well-meant advice:
"Wrench winter figs off the gray branch."
Hoarfrost, in the shade, reaches the wall.
Now the goldred landscape
slights all decor and grows dark,
and I, after all this walking
and looking and hours by the radio
pull the cold watch over my wrist
and start writing.
"In the shade, hoarfrost reached the wall."

(LOVE)

The house, too, like everything, is born
and explodes and dies. Even the history
of the wells proves it, and the river streams
into the sea, until it no longer is. Awash.
How we are incessantly persuaded
and idly find ourselves
with the talkers.
Darkness transports us back
through its suggestive sieve. With eyes
well repaired, and hard-hearted heart
we go through wailing walls, tumbler-
doll in the waking night.
Something, that has rolled over and leveled
everything before us (love), stands
a cold sweat in the corner,
gnawed and hard as cowry shell.
We don't buy any friends with it.
Only the air over the damp skin
glows, weak fireworks
at the end of beauty.

A FIG FOR THE WAY HOME

The horses trot, one shits,
and Anna says: as if it would
throw out tomatoes.
It is this sound, and
the gentle fog of the sawdust,
and between the planks
the sun, that goes down again.
The polo woman has a very tight
black suit. We pick
for ourselves out of the green bag
a fig for the way home.

Joachim Sartorius

TO A DOLPHIN IN BATUMI

A man walks along the beach, remembering,
over rolling black pebbles.
It used to be different, they all said.
So he says: No, to the photographer
with the wooden dolphin,
show me a single
live one here
and I'll let you take me.
Motionless, meanwhile,
they stand by the water's edge
and look out.

Days, years later,
they remove the streamlined
cadaver.

IN THIS BLACK STILLNESS

Poetry is a destructive force.
— Wallace Stevens

Fine oblivion dust
drifts over you, on the building site,
this site is you,
you sift the sand,
want to sift something
out of it, out of the grains:
dead grass, a fossil,
the fern of the old love,
for ever blurred, crumbling,
even in recollected light
of the excessive words,
as if the mirror were too large
its object very small,
no great credit to fame,
tiny, a dust crack,
veined grass of intonations

140

that now again in secret ways
trembles toward you, always in vain,
for ever enigmatical parlando,
confessed, indifferent:

"What to do with these obtrusive hands?"
"One folds them. Clasps them."
"Is it someone at rest or — ?"
"If you only have the ferry coin,"
says the one with a small red cross
over her face. (Her skin
was of leaves. You sift
for these leaves.) Finally
we cross, at the heart of speech.
There we are. The great mirror shines.
Sounds become fainter.
Flowers are heavy and green.
They wilt. Glass sparkles.
Glasses fall down and break.

He stands up to his glans in mud.
One last time butterflies flutter.
Bread dries up. The clock is taken apart.
The skin loses its shine.
Love is there. She is embraced.
She buzzes upward.
Her liveliness is nothing but decay.
The leaves are strong on thick bushes.
Their sap oozes from sores.
"In such a case," says the tourist leaflet,
"retreat to clarity is recommended."
Yet we will stay. In this black stillness.
We are left with the words.
The raw, the lasting words
buzz out of the capsizing boat.

". . . bleeds the fold" "It bleeds with gray lips"
"Wedge yourself tight why not though sing freely
glance under blouse" Penetrating: "guess"
"You know the color? Is it
the same gray green like you?"

141

"Of ancient fern?" Stunned?
We turn the droning blare of speakers off.
The neon tubes escape through glass
in the nocturnal sky,
an entanglement of very bright lines,
becoming denser and paler. Here, before you,
the building site grows immeasurably dark, crowned,
confined by boards and an end.
In the room then you wash yourself,
in each hand a small hotel soap,
down to the new nerves.
Your find: a thorn, a delicate lid
and more delicate bones, a wire,
a toy-storm in stone.
Veins therein like toad piss.

In the nocturnal *charnier*
three rows of shin-bones, so light,
a row of skulls; artfully layered,
released from a more saturated
different ground (once)
like cheap glances secretly
buried in the eye,
opened up,
— thawed.

In the nocturnal studio:
paintbrush, an arsenal of forms, a sieve,
hair, box, pail, sarcophagus,
Pascal's casting on Steinway black.
Yet you can and can and can and
can not put her together:
not with thread, the clay, the stone out of her womb,
the numbers of the dates, the wire, the dust,
you sift the dust, sift it
to her voice on the tape,
the most rigid lips.
Charnier from *chair?*
Yes, in the beginning she gave you her back,
so that you did not see her. Then:
she was there, completely, not as usual.

142

A second burning look. And:
her voice, tiny, from this crack:
"Who then loves mine?" and
all eye-bites turned again,
the little veins, clots, blood
(only through the voice, blood),
and leafy skin and leaf . . .
. . . a bed of gray leaves . . .
Yes, buzzing, stammering
we spread out, weak
as we are, and use the circumstances:
project some sinking clouds
onto a wall for an ascension,
or move, displace ourselves
like words on indulgent paper.
To the ending then: "It wasn't meant
like that."

Trust whom there? Eye, behold:

Nulla figura in the black sieve.
Don't sift yourself away.

*Translator credits: "Alexandrie, Boulevard de Ramleh, 1903," "Hoarfrostwatch"
and "To a Dolphin in Batumi" by Rosmarie Waldrop; "(Love)" and "A Fig for the
Way Home" by Sibylle Schlesier; "In This Black Stillness" by Sibylle Schlesier and
Nathaniel Tarn.*

———————————————

Joachim Sartorius

In Berlin, everybody seems obsessed with the Wende, the "turn," as Germans call the collapse of the Communist regimes and re-unification of Germany. The sense of having recently been at the hub of history is overwhelming. So I was almost shocked when I saw how casually Joachim Sartorius can put in a poem about being with a whore: "Someone /bawls about unity /and money."

The irony and, even more, the large, cosmopolitan perspective (which can reduce "the events" to mere noise) are characteristic of both the poems and the person. Joachim is quite literally a citizen of the world, having lived many years in Africa, New York, Istanbul, Cyprus, before settling in Berlin. And his poems breathe that large air; they too travel: across borders of history and geography, across levels of diction, areas of reference.

Even his influences are not Celan or Brecht, as I might have expected, but rather Rimbaud, Williams, Ashbery. (He has translated Williams and Ashbery as well as Malcolm Lowry.) So it is not surprising that, in the context of German poetry, he is no partisan of any one group, but has defined his aim as reconciling the school of the hermetic poem in Celan's wake and the "New Subjectivity" of the sixties and seventies, reconciling "text-obsession and life . . . darkness and the everyday, silence and experience."

In the same brief essay (in Sprache im technischen Zeitalter, June 1992) he sees the poet as "a rememberer, and the poem [as] a documentation which, if it has form, can become a stela that outlasts the ashes of the moment." Tradition is no help in this enterprise. The poet must move through "his own personal thicket toward a state of language that still would be absolute."

The poems in this issue are from his second book, Der Tisch wird kalt [The Table Is Getting Cold]. His most recent book, Einszueins, is a collaboration with Horst Antes, in which the painter painted dates (from 12/19/92 to 1/30/93) and the poet worked with a layering of journal entries for the same period.

— Rosmarie Waldrop

144

CONJUNCTIONS

GET A SUBSCRIPTION AND SAVE

"Each issue is on the cutting edge of American fiction and poetry."–*The Washington Post*

NAME _____

ADDRESS _____

CITY _____

STATE _____ ZIP _____

ALL FOREIGN AND INSTITUTIONAL ORDERS: $25 PER YEAR

❑ ONE YEAR (2 ISSUES) **$18**   ❑ TWO YEAR (4 ISSUES) **$32**

❑ CHECK OR MONEY ORDER   ❑ BILL ME

PLEASE CHARGE MY: ❑ MASTERCARD   ❑ VISA

ACCOUNT NUMBER _____ EXP. DATE

SIGNATURE _____ 22/23

CONJUNCTIONS

GIVE A GIFT SUBSCRIPTION TO A FRIEND

MY NAME _____

ADDRESS _____

CITY _____

STATE _____ ZIP _____

GIFT SUBSCRIPTION TO:

RECIPIENT'S NAME _____

ADDRESS _____

CITY _____

STATE _____ ZIP _____

❑ ONE YEAR (2 ISSUES)   **$18**

❑ PAYMENT ENCLOSED   ❑ BILL ME

❑ RENEWAL   ❑ NEW ORDER

PLEASE CHARGE MY: ❑ MASTERCARD   ❑ VISA

ACCOUNT NUMBER _____ EXP. DATE

SIGNATURE _____ 22/23

A GIFT CARD WILL BE SENT IN YOUR NAME. ALL FOREIGN AND INSTITUTIONAL ORDERS $25 PER YEAR, PAYABLE IN U.S. FUND

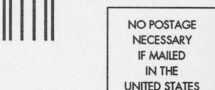

BUSINESS REPLY MAIL

FIRST CLASS MAIL   PERMIT NO. 1 ANNANDALE-ON-HUDSON, NY

POSTAGE WILL BE PAID BY ADDRESSEE

CONJUNCTIONS
BARD COLLEGE
ANNANDALE-ON-HUDSON
PO BOX 9911
RED HOOK, NY 12571-9911

BUSINESS REPLY MAIL

FIRST CLASS MAIL   PERMIT NO. 1 ANNANDALE-ON-HUDSON, NY

POSTAGE WILL BE PAID BY ADDRESSEE

CONJUNCTIONS
BARD COLLEGE
ANNANDALE-ON-HUDSON
PO BOX 9911
RED HOOK, NY 12571-9911

Special Troikas: A Corps
Nina Iskrenko

— Translated from Russian by Forrest Gander with Joy Dworkin

1.
Schlepping along the Siberian road
you go schlepping along the road when out of the blue
you are turning back

2.
Oddfellows
joined at the hands as if
nothing more than beheld

3.
A doughnut can't roll
like a glass into the full moon
It is too doughy and sorry-eyed

4.
Tiri-berikk
say the curtains   Aooop
answer the mailboxes

5.
If'n you don't snawl aroun fuckin sloaked
to the sklin, then a lotta things're going to fade to black
if'n you don't snawl around sluckin floaked

6.
Monday   Tuesday
Monday   TuesdayWednesdayThursdayFriday
Monday

7.
Think a bit about the fact
that already it's impossible to correct
Think   already impossible

8.
Tanks   my peaceful tanks
Minstryfinan   Minstryindust   Moscowboom
supply   distribu

9.
First line of text
second line a bit longer
the third li

10.
Past experience doesn't come in handy here
dot dot dot instead of unwritten words
little holes all around the 10 of the target

11.
/voice across the mirror/:   devil nilatS
                              sevil nilatS
                              evil lliw nilatS

12.
PRIVILEGE INC. is PRIVILEGE'S friend
his comrade
and brother

13.
Gosha, an anonymous citizen
yesterday, in the metro, laid, well, flat on the floor
overturned a pail of sawdust, stretched out his arm
to the cleaning woman   In private with you, he said, I'd

14.
Help! he cried, scumbag!   And she whacked him on the head
with a broom   Well, the people — you can imagine — saw everything
And so I'm on the bus to my daughter's   And my granddaughter's
    at home,
so I'm headed straight from work   carrying some pastries
Just now I'm off with every intention   of sitting with them for a
    cup of tea

15.
In the three-storied paper house
in the tinny, unnatural sky
in the fire-proof, insensible stream

16.
Respite for a response, for a reflux, for a repossession,
    for the bartering and parting of companies
make the call and take care
Haul it to the bank

17.
Well, how are things?
As they are
in a mudpuddle   No no
and no again

18.
Quickly and tastefully
elegantly profitably copacetically
skillfully

19.
The goal of language is language
МЫ   профессиональные жизнелюбы
The goal of putridity is putridity
ВЫ   любители
The goal of perestroika   is "the improvement   of the welfare
    of the workers"
ОНИ   нет

20.
Sew those sarafans and deliver more baby
machine operators!
In the village soviet, Wednesdays and Saturdays are for
    flogging the serfs

21.
The rude days shorten
as though they were starving the cuckoo
in some timepiece beyond the river

22.
In the clinic you take the form
Oh no we can't help, they say,
until you give us some pee-pee

23.
In general, there are enough plans
And big plans, comrades
Real big plans

24.
The goal of language   is language
Я снимаю шляпу Господи помоги Снег
It nullifies itself   Expense number one:
ТЫ падаешь на пол не шевеля ни рукой ни ногой   Ночлег
There are no casualties   no desolations
ОН и ОНА с помощью зеркала и ряда пластических операций и
трюков разрабатывают канонический сюжет

Nina Iskrenko

25.
la do mi do re
do so mi re la . . .
No need to unnecessarily complicate matters

Nina Iskrenko's letters begin Dear So and So, exclamation point. "Our life is full of impressions as always."

When I visit in Moscow, she takes me walking through Gorky Park. The ferris wheel, left over from a fairy tale, looms three hundred feet above us. We wait our turn and are hoisted to the apex where we can see to the river. "I went to school there," she says, pointing to the distant buildings. "Moscow University. Studying physics, some lives ago."

Most of my photographs of her are taken in a graveyard. She is standing before a larger-than-life statue of a robed muse. In her two hands, Nina holds a dahlia, grinning, her horse-black hair blown across her forehead. In the next picture, she grips the thick stem of the flower between her teeth.

In my clearest memory, Nina is taking off her glasses, leaning toward me the way she does with her eyes closed, developing her thought, translating it into my language, one side of her mouth barely smiling, the other side neutral, hair falling across her face. Even in casual conversations, she is plumbing her aesthetic, reconsidering, tracking something important in her thought. Her aesthetic, what she calls polystylistics, mixes incisive politics (in "Special Troikas" she is both blatant, satirizing that Russian brand of officialese, and subtle, as when she blurs the work days together) with word play and sensual lyricism. Her intention is to corrupt any unitary speaking voice, to distribute the authority.

Her first official book, Or, was published in the Soviet Union by the press Soviet Writer. A collection of her poems in English, translated by John High and Patrick Henry, is forthcoming this year from Three Continents Press. Other translations of her work appear in the anthology Third Wave: New Poetry in the Age of Perestroika, published by University of Michigan.

Iskrenko frequently performs as well as reads her work in Russia. But she has also twice toured the United States, most recently in May when she arrested audiences in San Francisco, New Jersey and Providence.

— Forrest Gander

149

From The Marx Family Saga
Juan Goytisolo

— *Translated from Spanish by Peter Bush*

GUARDA, Carlo!

(had he said that in Italian?)

che bel transatlantico!

his bejewelled finger pointed to the faint silhouette of a boat looming on the misty horizon, its luxury cabins, funnels, radar, aerials, bridge right opposite the select beach,

as if by some trick or special effect

from the depths of their parallel prostration, relaxing on striped airbeds that like the beach huts and awnings sported the colors of the national flag in the shadow of imitation Polynesian cabins or out under the sun, already protected by dark glasses and sun-screening lotions, the bathers

just did not seem to notice

they had paid a weekly or monthly contribution for their tiny slice of seaside delight

well beyond the pockets of most of their compatriots

(back-packing tourists into guide books, they grunted and scowled) or, like some privileged individuals, owned a season ticket that common mortals valued and coveted as much as a subscription to the annual repertoire of La Scala

(an incredible saving according to the lady next to them, a veteran visitor to that establishment frequented only by the famous where being cheek by jowl, rather than implying the smelly, physical discomforts of metro and bus, flattered the clientele with a frisson of much-prized togetherness)

allowing them to smile benignly, forgivingly when some near-naked kid flourished a bucket and spade, annoyed the neighboring family with his sand castles

oh, ce n'est rien, laissez-le s'amuser, il est tellement charmant!

quite entranced by the tender sprout exemplifying the virtues promoted by ubiquitous television advertisements for balanced infant

150

diets, swimwear, protein-based shampoos and beach-games
nobody there flaunting plebeian tastes, no strident, ghetto-blasting
cacophony, couples in splendid musical isolation, tuning into their
micro-headsets, as they sucked deliciously effervescent ice-cold
refreshment through straws and exchanged sleepy or blissful looks
dripping from the paraphernalia of sprays, moisturizing milks,
rejuvenating balsams, anti-wrinkle or hair-regenerating creams
just the thing on such a gloriously sunny day
(not to mention the playful, yapping lap dogs, their dear little
tongues hanging out, as they ran along the shore, wallowed in the
sand, egged on by their owners' snooty looks, pitting against each
other blue-blooded, tried and tested pedigrees)
occasionally, a young mama, with firm inviting breasts rehearsed
the ritual of mildly rebuking her hound, slobbered over her pooch's
snozzle, brushed and combed its wind-swept mane, showering words
of advice and wisdom on the smiling recipient who responded
with fervent licks, in a show of spontaneous innocence aimed at
demonstrating to the gallery the amatory charms and virtues of
the lady concerned, the dame with the golden tresses and erect
nipples, redolent of mouth-watering suction
one more summer's day, just like any other, in that zone insulated
against the cheap tans of the rabble by bellicose personnel experienced at guarding entrances and frontier posts, amiably servile
towards the high and mighty, harshly forbidding to intruders and
peeping-toms, this is a private beach, didn't you see the sign?
members and ticket-holders only, if you want a free swim, clear
off to the other side of the breakwater, where you'll meet up with
your own sort!
summer bliss, pure bliss of summer, succulent *après*-siesta lethargy,
collective slumbers, beatitude shared by somnolent couples who,
even when stripped of emblematic clothes and vestments, still
displayed badges of distinction, bags, hats, jewels, children, lapdogs and so many other symbols of their elevated status
(yuppies
bourgeois
landowners
mafiosi launderers of snow-white capital
arms dealers
high-class smugglers
NATO chiefs and bureaucrats
a plump, flaxen-haired archduke)

a dissipating dolce far niente, soothing them, cradling them,
how else could one explain that nobody had yet noticed the boat's disturbing,
threatening, massive presence?
the huge pile had sidled up to the beach run the risk of going aground, of toppling over, elegantly attired officers trained their binoculars on the shore from the swimming pool, luxury cabins and bridge, others ordered the crew to bring the vessel to a halt, the novel nature of the scene and liner's cardboard stiffness were cause for wonderment and consternation, why had they thrown their anchor onto that beach, that beach for heaven's sake rather than mooring in the nearby port or simply continuing their cruise? was it to enable them to enjoy the magnificent spectacle or perhaps they harbored hidden, devious intentions?
almost everybody had sat up on their airbeds, looked with surprise and apprehension at the pot-bellied liner riddled with bleary port-holes and picture windows, gangways, masts, safety rafts around which a strange, vociferous crowd was suddenly gathering
a number of Amazons had run to the sea's edge clutching off-spring and pooches, sunglasses pushed up over their foreheads like actresses in the latest television soap or following the words of wisdom from the oracles in *Marie Claire*, bikini triangles tailored to their pubic curls, bronzed bellies, lush breasts, studiously unkempt hair, cooing with the innocence of doves at the swarming male hullabaloo around the lifecraft and top decks of the model boat, an increasingly audible clamor of impatient immigrants, dazzled by the resplendent vision of Eden, that remote, inaccessible Promised Land till then only glimpsed through cyclopean eyes, plethora, abundance, riches, arrayed on the smooth well-groomed beach packed with beautiful, refined people, ecstatic before the immediacy of so many luminous creatures after an entire existence of ugliness, sacrifice, privation
and misery
the officers were trying to impose a semblance of order on the savage free-for-all broken out among the hopefuls for the boats to go ashore, the cry of land ahoy had gone up and through trapdoors and hatches, out of the boat's entrails, they streamed pallid, hirsute, anxious, clinging to one another, excitedly shouting each other on, the boats were clearly over-laden, but nobody was prepared to surrender a place won by sheer obduracy, new hopefuls kept jumping down hanging off the ropes in clusters, the most impatient

hurled themselves straight into the sea in life jackets and buoys
or held their noses and dived, entrusting
their destiny to the fates
they could at least swim?
no one could be sure they jumped into the water such spirit such
speed, through binoculars one could follow the frantically flailing
arms, the clumsy attempts to grab hold of top-heavy boats at the
risk of capsizing them, hands stretched out and spurned, generously
helped by the most adroit spattered by their waterlogged lungs,
as the liner relentlessly spewed out its human cargo and those
coming down punched their way to the remaining places, those left
behind (dozens, hundreds?) had no choice but to dive overboard,
singly or in groups, just like the shipwreck of the *Titanic* captured on
prints in books
and annuals
the spectacle of that bloated whale of a boat (surrounded by flimsy
craft and swarms of swimmers like a shoal of fish caught in the
nets of a tunny fisher, thrashing tails making the light shimmer
on the water, creating the sound of boiling water) was as ridiculous
as it was
alarming
who could those coarse, uncouth fellows be, gesticulating, hallucinating, with untold energy, now rowing at full pelt towards the
beach?
someone had let out a cry of alarm
the Albanians!!
and panic spread through the enclave of select, beautiful people,
among the couples dozing in the torrid torpor of a summery siesta,
the mamas went after their children and dogs down by the sea,
the male of the species improvised feverish confabulations not
knowing what stance to take in this emergency, even the lifeguards
and barmen seemed dumbfounded, how to confront and halt the
flotilla of packed boats, the serried ranks of swimmers advancing
on the beach? the management of the place had not foreseen such
an eventuality, had no firearms at its disposal! caution advised a
quick retreat and the mafiosi more expert in sliding out of tight
corners were already rushing their families and goods to the exit
determined to safeguard the lot against this unimaginable tidal
wave of barbarians while the majority of customers awaited with
sheepish fatalism the massive incursion of galley-slaves, dishevelled
little men in threadbare trousers or knee breeches emphasizing

with every movement of the oars the lines of their weak chests and protruding ribs, bushy eyebrows, bearded faces, an unquenchable spark in their incandescent eyes
some had been unable to resist the magnetic pull of the new Judea and dived out of the boats in order to reach the shore more quickly, sped energetically through the water, their heads floating ever nearer, spurred on by feelings of warmth and friendship towards the paladins of well-being and free enterprise, spitting images of those they had seen in television advertisements and serials set in Texas, paradise, paradise
tangible and concrete at last!
the first ashore had kissed the sand in an act of enraptured homage to a fraternal, welcoming land, had kneeled before a young mama complimenting her or blessing her, tongue-tied, trying to win her benevolent affections, looking longingly at the delightful child she held in her arms and, unperturbed by their coldly statuesque pose, tried to ingratiate himself with her lapdog, a rabid Pekinese squaring up to the intruder, fully aware thanks to a pukka training that the fellow didn't belong by a long chalk to his owner's class and lacked the necessary cachet of fame or fortune, gradually worked up by the genuflector's insistent caresses or finger snapping into a bristling frenzy, ferociously baring its canines, an outburst of true hysteria the newcomer didn't or couldn't understand, fascinated, bewildered, happy, smiling, pathetic, arms crossed, gently pleading, beady eyes fixed on the stone goddess's bikini triangle that drew an off-putting
but ever so precise
veil over her grotto or sanctuary
the beach had filled up with hairy-faced sopping wet Albanians, some smiled and kissed the ground, closed in on the appalled families and sought out a tangential, semiological relationship, with children and dogs, unable in their euphoria to grasp the frowns and reproving looks from those svelte, well-fed forms, consumers of the exact quantity of proteins required by their weight and height, surprised by the hurried flight of their more wide-awake brethren and by the impotent, outnumbered beach staff's vociferous insults, an out-of-control patently explosive situation, a catastrophe, they muttered,
absolutely unheard of
when would the forces of law and order turn up? the proprietor had called them. the bathers listened out for the wail of car sirens,

breathing a sigh of relief as soon as their deafening concert turned the corner, it was an invasion, an invasion no more no less and the State should adopt immediate defensive measures, protect its citizens, round up, arrest, deport the ragamuffin rabble, isn't that what the Community laws and statutes were for or were they just so much paper and ink put there for show?

(the man rabbiting on was a respectable arms dealer enriched by the providential outbreak of crises in the Balkans)

but the Albanians seemed unaware of the danger and pursued their futile attempts at fraternizing with families, mums, kids and dogs, smiled half-wittedly at those upbraiding their uncivilized behavior, gesticulated, looked lovingly and longingly at the counter replete with cold drinks and rolls, now into their third day of a pitiful diet, looking for food and help, not daring even to run their fingertips over the tempting fare, at most begging humbly, movingly, for a glass of water to slake their consuming thirst

the sudden arrival of truncheon-waving helmeted police literally stunned them

had they come to look after them, to take them to reception and welfare centers set up for refugees?

a few went to welcome them with open arms, but the grim faces and unbending manner of the men in uniform halted them in their tracks, made them keep together, hold back, visibly upset, wanting to explain their odyssey they pointed at the liner where they had been cooped up on the journey from the country of idols and false prophets, apparently railing against communism, and they showed off medals bearing likenesses of the Desert Lion, surely mistaking the Adriatic coast for the ranches of Dallas, their notions of geography being somewhat hazy, one had taken the wet photocopy of a dollar out of his pants and was repeating an almost unrecognizable God bless America!

much to the relief of those present they allowed themselves to be shepherded to the lorries, the police and military, having rejected the use of force, lined them up before escorting them to the parking area towards which army vehicles were now rumbling, keep calm, just keep calm! an interpreter bellowed through a megaphone, they would soon enjoy shelter and food, would get refugee status, would benefit from the right to attain with the fruits of their labor all the goods they had just glimpsed on the select beach, would be able to apply for visas and set up home in

Texas, sweet honey-dewed promises, with which they cheated them pacified them
the most wary, the cleverest had tried to scarper, but lifeguards and emboldened paterfamilias grabbed their threadbare clothes held furiously on till the police arrived
only the Archduke showed any interest, wrapping a sumptuous, imperially tasseled dressing-gown round his abundant rolls of flabby flesh, he welcomed two of the lads, no less well-endowed for being on the skinny side, into the inner sanctum of his beach hut, keep your hands off these two, he warned, they're mine and from now on will devote themselves to servicing my distinguished self, as he draped the mantle of power around them, drooled over their damp breeches, as if trying to weigh up their attributes, their cocks' normal size and potential for expansion
a masterly shot now panned the rows of Albanians herded by police and soldiers towards lorries and vans, hands tracing illusory victory signs, matrons with smelling salts, badmouthing lifeguards, lapdogs on the point of paroxysm, youthful mamas retrospectively aroused by their adventure until they center and deliberately linger, on the trio comprising the Archduke and his brood
final close-up of chubby, angelic cheeks and bulging blue eyes, a face licking its lips, winking at the camera like a saucy frolicsome Betty Boop.

What a hotchpotch! Sequences from a Fellini film mixed up with a live news flash from the port of Bari concerning a ferry packed with Albanian refugees!
Tussy's compulsive zapping, her unrelenting mania for keying in on the remote control, confused images, jumbled shots, moving from the sophisticated liner rebuilt in the studios of Cinecittá to the rusty, battered ferry and its exulting, jubilant human cargo, as ever Jenny had tried to reason with her, please for once make up your mind, this way you won't see one thing or the other! but Tussy carried on regardless, esconced in the sullen silence of puberty or personal disillusion, looking vacant,
in willfully distant mood
(how can one laugh in a world like this? she had responded the night before to her mother's affectionate reproaches contemptuously waving her hand)
they could do nothing but steel themselves, wait till the storm had passed, neither Jennychen Laura nor her father managed to wrench

her out of that state of mute impenetrability, her prickly suspicion of everything around her

More's arrival did not solve the problem, Tussy had been unable to escape the paternal kiss but immediately slipped out of the room and into the street without so much as a goodbye while he deposited his reference books on the shelf next to his manuscripts, slumped down with a deep sigh of exhaustion into the armchair she had occupied minutes earlier, and delicately refrained from asking about supper, faithful Lenchen was as busy as usual in the kitchen and the smell of boiled cabbage

(ephemeral hopes of a delicious sauerkraut wafted through his mind)

started to invade the house

a good day's work? (Jenny)

same as usual

(patently upset by Tussy's reserve and sulkiness

did he still remember the time he gave her piggy-backs and she put flowers in his hair chanting excitedly, faster, faster, pony, take me with you to the park?)

Jenny had finally got hold of the program changer and pressed the button for her favorite news channel

(Lenchen put in a brief, discreet appearance

did she need something?

she whispered in Jenny's ear who got out her purse and gave her a two-penny coin)

look! the deserters from paradise!

(did she say that on purpose, knowing how for months he had been taking refuge in the solitude of his books, avoiding the triumphant television news broadcasts and raucous headlines of the daily papers?)

the camera gave a wide angle of the port, hundreds of men jam-packed on the quaysides, seething, writhing

under a merciless sun

most wore just pants, a rag or handkerchief tied over their heads, some had a picturesque piratical appearance, with bandages down to their eyebrows and matted beards, snared in that trap after their hopes had been raised by promises of asylum and visas, surrounded now by a cordon of soldiers armed to the teeth while helicopters whirled, skimmed over them in intimidating flight, the dream cherished for so long had been shattered by the joint impact of the Special Operations Group and the loudspeakers barking out

slogans, one by one they had been stripped of knives, teaspoons, scissors, of anything that could be construed offensive and for days they had been waiting on the sodding ferry that was to return them to where they'd come from, their adventure thwarted amid the din of propellers and their own hoarse cries, from time to time they tossed them fodder and drums of water which unleashed bouts of fighting and snatching, only the fittest and strongest got their hands on the meager booty leaving the majority sweaty and hungry, wracked with pain and tears, others looking spaced out, wandered aimlessly, grinned learily, pleaded half-heartedly, pissed or shat indifferent to the protests of their neighbors, noise from the enclosure increased by the hour with the heat, stench and squabbles provoked by feeding time, the film registered the howls of despair of those who dared ask their guards for
explanations
why are you treating us like this? aren't we human like everyone else? I've seen cats being fed on television from silver spoons!
body after body parched, scorched, cracked by the sun, wild-eyed, blind looks, moving like wild animals in a corral, still not resigned to the inevitable, to the inflexible law shutting them out, like Jews or Bosnians heading for some future holocaust, old tales from a Mediterranean fertile in persecutions, massacres, fanatical oppressive doctrines, carefully planned mass deportations, Mediterranean! Mediterranean! all-embracing mother, seed and cradle of civilization! patron of classical art and beauty! crucible of cultures! yet so alien and cruel, Mare Vostrum, theater of wars, crusades exterminations of whole populations, crucifix bearing swords, ecclesiastical blessings upon blood-stained caudillos, tyrants deified by statues and books, purifiers of dynasties ethnic cleansers, the whole magma of horror and detritus accumulated in its basin over the centuries!
(who could have let that speech out of the bag?)
and now a quick flurry of camera shots, the quayside covered in shit, bits of paper, variegated leftovers, Caritas bags, as the last invaders were hustled on the ferry, dragged or hoisted up the gangplank, confused, exhausted, furious, out for revenge, despondent or demanding their ticket to Dallas, recalling the coldly calculated promises from the society they had glimpsed under the awnings and on the airbeds of that select beach, a paradise of well-fed athletic bodies, mamas with quivering come-on breasts, playful children and dogs, delicious plenitude of gods who, clinging to the

ferry rail, they contemplate, still contemplate, staring, hypnotized, convulsed in sorrow, misty-eyed
as the program presenter said, who the hell cared about the tears of an Albanian and his enforced return to the debris of a demented utopia?
to salve their consciences and show their grief at that stern but necessary cleanup operation, were they supposed to sign up all the divos and divas from La Scala to console the distraught ferry passengers with their art?
Tussy wasn't there to press the button and regale their eyes and ears with the Felliniesque version of the second scene from the third act of *Nabuco*

> *Oh, mia patria si bella e perduta!*
> *Oh, remembranza si cara e fatal!*

the pair of distinguished exiles from Treveris remained silent transfixed by the final images of the ferry and the by now blank screen of the television

It was called water off a duck's back!
for months, first to their surprise, then their shame, finally to their consternation they had witnessed via the television screen and the newspaper headlines in the street the dismantling of the systems supposedly based on his thought, the collapse of walls and watch towers, the outbursts of jubilation of those the pundits of the London intelligentsia dubbed guinea pigs in his sinister laboratory, the astonishing metamorphosis of impenitent dogmatists into wheelers and dealers on behalf of
the universal panacea of privatization
at once they began to burn their portraits and effigies, boisterously demolish statues
attaching them by cables to the very same tractors which years before had symbolized Socialism's resplendent victories on paintings and murals of harvests and peasants and, after a long wait, giving the volunteers time to undermine the pedestal's foundations, the entire weight of the giant, leaden mass came crashing down
to the cheers of the populace
an interval of thirty or so years, and the Trimurti of scientific socialism encountered the same fate as his wily, moustachioed descendent!

weren't they already calling them, ironically, the Gang of Four?
(a droll journalist had won fleeting notoriety by dubbing Engels "Mao's latest widow"
that day, Laura was unable to quell her anger, burst into tears, as she left slamming the door behind her)
what remained of the dies irae that would disrupt the whole of European industry, throttle its markets, ruin the property-owning classes, spark off the total bankruptcy of the bourgeoisie?
ironically hadn't the sudden acceleration of history worked against him?
if communism was to be the last stage in the epic of humanity, if materialism was right and the labor theory of value cunningly concealed that nth degree of usefulness, how could one explain the incredible brutal leap backwards?
in the light of what has happened, how is one to interpret the business of the weapon of criticism not being able to replace the criticism of weapons, material force having to be crushed by material force, but theory also being transformed into material force as soon as it is embodied in the masses?
the perverse and twisted application of his doctrines in order to restore Tsarist idolatry and the most loathsome trappings of power of Asiatic despotism had plunged him into decades of silence, embalmed alive by those who had suppressed cruel exploitation by the bourgeoisie and governed
in the name of science and right thinking
a pathetic exile on Dean Street, what could he do against the engines of omnipotent authoritarianism and the publicity machine of a superpower? could Jenny, who had stoically borne all the travails of their precarious nomadic existence, withstand the final blow, the discrediting of this system and loss of status?
as the heralds of the free market chorused, his work was now reduced to a heap of rubble no rag-and-bone man was offering to buy up even at knockdown prices!

It was just like the day he burst into Bishop Policarp's quarters, intoning a sacred hymn in that beautiful bass timbre persuading him of his attachment to the ancient rites, allowing himself humbly to be catechized by the man he in turn gradually converted, as he gained his confidence, to the logic behind his cause, the destructive-creative spontaneity of the masses and then he had put in an appearance via the last door to the last carriage on the train

on the number 4 line of the metro, Porte de Clignancourt to the
Porte d'Orléans, departing from the platform in the Gare du Nord,
after the hustle, jostling and elbowing of rush hour, when customers,
strewn over the seats, read their newspapers, consulted the list of
tips for the afternoon races, solved crosswords, looked at the floor
or exchanged bovinely neutral glances, from the heights from
which he always looked down on any gathering now extended by
a top hat, an immaculate cylinder of black felt, elegantly perched
above spellbinding locks, a torrent of curls cleverly orchestrated
to the vibrant rhythms of a majestic Romantic score, capping his
consummate orator or actor's face, his cheeky-chappy, cunning
eyes
(a tremulous glint, ray of light piercing the heart of the fountain
deep in the shadows, magnified in the left socket by a Prussian
officer's monocle where the carriage lights now danced mysteriously) his energetic manner, the pretense of vulgarity, of someone
accustomed to rousing the passions of the rabble, well-fitting,
gleaming dentures, chin and double chin constrained by white
collar and bow tie, starched shirt front, frock coat opening over a
pearl gray waistcoat with diamond-encrusted buttons and dainty
gold chains shades of the bourgeois patrons of Dutch painting, a
concave belly of unconcealed proportions, long funereally mournful
or dismal coattails, natty dark pin-striped trousers, rounded off by
shiny patent leather half-boots, encouraging mental nirvana and
numbness in the beholder
his large, hairy hands, painstakingly manicured, displayed an
untidy garrulous assortment of gold rings
ladies and gentlemen!
(he cleared his throat)
allow me briefly to introduce myself to you!
(he delayed for a few moments, making sure the gaze of every
traveller was focused on him)
I am the owner of a most powerful multinational
(pause)
am rich, very rich
(pause)
unbelievably rich
(fresh pause and sigh)
I own farms and ranches in several states of North America, tower
blocks and apartments in New York, Rome and Buenos Aires,
summer palaces in Montecarlo, Capri and Marbella, a personal

fleet of airplanes and yachts, I am an associate of Lebanese magnates and Arab petrosheiks, manage consortia and holdings tucked away in remote tax havens, buy and sell on the stock exchange speculate on the black market, am a past master in the art of trafficking influences, evading the revenue men, soaking away capital, I launder the money of my wheeler-dealer friends, supply arms to Croats and Serbs, Tamils and Ceylanese, Kurds and Armenians, take advantage of a submissive, cheap labor force to create profitable enterprises in the countries of the Idiot World and, ever since the demise of the detestable system in the USSR and satellite countries forged according to the norms of my mortal enemy, I am the promoter-in-chief of free enterprise in his ruined dominions buying job-lots of railways, newspapers, factories, entire cities as easily and profitably as that fellow with multiple activities and diverse interests, capable of smoking a smuggled cigar under the noses of the customs men, portrayed by my very good and distinguished friend Mr. Dickens! (he ran his eyes over the hypnotized audience in the carriage, noting that nobody got out at the next stop, as if these paying customers had unanimously forgotten their destination
new passengers got in, at each station swelled the silent ranks of enrapt admirers) it would be a thankless, interminable task to enumerate a complete list of my possessions, the last edition of *Who's Who* devoted a special twenty-page section to me and in the present state of the market, responsive to every kind of initiative, my wealth, ladies and gentlemen, is increasing by the day!
(he took a cotton handkerchief from his pocket, wiped away the sweat and waited for the doors to close)
but it's not enough!
(in Strasbourg Saint-Denis the carriage had welcomed in a fresh lot of colorful travelers he was complacently giving the once-over)
no it's not enough!
(he was no longer talking, but shouting)
I couldn't care less if the global income from my wealth earns me six hundred dollars a minute! I'm voracious, I need more! night and day I'm tormented by desire for everything I don't possess, that's why I've come here to ask for your help so I can get richer, if you've got a hundred francs, a hundred francs! if it's only five, five will do! a generous gesture, however small, will increase my capital momentarily relieve my omnivorous appetite!
(he stopped to admire the impact of his words, seeking out applause

and approval, but they all seemed to be undergoing mesmerizing treatment, looked taken aback) be proud of your wholehearted cooperation in making me even wealthier! place your mite in my fraternally outstretched palm! preferably notes and, if not, coins, whatever amount, however modest, will contribute, if only an infinitesimal part, establishing my presence on the Olympus of the Croesus worshipped in your magazines, don't pretend to be deaf, blind or dumb, don't slip off! think how your gift will resonate in my glorious person and, on the rebound, on yours, look me straight in the eye! if your personal situation isn't exactly buoyant I'll accept a minimal offering! take a lead from this honest African immigrant collaborating humbly in my aggrandizement with a symbolic franc! go to it, ladies and gents, give me the biggest note or coin in your purse or wallet! times may be hard and the future uncertain, but poke those fingers right down inside your pockets!

Juan Goytisolo loves to remind his readers of Jean Genet's dictum that writing should be an adventure taking the writer along unknown paths, not a bus journey to a routine destination. And yet originality is a return to origins, according to Gaudí, another figure in the pantheon, and he has recently spoken of having the time only to reread the works he considers to be true works of literature as opposed to the fast-food produce favored by so many publishers, prose that goes in and out and down the pan, never disturbing or infecting the reader.

Although some reviewers love to dwell on what they see as a fascinating avant-garde labyrinth, there is always in Juan Goytisolo's writing a sense of present historical crisis, of the writer and his writing being shaped by and wanting to have a stake in the wider world. A child of the 1930s, he once remarked that the Spanish Civil War destroyed his family — his mother was killed while out birthday-present shopping in Barcelona during a fascist bombing raid — and that he was educated under the shadow of a perverse spiritual father, General Franco. From before his departure to exile in Paris in 1956 he felt drawn to the harshness of other people's realities and their struggle for justice. I was first drawn to his early writings, which explore the barren, North African landscapes of Murcia and Almería in southeast Spain, the source of the cheap labor that was slotted by the Francoist Ministry for Emigration into the production lines of Barcelona, Düsseldorf or the kitchens of London hotels despite what the rim of the peseta coin said about Spain being One Great and Free. The narrative had a sympathy and a disturbing edge not to be found in the travel writing of Cela: no peasants patronized as so many picturesque plants in a Spanish rural backwater. Coming from the cabbage and potato flatlands and different working-class culture of a Lincolnshire ignored by the English literati I felt a point of contact.

In the early sixties at the height of the struggle for Algerian independence the subversive hue of Juan Goytisolo's politics led him into the cafés of Algerian and Moroccan migrants in Paris and to a physical, sexual epiphany that was to pitch his life and writing into the Realms of Strife (1986) described in the second volume of his autobiography. An erotic attraction to the physical beauty of these migrant workers triggering off the desire to learn Arabic in Tangier and Marrakesh and Turkish in Paris initiated "the alchemy of converting passion felt towards a body – a physical, cultural exemplar of a body – into a voracious form of knowledge, capable of turning the lover into a linguist, researcher, scholar or poet" (Saracen Chronicles, 1981).

For him what distinguishes a colonizing Flaubert from a liberating Genet is the personal perspective, the movement from the individual to the collective propelling the writer into the ranks of the anticolonialist movement "to penetrate the language, literature and thought which the body of the beloved evokes and represents."

The particular literary gold which Juan Goytisolo discovered through his exploration of Arabic and Islamic culture was the series of Spanish classics that was a consequence of the coexistence of Arab, Jew and Christian in medieval Spain. These works from the Archpriest of Hita to Góngora had been buried under a welter of fascist rhetoric and academic pedantry as had the Spanish language itself. The literary language, the playful and venomous baroque of the writer's transcultural consciousness was now to take pride in its hybrid state and freedom from any narrow identity of self based on the singularity of nation, gender or ethnicity.

From Count Julian (1970) onwards flows a series of texts creating an original Spanish voice that is simultaneously poetry, politics and literary criticism. Translating Juan Goytisolo for Anglo-Saxon readers is likewise an adventure, stretching and expanding that language and culture in different directions at the same time, attempting to grasp the surreal unity of the apparently disparate: what, for example, in the penultimate text, Quarantine (1991), is the connection between the Sufi Ibn Arabi, Dante, the Gulf War, a Gitane-smoking student in New York and a variety of parodic and rhapsodic styles?

The present passage is from the opening sequences of the latest text, The Marx Family Saga (1993). On this occasion, and this is part of the novelty, the immediate literary inspirations are the writings of Karl Marx and Charles Dickens, two authors some might think unfashionable in this postmodern day and age, yet whose Victorian truths could still have a contemporary ring in the chaotic world beyond the fashion-makers. One of Goytisolo's most comic texts, it enjoys a host of bit players: the writer pursued by his publisher for the one that will sell a million, a feminist sexologist from L.A. vying on a TV chat show with Bakunin reincarnated as a clown, a film crew setting up their shoot of the house-warming party Karl & Co. are giving to launch their new pad in Hampstead. . . . This literary journey to North London was sandwiched between two real journeys to report with political passion from Sarajevo and Algeria. Juan Goytisolo's literary and political writing remains in the eye of the storm.

— Peter Bush

165

Two Stories
Can Xue

— Translated from Chinese by Jian Zhang and Ronald R. Janssen

A DREAMLAND NEVER DESCRIBED

THE RECORDER SAT in his roadside shed writing down the various dreamlands described by passersby. This had gone on for many years, and he had recorded a nearly infinite variety of images. Usually a session went like this: the passersby — all ordinary people who appeared a bit confused as they entered the shed — walked in and sat down on the floor. Their descriptions differed from person to person and ranged from vivid to dull and mechnical, confusingly meditative or obscure. The Recorder sat before them showing no facial expression. He copied verbatim, collecting everything into a black notebook. Then the passersby would leave sullenly.

Gradually the number of people with dreams to report decreased, and the Recorder felt more and more lonely, yet he continually stretched his neck out stubbornly and stared toward the end of the road. He was hoping for a dreamland that had never yet been described, one charged with heat and blinding light. He was not even sure its image had occurred in his own mind clearly. He only believed firmly there was such a dreamland. He could not by himself write this dreamland directly into the black notebook but had to wait for someone to come in who could set it forth as it had appeared in his own dream. Then by the roadside he would describe this dream to the Recorder, and the Recorder would copy it down for him. Because existence travels in zigzag paths, all the Recorder could do was wait.

Day after day, the people who arrived could never describe directly the image in the Recorder's mind; therefore, this image could never be established. As a result, the Recorder became disheartened day by day, yet he still stretched out his neck stubbornly. His hands and feet cracked in the bitter wind of winter, and in the dampness of spring his joints swelled like little steambuns.

In addition, the run-down shed by the roadside started leaking. Most passersby no longer stopped to describe their dreamlands; instead they flung cold glances in his direction and continued on their way. The Recorder observed every one of them carefully, and his heart pulsed regularly between hope and disappointment. Sometimes a whole day would pass with only one or two people coming into his shed. And their dreamlands were nothing out of the ordinary, although they were filled with the mad joy of wandering in the vast universe; or with a conceitedness like a person who locks himself inside a cave deep within the shell of the earth; or with the horror of being captured by some beast of prey; or the ghastly feeling of being in the process of dying. However, no one ever dreamed the image that appeared in the Recorder's mind.

Maybe this was nothing but a kind of torture? The Recorder had asked himself numerous times, and numerous times had failed to find the answer. But just at the moment when the passersby with dreams were leaving, the light of that dreamland that had never been described would make his body tremble all over. This trembling — the trembling itself — confirmed in him the existence of that image. So he named that image that had never been described nor had ever occurred clearly in his mind "the wind." "The wind" always arose when the person with dreams was leaving. Now what he was expecting with his stretched-out neck was more than merely the dreamers, because he knew when they were leaving that light would appear. He had begun to see this more and more clearly.

Then in the rainy season there came an old woman holding a huge umbrella. Her snow white hair had been tousled by the wind. The eyeballs inside her long, narrow sockets had no vision, yet she was not blind. She entered the shed and let the Recorder touch her ice-cold fingers, then she went on her way. It was on that day that the Recorder stopped writing down the descriptions of the dreamlands of the passersby. Nor did he stare down the road anymore with outstretched neck. However, he was still waiting, and he seemed to know what he was waiting for. With the passing of time, that image of his had changed gradually into something less definite, and his hearing had deteriorated daily. Very often when a passerby entered the shed, the Recorder was still in his reverie. Only one thing was clear: at a certain moment his heart would throb in response to that invisible light and that empty image, and his blood would surge like a herd of running horses.

167

Once in a while there were still people stopping by his shed. The dreamlands that they described had become more and more outrageous. Everyone complained that the thing he had seen was indescribable. And because it was indescribable, they sometimes left, disheartened, in the middle of their account. The Recorder, understanding all this, held his black notebook and pen in his hands and pretended to be listening carefully. As a matter of fact, in his mind's eye there still appeared the image that once had made him tremble, yet it had faded into a blankness with something like shadows swaying back and forth within it. He couldn't confirm it, yet he was satisfied. Closing his notebook he sat on the floor for a break, and the instant of the break was sweet.

The following is a dialogue between the Recorder and a person reporting a dream:

Dreamer: "What have I been talking about? What I have said is not even as much as one-tenth of what I saw. That feeling could never occur again. Why can't I describe it? It's so disheartening! The wind is too strong here."
Recorder: "Uh-huh."
Dreamer: "Whatever you have recorded here is all rubbish. Yet we still come to you because everybody knows you are the only person who is doing recording here. I really want to describe it. Please tell me. Is it because I am not verbal?"
Recorder: "What you've said is really interesting."

After the dreamers left, they never revealed to others the image that they had described to the Recorder, as if it were an unspoken agreement among them. After they had described their dreamlands to him, they felt they had left a piece of valuable property in his run-down shed. As a matter of fact, they seldom reflected on what they had described, yet they remembered making the description because that was their property. They paid no attention to whether or not the Recorder had written anything in his notebook. What they did pay attention to was their own act of describing inside the shed. Although during their descriptions they were also continually grumbling and complaining, as if impatient or totally bored, deep inside they were quite satisfied with themselves. Once they left that shed they felt they became mere ordinary people. They tended to consider the unique communication between themselves and the Recorder as a supreme secret. They also tended to see that black notebook as something which made them feel intimate and committed to something in their hearts.

Nobody had expected that the Recorder would abandon his black notebook, because it contained such a quantity of unique and strange dream images, and it was therefore considered by many people as the property of numerous dreamers. But now he had thrown the notebook away, and he explained this only indifferently: "Flew away without wings." And he refused to raise the issue again.

Random passersby continued to enter his run-down shed. As usual he sat on the floor, straight and solemn, listening to their descriptions without making a sound. The disappearance of the notebook hadn't affected the unique communication between them. Among those random passersby were some who had visited him before and others who had never been there. Without mentioning it, they all experienced the benefit of not having the notebook because now they could talk about whatever they wanted without worrying. After they had arrived at the Recorder's shed, every one of them would speak, whether for a long time or a short time. So they started talking, yet who could hear clearly what they were talking about? That was impossible. It was not until today — this is quite a few years after it happened — that we realized that those people had never said anything meaningful. Instead they were only pronouncing some syllables willy-nilly to pass the time. And the Recorder was not listening carefully but only pretended to pay attention. As a matter of fact, he was thinking of something else. It was certain that he was thinking of that blank image and waiting impatiently for its arrival. Yet he knew that one cannot rush this sort of thing. Therefore, he had to pretend to be listening to the dreams. It was with such purposeful procrastination that they passed the endless time, repeating the same thing again and again, patiently.

From the Recorder's point of view, throwing away the notebook was of course free and easy, perfect. However, it also had some drawbacks, one being that he was more and more dependent on the dreamers. He had classified his life into several periods on the standard of the arrival of the dreamers. He no longer remembered how much time he had spent in the shed. In fact, his concept of time had completely disappeared. Whenever he was recalling certain events he would think this way: "That's the day when that dark, skinny-faced man arrived . . ." or "That afternoon when the woman with butterfly freckles arrived . . ." or "That day without anybody stopping by . . ." or "That morning when the person came then left without saying anything . . ." et cetera. Such classifications appeared very convenient, yet because fewer people were coming to him, his memory was deteriorating gradually. This method of classification, as a result, embodied great vagueness and even falsity because it distorted sequence, and very often vague things would happen. Fortunately, now he didn't care that much about such things, and he had become increasingly casual.

If within one day more than two passersby arrived, the Recorder would consider that day as a festival. When the dreamers had departed, he would still sit in the shed with his back straight and with his solemn facial expression. His whole body including his heart was trembling amidst the light that nobody, not even he himself could see. Such an event was not common, and the Recorder knew it himself; therefore, he didn't appear anxious. He also knew that the dreamers did not come of their own free will. The will that determined their arrival was in fact inside his mind. Now that he had stopped stretching out his neck to stare down the road, most of the time he felt calm. His only hint of impatience would occur at the moment when a dreamer arrived, because he already knew what the consequence would be. Afterwards, he could be seen creeping about, shivering in the cold wind and blowing warm air onto his finger joints, which were as swollen as little steamed buns, yet in his eyes there danced indescribable ecstasy.

Many people say that the Recorder was a fictitious being because he couldn't even prove his own existence, and they are right. There was no proof of the existence of the Recorder himself, at least for the middle and late periods of his career in recording. He was shrinking into his strange and unique shell, until finally nobody could see any trace of him. What they saw was only an empty shell that had been abandoned by the roadside. The shell was similar to the most ordinary shell of the river clam. Once in a while someone asserted that he could hear the sound of the Recorder as though from an extremely deep rock cave, but because that cave was so profound, when the sound arrived at his ear it was almost like the weeping of an ant. Such assertions were of little use.

It's true that every day we saw the Recorder sitting in the shed by the road in the same posture and behaving in the same way. The strange thing was that whenever we intended to consider him as being of the same species, there would arise unexpected doubts about his personal life as we have described it as well as the mysterious communication between him and the passersby. But these were things that had been explained from his own personal perspective. Without that, everybody felt it would be impossible to make an adequate analysis of him. Almost nobody could remember any specific details about him, such as a word or phrase, a facial expression, a gesture, a line he had written and so on. Everything about him existed in his own description, yet that description was only dimly discernible and lacked continuity. The key here was that nobody could recreate his description in their own language.

Nineteen-ninety was the tenth year after the Recorder set up his shed by the roadside. There was an unparalleled snowstorm. After the big snow, all the inhabitants swarmed onto the streets, stamping their feet, blowing warm air into their hands and discussing the storm. When they walked into the run-down shed of the Recorder, they saw that the storm had blown away half of the roof, and inside the snow was piled up more than two feet deep. People found the Recorder sitting quietly in the snow drifts. His eyebrows and hair were piled with snowflakes. No one noticed that a cloud of warm steam was rising high from the back of his neck. What kind of energy source was steaming inside his body?

"From now on nobody will come to discuss their dreamlands," the Recorder declared to the arrivals in a firm tone. "That era has passed. I have decided this just now." Nobody was listening to him. Nobody was noticing him. Nobody had ever thought of noticing him.

The Recorder was still sitting by the roadside waiting. Now there was no longer anybody to come to him. That is to say, what he was waiting for was no longer those dreamers. His body was seated straight. His dried, skinny face was always inclined toward the north, and on his face there was an expression of having abandoned everything. He was still indulging himself in that empty image, yet people could no longer discern his reaction toward it. What people saw was a person in rags, a figure close to an idiot, wasting time sitting in a tumbled-down shed by the roadside. Such unconventional behavior did not arouse people's good feeling toward him; instead now people cold-shouldered him. When they were passing by, they would turn their heads away intentionally, or they would raise their voices, pretending that they did not notice that shed.

171

Thus the external time classification of the Recorder had stopped. Pretty soon he had lost the feeling of time. Once or twice a day he would walk out of his shed to look at the vehicles passing by, the pedestrians and the sky above him. Of course it's more likely he did not see anything but only pretended to be observing. There was no set time for his walking out of the shed — sometimes it was in the morning, sometimes in the afternoon, sometimes at midnight. At the beginning he didn't know what he was doing himself. It dawned on him after several days that he was classifying time again according to his own subjective will. This was a brand new kind of time. From then on he was going to live in this kind of time, and he had decided this himself.

Once upon a time there was such a Recorder. Yet this was not a very important thing because for us nothing that cannot be proved is important. We only recognize that there existed this person, we saw him and remembered him — we said so in 1990.

The inner world of the Recorder was more and more carefree. He could hear ten thousand horses galloping in his chest, and he felt the temperature of his blood rising and rising. Every thump of his heart would make him intoxicated in the extreme. He still could not see that miraculous image. Even if he had seen it, he could not have described it because he had abandoned his skill and he no longer knew how to describe. That was the source of his secret sorrow. Yet this sorrow itself was the spring for happiness, and this could never be known by others.

As he walked out of his shed, his whole body and heart felt vaguely that he was walking into that image. He could see nothing, but people saw him watching the passing cars. Thus the time that he calculated subjectively was increasing. He felt deeply that there would no longer be any recording. Yet in comparison to his former recording career, he felt that the present life was fixed, like an iron railroad which drove straight into the emptiness ahead. Although the forms in his imagination were still obscure, he was no longer bothered by this because he didn't need to express anything. He was only recording inside his own mind. This was only our guess because nobody knew.

The white-haired old woman had come several times. She stayed longer and longer in the shed. People saw her touching the Recorder's forehead with her ice-cold fingers, but that's all. Both sides had kept their silence. This was something that people noticed in passing but forgot about immediately afterwards. Every time after the old woman left, the Recorder would go out of the shed at a quick pace. He would stand up straight on a rock placed by the roadside for road construction and focus his glances on the sky, searching anxiously for something. What was there in the sky? Of course, there was nothing. The Recorder would descend from the stone disheartened. He would ponder gloomily for a while, then become cheerful again.

On the street, cars streamed by; the battered shed, resembling a lonely island, endlessly shuddered.

ANONYMITIES

She never arrived when he expected. To put this another way, she always appeared in his apartment just at the moment he thought she would. Every time she arrived he saw in his mind's eye a clear image — a triangle with a grayish white fog along its edges. Now she had arrived once more. Sitting lightly on the table, she was jabbering something to him. When she sat down, the table did not move the least bit, though her glance was as blazing hot as it had been on other occasions, enough to make him feel a pressure he was very familiar with. She took his cup to get herself a drink of water. After she finished, she tilted the mug toward the sunlight and examined it for a long time. Then she waved it in the air as if she were ladling something. "*Gudong-gudong-gudong,*" she gurgled, and his Adam's apple bobbed twice accordingly. Usually every gesture of hers would lead directly to some physical response from him.

Perhaps because she had walked very fast when she came, he could smell the faint sweat on her body. This displeased him a little bit. Oddly, she had seemed never to perspire when she was young, and he had gotten used to her without perspiration. As soon as he sat down, he sank deep into memory. Yet this memory was constantly interrupted by the sound she was making. That sound came from her riffling through sheets of paper. She had picked up a stack of white paper from his drawer and was shuffling the leaves over and over as if she had found a way to entertain herself. Her pointed nails were pressing into those sheets, her shoulders were trembling and her nostrils emitted a faint whistling full of satisfaction. So he stopped his reminiscing and stared at her playing her game as if he were somewhat fascinated.

173

The fact is he had never considered her age seriously. Somehow he felt he had known her for a relatively long time. Therefore, she could not be very young. But from the very beginning, he could not figure out her age. When he asked her, she replied that she didn't know, and she added that it was because there was no way she could know. As for him, at the time he was in his prime. Generally speaking, it had never occurred to him that another person's age could become a problem. However, the relationship between them grew in phases. Under careful analysis, it was very similar to the growth process of a plant from the time of its sprout breaking through the earth until the time of its withering away. But he could barely distinguish which period in their relationship corresponded to which stages of the plant's growth. He always felt that the whole matter was very vague and wouldn't be clarified until the last minute.

At present, her calmly turning over the pages gave him a feeling of perfect peace. In the distant past, she used to be impatient. Sometimes she could even be rude. He still remembered that she had thrown his favorite blue-flowered porcelain mug out the window. Besides that she had thrown away some other things. That day, when outside the window the sky was filled with galloping clouds, the two of them had lain on the bed side by side for a long, long time. Their bodies had turned bloody red. Suddenly she had crawled over him and thrown out that porcelain mug. They both heard the cup shatter. After she had gone, he went downstairs looking for the broken mug. He saw that the thick grass in the garden had become blackish green and as tall as a human figure.

She had also criticized his residence. According to her description, he was jammed amongst crowded skyscrapers and everywhere surrounded by irritating noise. He was not very clear about his own environment. He was born in this apartment, and had been living there ever since. There was a period when she sealed all the windows and doors with thick craft paper, turning the room into a dungeon filled with body odor. After doing this she disappeared for a fairly long time. When she arrived again, it appeared that she did not even notice that he had torn away all the craft paper. It was at that time that he knew she had a problem with forgetfulness.

The moment when he thought of this, her hands stopped flipping the paper. With her shining glance she stared at his forehead. Stretching out her hand, she picked up the empty mug and made another gesture of ladling water.

"You are reminiscing about something." She said these words clearly. Then she jumped down from the table and walked toward the corner of the room. She stood there silently. He heard the clock at the station chime three P.M. Outside the window the air was a bright white.

"You have come and gone, gone and then come, numerous times. Now I don't even care whether you are coming or going. Sometimes I don't even know whether you are going or coming." This he said while facing the window. He didn't want her to hear too clearly. When he turned around she had disappeared, leaving her faint sweaty odor in the air.

That was the longest night. He paced up and down in the dimly lit morgue of the hospital, uncovering every corpse for identification, once, twice, three times, four times. . . . At four o'clock in the morning he returned to his apartment, cold sweat covering his body, feeling dizzy. She was already waiting in the shadow at the turn of the staircase.

She threw herself on his bosom, trembling. As soon as they entered the room, she closed all the curtains and refused to turn on the light. Her hair gave off the heavy odor of the morgue as well as the odor of the frosty wind of early morning. She made him smell those corpses again.

"There were altogether fifty-three," he whispered into her ear.

After she warmed up, she groaned faintly. Then she said confidently: "It's all in vain. You! Why didn't you recognize me? You repeated again and again without even knowing it. I know in your mind there is another person, yet it's all in vain!"

That morning both of them were so ardent. In the dim light he noticed that her eyebrows had turned a deep red and her pointed nails were glittering.

"I have looked and looked, looked and looked, oh!" he groaned, falling into that bottomless cave, his whole body entangled by tentacles. His thumb had started bleeding. "Now my whole body is covered with that odor. I never expected it to be like this. Maybe it's been this way from the very beginning. Is it true that my sense of smell is developing day by day?"

"Let's analyze it together," she said, flipping on the light. He dared not look at her in the dazzling light, so closing his eyes he turned around to face the wall.

"So you haven't recognized me even once?" Stroking his back

tenderly she continued, "Do you feel that's difficult? It's not really! You know that there's a tiny mole under my left ear. Why did you forget to check their ears? Altogether there were only fifty-three people, yet you wasted a whole night. Ever since we departed last time I just knew you would go to a place like that. It can be said that you have been looking for that person ever since you were born. But you didn't know it when you were young. That's all. Next time make sure that you don't forget to check those ears."

He woke up when the big clock at the station was striking nine o'clock. He could hear the rustling sound she was making in the room. Forcing his eyes open, he saw that she was pasting up the craft paper again. One of her long legs was planted on the table, the other on the window sill. Her shoulders rose and fell. She was completely focused and meticulous. Without turning her head, she knew that he had awakened. With one forceful jump, she sprang to the bed, then rolled over his body to the floor. She crawled to the door quietly, opened it and disappeared into the darkness.

Waiting is unbearable, especially that kind of waiting for which there is no clear termination. In those protracted days he realized the full benefits of the craft paper. Sometimes he would not leave the apartment for a long time. In the darkness he completely forgot how many days had passed. In addition, once he closed the door and breathed only the air of the two of them, this made him calm down. With the craft paper on the window and the door, he imagined himself as a mole. Occasionally he would be lured by his fantasy, then he would open a tear in the craft paper to look at the bright whiteness outside the window. Every time he would be startled and his heart would thump.

He only went outside deep in the night when the station clock struck twelve and when there were scarcely any pedestrians on the street. As a result, it was almost natural that he should participate in the murder. This he did with a fruit knife in collaboration with a tall masked man. It was on the ground floor of his apartment building that this person struck an old man with a stick. As the victim was falling slowly, he dashed over and stabbed at the position of the old man's heart in his left chest. He couldn't pull his knife out. With the knife in his chest, the old man mumbled something. Hurriedly, he turned back the old man's ear. Without a doubt, under his left ear there was a mole. From it spurted a drop of blood. The big masked man shouted, pushed him aside, lifted the corpse and walked toward the riverbank at a quick pace, leaving him standing there alone in a daze.

"This is your first time to do such a thing," the masked man sneered at his back. "You are looking for some kind of proof. Somebody told you a certain method, yet it cannot bear any result. I've seen this kind of thing so often. Don't believe anybody's method. You'll get used to it if you do it more often."

The whole matter drove him to distraction for a long time.

Whenever he returned to his apartment early in the morning and passed that long, pitch-dark corridor, he would hold his breath to listen closely, hoping she would jump out from her hiding place, yet every time he was disappointed. She hadn't been to his apartment for three months. He knew she had very casual habits; therefore, this time maybe she had forgotten. More and more carefully, he opened and closed the door, attempting to keep her odor in the room for the longest time, although amidst that odor was the sweaty smell which had once aroused his unhappiness.

One night as soon as he lay down, someone knocked three times clearly on his window pane. Jumping up he opened the window, yet there was only the wind blowing outside. At that moment he remembered that he was living on the tenth floor and a person couldn't possibly hang outside the window. At that instant there flashed in his mind's eye that triangle, now with red light along its edges. It was humming. Unexpectedly she did not appear.

The last few days of waiting, he was full of hatred. He tore away all the craft paper, smashed the window glass, crumpled up the paper that bore her fingernail marks and disassembled the bed in which he had slept with her. Then he left the apartment and wandered aimlessly along the river early in the morning.

All of a sudden he saw her standing on a boat filled with passengers, one long leg on top of the rail along the deck. Her torn clothing was streaming in the wind, and she was staring into the water. Afterwards she saw him and smiled blankly. She pointed at her temple and then at the river. He didn't understand her meaning, yet he became extraordinarily annoyed by this lack of understanding, so all he could do was wave madly and fruitlessly at her while he was running breathlessly with the boat along the river bank. He must have appeared to be overrating his physical abilities ridiculously. The boat was pulling away gradually. She had left the deck for the cabin. The whistle blew twice wickedly.

He stopped. Was this boat going back to the city or leaving it? Clutching his head he pondered and pondered. Finally he felt he should clarify the matter at the dock. He had been to the dock several times, yet at this instant he couldn't remember which direction he should go. Then he recalled that he had discussed this problem with her late at night. She had insisted that this was a permanently unsolvable puzzle. As she was saying that, she made a boat with her palms sailing back and forth in front of him and blowing the whistle with her mouth, a sound not unlike the two he had just heard. It seemed that he should not go to the dock but rather to any other place of his own choosing. Right. He should go to that park in which they had first met. It was by a fence on the lawn that he had discovered her sitting in the open air. At the moment he had been overjoyed by the discovery, but now when he thought about it he found there were some doubtful elements within the emotions of the time.

He walked all day except for stopping by the roadside to eat two pieces of bread and some ice cream. It was not until dusk fell that he entered the park. There were great changes in the park. He couldn't recognize that section of lawn. Perhaps there had never been a lawn. Nor flower beds and gardeners. Everywhere there were low wooden houses resembling each other with their doors tight shut and people rattling the same thing inside each house. Between houses there were only very narrow walkways. Without care one might brush against the dirty, damp brick walls. He wandered back and forth among the houses, hearing those monotonous rattling voices rising up into the silent night sky forming a gigantic wave of voices rumbling over him.

Finally one door opened and there appeared a dark shadow. Quickly, he walked over and recognized the figure as the old man who patroled the park. He appeared much older now. He asked the old man the direction of the original lawn and how he could exit from this group of houses.

"You can never find it, nor can you exit because it is night now." He guessed that the old man was laughing at him with a bit of contempt. "At night everything looks exactly the same, and you might feel that if you came oftener. There haven't been any tourists for quite a few years because it's too monotonous. Perhaps you're the only tourist who's been here for many years. Yet that's no use. You can't stay on. I'm going in. I can't stay outside for too long." He closed the door sharply and snapped off the light inside. In one instant all the lights in all the wooden houses were turned off and the chattering stopped. It was dark all around except for the vague silhouettes of the houses. He felt his way along the brick walls.

"It's too monotonous here. It's easy to divert your attention. Please watch out," the old patrolman said, although where he was standing could not be made out. Yet his words were reassuring. Standing for a while gazing over those vague, dark mushrooms in front of him, he realized it was time for him to return to his apartment.

This time she was waiting for him at the front gate of his building. In the glow of dawn her smile was as fresh as a new leaf.

"I went to the place where we met for the first time. It's so strange that it turned out to be a stone pit, but what I remembered is so much richer," he said, feeling bubbles rise in his lungs. "I hadn't realized until now that this whole thing has had a decisive influence on me."

"No individual thing has decisive significance for you," she said.

The door had been blown open. Wind blew in through the broken window glass. She tittered. Picking up a fairly big piece of broken glass, she stared at it, facing the sunshine. The edge of the glass cut her finger. Blood dripped onto the other glass. The sun shone on them. They appeared gaily colored.

"It's not necessary to go to that park or stone pit often. We only met there incidentally. You only need to think of one place in your mind, and that place becomes your destiny." Putting her cut finger into her mouth, she sucked with force. She said vaguely, "That's all it is." After she finished the sentence, she spat out a big mouthful of blood, making the whole room smell of blood. Her finger was still dripping. Suddenly she said, "I'm leaving." Turning around, she walked out. Like a gust of wind, she ran down the staircase, leaving a trail of blood in the corridor.

Returning to his apartment, he covered the window again with craft paper and assembled the bed that had been dismantled. Then he lay down deep in thought amidst the thick smell of blood.

He remembered the time when they had gotten to know each other. She had been so full of vigor, indulging in fantasies. Every day she never tired of looking for something new. Once they had even climbed to the top of the commercial building in the city and thrown a bag of garbage onto the crowds below. When they descended the building she was giggling endlessly. Now when he reminisced about it, the memory seemed unimportant. But at the time it was full of joy. Often there had been partings, but every time he had been full of hope and imagination, not the impatience and hatred that now possessed him. Since when had she turned so gloomy and rigid toward him, become so indifferent toward the things that he cared for? Once he had thought her to be a warmhearted woman. At the beginning he thought she was just worn out and would not come again. Yet after a while she had come back. Maybe the time between two visits grew a little bit longer, but she had never left without looking back. This morning was the first time in a long time that he had seen her laugh. He had doubted if she could even smile.

Before he fell into sleep he struggled to the window and looked down by raising the craft paper. He saw her standing on the street in front of the grocery store raising her injured hand. She also saw him, so using the other hand she pointed at her feet and nodded her head. He didn't understand the meaning of her gesture, not even once. Whenever he thought of that he felt very disheartened. He fell into sleep dejected and slept very deeply.

When he awoke he noticed many bloody finger marks on the wall put there by her the day before. At the time, he hadn't noticed, but after one day the blood marks had turned a bit black. They looked like leeches crawling on the wall, making him uneasy. Watching those leeches — her masterpiece — he remembered she had always been against him, and she was always mysterious in her ways. Nobody could predict what she was going to do in the next minute. With her back towards him and her face towards the wall, she said in a harsh voice, "People like me had better hide themselves in order not to upset people." He turned her face back and saw an expression similar to that of a little deer being chased. He was so touched that he almost cried out. That time they stayed together for three days without leaving each other for one minute. At dusk, they would open the window and watch the sunset. Standing at the window hugging tightly against each other, they exchanged breath. She even leapt into the air naughtily. Every time she did so, he would be so frightened that his face turned pale and he would pull her down tightly. In the short three days, she forgot about things like the craft paper. She was jumping up and down and saying crazy things. Perhaps it was because both of them were young at the time, and also they were confused by the emotion caused by pity. That was the longest time she stayed. It was so long that he even had some illusion that she would stay forever. But, of course, this result was not to be.

Later on they could no longer share such intimate talk. Instead, they would talk vaguely and exchange evasive glances. When they met on the street, they would greet each other with some vague gesture the same way she did in front of the grocery store. This method was decided on by her, and he went along with it. It appeared that they had a tacit understanding, but in reality they were very distant. Even at the climax of making love, the feeling was vague and ambiguous as if they were thousands of mountains and thousands of rivers apart. It was totally different from love-making with other women when he was young. Every time when it was finished he would be overwhelmed by an infinite confusion, his head feeling as if a bird's nest had grown there. At those moments he meant to dash out and chase her, yet he had no confidence whatsoever. Finally he would drop the idea. It was not because of his self-esteem, but just because he felt it would be in vain.

As she got older, her tone and glances became colder, and their distance and grievances grew deeper until they began holding grudges against each other. Once she revealed to him that their present situation was the best, exactly what she wanted, because it reflected the truth of their relationship. If they were, instead, to do nothing but stand at the window enjoying the setting sun, she would have to jump down and never return. However, such a relationship was horrifying. He couldn't remember how many times he had sneaked into the morgues of those hospitals to check the corpses, feeling exhausted from anxiety and fear. And he never dared to doze off in the morgues because there was always a red-eyed cat glaring at him fiercely. The days of waiting were endless spiritual torture because there were no lines or color there, just complete emptiness. It was during that period that his mouthful of strong teeth started to loosen.

Then an odd thing happened — she bit a small piece of flesh from his arm. According to her, she did it unintentionally, and she promised that nothing similar would happen in the future. The wound was not deep and healed quickly, leaving only a tiny scar. But whenever he thought of it he shivered with fear. When he inquired as to where the flesh that she bit off went, she replied that she had swallowed it. When she said that, she appeared furious, sending a chill up his spine. Yet he missed her every minute, every second, even missed the long bench by the fence on the lawn. It was there that she sat in the open air and gave him that magnificent talk. Besides there was that warm, sliding sun, the rising warmth from the earth, making him mistake her for a fine young maiden. She had forgotten all that long ago. Whenever he raised the issue later on, she appeared bored. Using her strong index finger, she would make a decisive gesture to stop his story. "I was only waiting for a boat there," she would say shortly and drily. He couldn't help feeling very indignant.

It was fairly recent that she had gone to the extremes in her appearance. In the past, she had never paid much attention to her appearance. Yet she always dressed simply and comfortably. Her clean underwear gave off a fine fragrance. But recently she had put on a set of extremely ugly men's clothes and refused to change. They had become dirtier and dirtier, shabbier and shabbier. Yet she even boasted about them, saying they were so convenient. In the past, time spent washing clothes was nothing but trouble for her, and so on. Then she would say that since now she could no longer smell the odor of the dirty clothes why should she spend time pursuing formalities. It was even acceptable that she would not take a bath from now on. The only reason she kept taking baths and washing her hair was as compromise with his strange habits, despite the fact that she felt they were vulgar. This took place in the third month after she cut her finger. They saw each other at the dock. Both appeared a little bit wan and sallow, a little bit melancholy. He told her he had heard someone knocking at the window of his apartment late at night. Could it have been her?

"That's impossible. When I'm outside I never think of you. You've known for a long time that I don't have a memory." She wrinkled her nose slightly. "Can you guess if I have just returned or am planning to leave? An eternal puzzle." She pointed at the passing boats and asked him to look. The river appeared vast and endless with boats floating as if in the universe.

He did not answer her question because he knew it had no answer. It was she who had told him that. Lowering his head, he saw that her bare feet wearing the sandals had turned a bit rough.

"Shall we return to the apartment?" he asked.

"No," she said harshly. "From now on let's see each other here. It's very convenient for both of us. Of course, there's no way for me to arrange the date ahead of time. You'll just have to come often and see if I'm here. That shouldn't be too difficult." Arrogantly she threw back her short hair, putting her hands into her wide pockets.

"I turned over a person's ear, and I saw that mole," he said. "At the moment I was in a unique situation."

"There are such cheap marks everywhere," she sneered in contempt. "Now you'd better go. Let me see you disappear among the crowd."

"It's you who has raised the issue."

"It's possible that I have said so. Don't always remember. You should forget along the way. Why don't you go?"

At that moment a gray boat was anchoring. She raised her long legs and boarded the ship. This time she did not look back. The boat gradually sailed away as if it were departing into the vast universe.

But he knew there was a thread linking him with that boat. He turned around and walked away. At every step he felt his chest being pulled at painfully by that thread. At the same time, that triangle in his mind's eye was shooting out gold sparks.

I once watched a student slam her Godot on the desk and stalk out muttering, "When I wake up in the morning, all I want is a cigarette, and somebody friendly to talk to!" Can Xue is another writer capable of spoiling the morning coffee.

Some readers can't scan more than a few lines of her work before shaking their heads in bewilderment and putting the text aside. Others manifest verbal spasms resembling those of Can Xue's own most extreme characters. One sinologue claims (in print, for everyone to see) to have read all of Can Xue's stories backwards without finding any sense in them. But Li Tuo, one of China's best literary critics, includes her among those recent writers who have created the languages and forms necessary for perceiving newly emerging realities.

By Flaubertian standards, writing for Can Xue is not a true craft. Language is a barrier and makes her impatient. Her work is, rather, a kind of stampede through arenas of feeling that are, in most Chinese people, pent-up frustrations and passions. But even in her eruptions of incoherence and eccentricity, one easily perceives zones of attention that govern her diction and images and act as substitute in her idea of style for close attention to verbal craft. Largely, these are matters of tone. In her comic mode, she writes like the village gossip might — obsessed, acerbic, spiteful, hyperbolic, self-absorbed. In her tragic mode, she grinds the world to bits; in her lyric mode, she sings of flowers and sunshine and childhood.

In the United States, Can Xue's work is recognizable to all who care to sit still for a moment and reflect. Her character types crowd the main roads and byways of our fiction from Cooper forward. In our part of the century, writers like Kerouac have idealized them. Thomas Berger has seen their individual and private fanaticisms as contiguous with public and national ones.

It's been eight years already, but I still remember vividly the original force of "The Hut on the Mountain" when one of my graduate students in Shanghai offered it as "something you might be interested in." One of the first qualities that impressed me was the story's imagistic power, and one of the images that has stayed in my mind is that nest of blazing stones as the narrator makes her climb up the mountain. Stones I love, and the deep convulsions that spew them across the landscape. For me the "dry rock" portions of The Waste Land are the equivalent of pastoral nature imagery. Ruskin, Pound, Guillevic, Ian Hamilton Finlay, Paul Caponigro, Emmet Gowin. The splintered, the broken, the disrupted. Karl Orff, Tan Dun, Susan Howe, Can Xue.

The function of such art and artists is to keep our feet on the ground. Compared with their methods of narration and visualization, our customary modes of telling are wildly utopian in coherence and logic and harmony. In the metropolis of the dying years of the twentieth century, the bourgeois idea of order and reason is a mere dream of a dream of a human childhood that never existed anywhere anyway. Our artists come to call us back to our authentic and quite hopeless madness, a subject for which Can Xue is something of a specialist.

—Ronald R. Janssen

From Walking Words
E*duardo Galeano*

— Translated from Spanish by Mark Fried
With illustrations by José Francisco Borges

STORY OF THE FATAL ENCOUNTER BETWEEN THE DESERT BANDIT AND THE REPENTANT POET

HE WAS the survivor.

Firmino, old master in the art of banditry, was fleeing toward the countryside near Pernambuco. In an ambush at the foot of a precipice, army bullets had done in his woman and all his friends. He had been mutilated inside, and his remains wandered sadly in solitude.

That night it rained hard in the desert, something that never happens. Lightning revealed several skeletons dressed in military uniforms and hats, kicking in the air. The victims of many years of outrage had come to collect from Firmino the time he owed them for having dispatched them too soon. And their ghostly howls clamored for vengeance.

Waving his knife and swinging the butt of his rifle, Firmino fought the army of bones that rose up with the storm.

At last the rain stopped, as suddenly as it began. And in a moment, all the moisture evaporated and the dead went back to sleep under the dry ground.

Firmino, greatest scoundrel of the kingdom, could continue his flight.

After a long march, he cut some branches to make a fire and the bushes bled.

Firmino understood. But he pushed on.

The lost will be the found, sang Sabino the poet, and the earth will give birth to stars that will humble the heavens. The dumb will be radio announcers and we will have hospitals without sick people where today we have sick people without hospitals.

Reciter of verses in marketplaces far from the coast, Sabino the poet sang the prophecies of the red cow. The cow, which flew in his dreams, told him that the desert would be sea and fields of stone would burst with verdure, and that those in the know had seen birth without death and weeks full of Sundays.

This he sang until he grew weary. The poet Sabino got sick of reciting and waiting. And he repented having spent his life on a pilgrimage amid the poor and the damned in a hell of stone. He discovered that things are the way they are because they've always been and always will be the way God wants them. And he gave up his nights with the crazy cow that dreamt him rubbish. And he went over to the government. No longer did he raise his wooden sword to vent the serpent of sadness, but to punish the enemies of the established order.

Firmino continued walking toward the countryside of Pernambuco or wherever his legs would carry him.

One morning, not far from some hamlet, footsteps awakened him. He leapt up and pulled out his knife. But when he saw Sabino, a boiled chicken in suit and tie, standing in the middle of the thicket, the bandit calmly started shredding tobacco.

The poet introduced himself: Sabino, humble rhapsode at your service; he said that he had always dreamed of meeting the atrocious scourge of the desert, the lord of evil, and today destiny affords me this surprise which I certainly do not merit and which for me means more, much more than . . .

Firmino rolled a cigarette and lit up.

"A great honor," whispered Sabino, swallowing hard.

A few flies were the only audience.

The bandit sent a few smoke rings skyward, and sized up the stuttering bookworm before blowing him away.

Sabino, his face down, counted ants; but suddenly he drew his sword.

The wooden saber trembled in his hand. His voice shook even more: "I'd like to ask you a little favor," he sighed.

He wiped his forehead and eyes with a handkerchief, and he mouthed his entreaty: "Allow me . . . to cut off your head."

Firmino laughed out loud, a great belly laugh that rolled and rolled until he had used up all the laughter stored away since the last time he laughed so very long ago. Then he coughed.

And then he stretched out his neck: "Proceed, doctor."

The poet Sabino held the wooden sword with both hands and hung on for dear life.

The bandit Firmino stood up and stroked his neck.

The poet blinked. A rabbitlike groan escaped him and at last he was able to plead: "Say no."

The brigand did him the favor. Why not? You don't deny that to anyone. So the terror of the Northeast said: "No."

But the poet muttered: "Say no . . . with your head."

And then, when the bandit shook his head, it came loose and rolled on the ground.

The victory of Civilization over Barbarism made headlines across the front pages of the local, regional, national, continental and global press. In a public ceremony carried live by the BBC of London, Sabino received the reward and donated it to charity. The book that narrated his feat was translated into English, French, German and Esperanto, and the poet Sabino was chosen Man of the Year by *Time*.

Firmino's soul went straight to heaven.

On earth his corpse was split in two. The body was thrown to the vultures and the head to the scientists. Before his mummified head landed in a case in the Museum of Cangaceiros, the scientists proved that Firmino had been an ectomorphic-type higher mammal belonging to the Brazilian-Xanthodermic group. Their analysis revealed a psychopathic personality evidenced by certain bulges in

the skull characteristic of cold-blooded assassins from the mountains of obscure countries. The subject's criminal destiny was also apparent from one ear that was nine millimeters shorter than the other, and from the pointed head and oversized jaws with large eyeteeth that continued chewing after he was dead.

Firmino went to heaven because that's where his woman was, and because someone had told him there would be room up there for errant knights fallen in the noble art of warfare.

He was a knight without a horse. He went to heaven on foot, all the way up the high road to glory, with his Winchester as a walking stick and a silver dagger at his waist. A measured gait, elegantly armored. Bathed in perfume, glistening with brilliantine, rings shining on every finger, Firmino wore a large cross of glowing bullets and a Napoleon hat dripping medals and pounds sterling and other trinkets. After a long ascent, he arrived at the gates of Paradise. And Saint Peter would not let him in.

God himself sent word to forbid him entry. The Supreme Being could not close his ears to the unanimous clamor of angels, archangels and saints. Firmino's woman, who got into heaven by mistake, sleeps with them all. She is the only fire burning in eternity. When she makes love and dances, sparks shoot from her belly and the immortal tedium of celestial peace is relieved.

So Saint Peter didn't let him in. And Firmino did not beg, or say a word. He stood waiting in silence.

A long time has passed and Firmino is still there, waiting hat in hand, standing firm at the gates of Paradise.

From his observatory in the depths, Lucifer contemplates the situation with some consternation. Lucifer sees it coming; he groans: "I always get the worst."

STORY OF THE PARROT'S RESURRECTION

The parrot fell into a steaming pot. He stuck up his head, felt dizzy and fell back in. He fell in because he was curious, and he drowned in the hot soup.

The girl, who was his friend, cried.

The orange peeled off its skin and offered itself to console her.

The fire under the pot repented and went out.

The wall released a stone.

The tree leaning against the wall trembled with grief and all its leaves fell to the ground.

Like every other day, the wind arrived to comb the leafy tree, and found it bare. When the wind heard the story, it expelled a gusty sigh.

The gust opened the window, blew about the world aimlessly and went to heaven.

When heaven heard the bad news, it grew pale.

And seeing the heavens go pale, man was left speechless.

The potter of Ceará wanted to know. At long last man recovered his tongue and explained that the parrot drowned
   and the girl cried
   and the orange peeled off its skin
   and the fire went out
   and the wall lost a stone
   and the tree lost its leaves
   and the wind lost a gust
   and the window blew open
   and heaven was left without color
   and man without words.

Then the potter brought together all that sadness. And with this material his hands managed to bring back the dead.
   The parrot born from grief had red feathers from the fire
   and blue feathers from the sky
   and green feathers from the leaves of the tree
   and a beak hard from the stone and golden from the orange
   and he had human words to speak
   and water from the tears to drink and feel refreshed
   and he had an open window for escaping
   and off he flew in the gust of wind.

STORY OF THE SHADOW

The first taste he remembers was a carrot.
  The first smell, a lime cut in half.
  He remembers that he cried when he discovered distance.
  And he remembers the morning he discovered his shadow.

That morning he saw what, until then, he had looked at without seeing: stuck to his feet lay a shadow longer than his body.

He walked, he ran. Wherever he went, no matter where, the shadow pursued him.

He wanted to get rid of it. He wanted to step on it, kick it, beat it; but the shadow, quicker than his legs and arms, always managed to elude him. He wanted to jump over it, but it always jumped ahead. Turning swiftly, he got rid of it in front, but it reappeared in back. He hugged close to a tree trunk, leaned up against a wall, ducked behind a door. Wherever he hid, the shadow found him.

At last he managed to break free. He took a flying leap, stretched out in a hammock and separated himself from his shadow.

It lay under the net, waiting for him.

Later he found out that clouds, night and noon suppress shadows. And he found out that shadows always come back, coaxed by the sun, like a ring in search of your finger, or a coat traveling toward your body.

And he got used to it.

When he grew, his shadow grew with him. And he was afraid of losing it.

Time passed. And now that he is shrinking, in the final days of his life, he is afraid of dying and leaving it alone.

196

STORY OF THE FEMALE AVENGER AND THE ARCHANGEL
IN THE PALACE OF SINNERS

Dear Mr. Writer:

I am moved to write to you not out of admiration but out of pity for your minimal inspiration and limited imagination. In your prose, which is as proper as it is pedestrian, readers never find anything they haven't already read.

This letter offers you the chance to reveal your normally hidden talent, that is, if you have some hidden somewhere. Believe me, you don't need to be a genius to cook up a good story with all the ingredients I'll give you. You may be wondering: Why me and not another? In the first place, someone gave me your address. In the second place, all writers worth their salt are six feet under where the postman doesn't go.

Let's start with the scene: high on a hill, in a white tower that reached the stars, stood the brothel of Comayagua. The church was below. Half the town went to the brothel, the whole town went to mass and the processions. That's how Comayagua yawned its way through history.

197

Eduardo Galeano

In case it's of any use, I'll transcribe a traveler's summation of the attitude of the respectable ladies: *The scandal began here after Independence when close dances hit town. In the times of the Spaniards, people danced apart without touching, the minuet from France, the jota from Aragón . . .*

The brothel belonged to Don Idilio Gallo. The girls worked night and day without a moment's rest. Don Idilio drained their youth to the last drop. When they were bone dry, he sent them back to the street. I beg you not to spend too many words on this point, dear writer, given your notorious tendency to preach, and do allow Calamity Jane to come on stage right away. After all, while their treatment may have left something to be desired, Don Idilio Gallo's girls didn't have it so bad — compared with the rest of the frogs croaking at the bottom of that hole.

Calamity Jane arrived in bad shape, slumped over the back of her horse Satan. She came from the Far West, chased by the echoes of Apache drums. She crossed the mountains of three countries, guided by the reflections of her diamond ring on rocky canyon walls. Calamity brought along the ring, which disappeared the first night. And she also brought along her well-earned fame of having a mother's heart, a happy trigger finger, an infallible lasso and marked cards.

The girls took her in without Don Idilio knowing. She slept for a week. When she awoke, she faced him: "The hat," she said.

Instead of uncovering his head, Don Idilio, who wasn't much of a gentleman, pulled his Stetson down to his eyebrows. Calamity drew her Colt and blew it off with one shot.

Eduardo Galeano

Continuing to shoot, she kept the hat in the air. When the hat-turned-colander finally came down, Don Idilio Gallo let out a moan and Calamity blew the smoke from her gun. "That's why I didn't stay in Rapid City," she said. "They kill a lot in that shit-hole."

Does mentioning the names Colt or Stetson seem superfluous? I'm not surprised. But a professional writer ought to know that in a credible narrative the smallest details matter most. And by the way, I suggest you take into account that Calamity used a Springfield rifle, not a Winchester as some idiots claim.

Let's continue. They played poker. The bets went up as the bottles of Jamaican rum went down, until Don Idilio lost the brothel and everything else. That overbearing pitiless man didn't even blink. He accepted his ruin with the fatalism characteristic of the Gallos, descendants of sentries who in earthquakes would sit and wait for the house to fall in on them. Calamity gave him a letter of recommendation for Buffalo Bill's circus. With nothing else in his pockets, Don Idilio left for Paris. There he put on feathers and dressed up as a redskin chief, posed for profile shots and died of pneumonia.

The brothel, which had been cold as a hospital and hard as a barracks, became filled up with birds and guitars, plants and colors. From dusk till dawn the girls opened their legs. But by daylight, and until the first bells of Angelus, they opened their ears. Experience gave them the idea. They knew that behind every macho

Eduardo Galeano

with balls hides a shipwrecked sailor begging for refuge. Their confessional was so successful that it overflowed with multitudes from the enemy city of Tegucigalpa and from everywhere else. On the sides of the hill, long lines of men waited their turn to pour out doubts and secrets and hidden fears, dreams and nightmares. The church couldn't compete. Priests, as you know, only hear the confession of sins, which is what people least need to confess.

Meanwhile, Calamity got busy straightening out her papers with Mr. Government. Having always worn pants, she tried on a skirt. She tucked a Collins bayonet into her garter and money into her undershirt.

"In an envelope," instructed Mr. Government when Calamity slipped him a fistful of hot bills. And by decree the brothel, nonprofit cooperative that it was, was exempted from all taxes and new whorehouses were prohibited in the entire national territory.

In that year of crazy prosperity, the archangel arrived. According to tradition, the palace of sinners closed its doors every Friday during Lent. And according to tradition, after Jesus of Nazareth had traveled Calvary Street on the shoulders of pious women, and the last echoes of passion canticles and Via Crucis prayers had faded, a headless horseman would appear at full gallop from the mouth of the night. The horse would kick the brothel doors, give a few terrifying bucks and tear off, chased by whirlwinds and puffs of sulfur. Then, according to tradition, one of the wayward

sheep would repent and tearfully abandon her lustful ways to begin an honest life.

That Friday, the headless horseman galloped in, blind with fury like every year, but this time the doors were open wide. The black horse went right through the brothel and disappeared in the distance; the horseman rolled onto the ground, knocked into a Tiffany lamp and crashed against a wall. He woke up in a woman's arms. "Listen señora," he protested.

"Señorita," Calamity Jane corrected him.

The horseman was an archangel, an elderly dwarf with a red nose and the voice of a child, dressed by God to look like a headless devil and frighten licentious women.

Eduardo Galeano

There was lightning and rain all night and the world awoke more luminous than ever. Morning surprised the archangel in the midst of a sitz bath, sitting in a pool of green papaya milk. The poor man had hurt his ass when the rope that lowered him from heaven broke. Beside him, Calamity, mouth open, let him do as he pleased. With honey and cinnamon, the archangel cleansed her tongue soiled by insolent cursing.

Please, I beg you, don't offend me by asking if this really happened. I'm offering it to you so you'll make it happen. I'm not asking you to describe the rain falling the night the archangel arrived: I'm demanding that you get me wet. Make up your mind, Mr. Writer, and for once in your life be the flower that smells rather than the chronicler of the aroma. There's not much pleasure in writing what you live. The challenge is to live what you write. And at your age it's time you learned.

I'll continue. As you know from the available iconology, archangels have no sex but they do have stomachs. If Adam fell for a plain old apple, how was the archangel not to give in? The brothel offered him the delicacies of its orchard: the golden flesh of the mango, the dizzying breath of the passion fruit, the freshness of the pineapple, the softness of the guanábana and the avocado.

And, as everyone knows, archangels have souls; and a soul needs to confess, even if it doesn't sin. Calamity complained about the Wild West and the archangel complained about Heaven. Chocolate kept them company by day; rum by night. She said that if she owned Wyoming and hell, she would rent out Wyoming and live in hell. And he said that having spent all eternity serving the Lord in Paradise by doing the hardest chores, the Ingrate thanked him by sending him to earth to redeem drunks and whores. She told rude secrets about General Custer and Sheriff Wild Bill Hickok, and he railed against the advisers of the Holiest One. And talking, they discovered they had spent their entire lives alone and hadn't realized it.

Some afternoons Calamity took the archangel out for a walk in the streets of Comayagua in a baby carriage. They walked proudly, impervious to resentment and envy. They were pursued by the evil tongues of anti-imperialists, atheists and the advocates of virtue and good manners. And there were always skeptics who would elbow each other and ask under their breath: How come Calamity Jane doesn't understand a word of English? What kind of an archangel doesn't have wings or a sword of fire and doesn't know a word of Latin? How come the two of them talk with accents from around here?

I don't know if this happened: I only know that it deserves to have happened.

The rest is the least of it. Time covered all tracks. You might imagine that the archangel had a fine time, life was a lot more fun than salvation. But you might also suppose that in the end Calamity tired of it all. You could suppose that in a palace wallpapered with mirrors that gave away her age she would find no place to hide. Imagine the brothel in its glory, with the National Symphonic Orchestra playing till dawn, and one night Calamity dances the belly dance, naked under a red negligee, and the audience applauds with cackles and sniggers and she fights back the tears. And the next day she leaves. She leaves without saying goodbye, when no one is looking. Her horse Satan kneels down to help her mount. She doesn't go north, back to her origins. She continues the trip south toward her destiny. Someone must have heard the sound

of hoofbeats and the whistle. She was whistling. To keep herself company? To get up her courage? You choose.

And the archangel? Did Calamity take him along in her lap? Did he go back to heaven? Did he try? Did he become a man at last, a new Idilio Gallo? Don't bother asking. No one could answer, not in Comayagua or in any other town on the planet. Sorry Mr. Writer, *homo scribere*, you have no choice but to make it up.

Yours,

(Signature illegible)

The tenderness of his anger is what first struck me. I had arrived in Mexico for the first time — it was 1973 — and Cedric Belfrage's translation of Galeano's Open Veins of Latin America had just been published: a treatise on political economy written like a novel about love or pirates. He begins: "The division of labor among nations is that some specialize in winning and others in losing. Our part of the world, known today as Latin America, was precocious: it has specialized in losing ever since those remote times

when Renaissance Europeans ventured across the ocean and buried their teeth in the throats of the Indian civilizations." And as he tells stories of the rogues and heroes who helped Latin America perfect its role, the fury builds, his (and our) blood rising at the derisively prophetic games history plays.

His is a wry, black humor that not only indicts the powerful, but incites the reader. In an afterword to the 1977 edition he tells of a girl quietly reading Open Veins on a Bogotá bus who suddenly stood up and read it aloud to all the passengers; a woman who fled Santiago in the wake of Chile's bloodbath with the book wrapped in her baby's diapers; a student who spent a week going from one bookstore to the next in Buenos Aires, reading bits of it in each store because he hadn't the money to buy it.

While I was discovering Galeano, he was in jail in his native Uruguay, arrested along with a fifth of his countrymen for the crime of spreading dangerous ideas. By then he had also published a book of short stories and a novel, but was better known for his intensely political essays and opinion pieces, and actually began his career as a cartoonist. Released after a few months, he fled to Buenos Aires, where he founded and edited a cultural magazine until a coup d'état swept Argentina too. His name turned up on the death squads' lists. As he says, "I don't like being in jail; but I like being dead even less." He fled to Spain, and lived there in exile for eight years.

Galeano thanks the Uruguayan and Argentinean generals for the time and perspective to return to literature. The first result was the marvelous trilogy Memory of Fire, an epic mosaic of the Americas' past, which combines his delight in steamy language and the short short story with his driving need to dust off history and celebrate our collective striving for freedom.

The fury has grown ever more tender over the years (his next work, which applied the style of the trilogy to his own life, is called The Book of Embraces) but the earnest eloquence, often fashioned in delightful aphorisms — "Street violence is the continuation of television by other means" — is undiminished. If he weren't such a maximalist, one would almost call him a minimalist.

"I'm always trying to undress the language, to pull the clothes off rhetoric that muffles and conceals the naked word," he says. "When I write I also try to marry the divorced, to put together pieces of myself: thinking and feeling, wakefulness and sleep, body and soul. I don't believe in borders that separate literary genres, and I enjoy violating them. I also love to make fun of the customs officers who keep imagination and reality apart and raise a wall between literature called intimate and what they call socially conscious. The wars of the soul look too much like the wars of the street."

These stories are from a new book I have just finished translating, Walking Words. Here tenderness nearly obliterates anger and Galeano's obstinate black humor becomes more a framework than a weapon: bitter twists of fate are the given, fleeting glimpses of joy the payoff for people who harbor no expectations, but whose hope is a source of undying sustenance.

— Mark Fried

Travail Vertical et Blanc
Anne-Marie Albiach

«*elle s'ignore, elle s'éblouit face aux données*»

des racines un souffle adjonctif travaillait dans
la force   d'une mesure

        il est au revers immédiat
ou longiligne, il prend les chevelures au plus noir
d'un destin instaurant les énigmes en son parcours
de   jeux de scène à peine perceptible
      sa venue étreint les genoux et effleure
      les mains proche d'une innocence

        «*et dans la lumière interne ils
        exercent un rapport de reliefs*»

dans une préhensible vulnérabilité; le regard soumis
aux couleurs

      l'obscur se double
      dans le mineur, cette mémoire
      tactile
   «*tu es là
      sombre*»
*dans une ligne médiane ils cherchent leur corps;
«tu effectues des gestes par lesquels tu t'approches
ou te retires»*   *il n'est pas en ton pouvoir
d'annihiler le contour*

    cette opposition se précise aléatoire;   muets
dans l'acidité de l'air se récidive telle douceur leur
absence

empreints d'une ardeur qu'ils auraient tenté
de concrétiser,

cependant elle se remémorait des
tissus, des parfums, des chaînes — là
où les oiseaux de nuit émettent leurs
cris dangereux pour qui les ignore :
l'exacerbation qu'ils
donnaient à ce lieu;

lèvres ouvertes, taches, brûlures :
cette   représentation corporelle
devenait interdite

«*ces gestes qui animent;* se détourne encore
d'une infime trace sur la poitrine»

elle tremble devant leur nudité; nos paroles
divergeaient dans un écart, le dernier mot au
jour incertain   ce
qui oscille

l'indistinct remonte vers l'angle

                le hasard les prend

sous   une trajectoire

        «blanche, elle s'éblouit
            elle s'atténue»

     à cet endroit où les images s'effacent
s'avère une terre;   dans
une étreinte une réminiscence comme
si l'on attendait dans l'épuisement le
lever du jour

    elle abstrait l'objet; elle dévie le geste qui se
prend à l'écart du geste, face aux nourritures et
leur nom dans l'extrême; une avidité de l'offrande,
paroles sacrificielles

   «ainsi s'adonne l'image tellurique, une disparité»
    *«elle engendrait son fils dans le mutisme ou
l'engendrement d'une figure de style»*   et une
mémoire apte à se dénouer à la moindre altérité
dans les voyelles, une abstraction des origines; son
visage reflétait l'homonyme d'une perte antécédente
   les répliques
      cet épisode archaïque s'accentue

      la loi de la succession la blancheur des
signes une distance vertébrale
        ils blêmissaient
et brisaient telle logique

Work Vertical and Blank
Charles Bernstein

working around and through "Travail Vertical et Blanc" by Anne-Marie Albiach

«*she ignores herself, he obliterates, face to the given*»

a breath adjunctive has worked in
the force   of a measure

he is reversed immediately
or longingly, takes the dishevelled lures to the most black
of a destined foundering the inscrutability in the run
of   play of scene at pains to be perceptible
grasp knee, brush
hands near an innocence

«*and in the luminescence interned they
exert a rapport of reliefs*»

in a prehensible vulnerability; regard subsumes
its colors

the obscure doubles
in manure, this memory
tactile

«*you are there
somber*»
*in the median line they search for their bodies;
«you effectuate the gestures by which you approach
where you retire»   he is not in his ability
to annihilate the contour*

this opposition aleatorically precise;   mutes
in the acidity of the air, repetition of an offence
such swell lured absence

imprints of an ardor that they will be tempted
to consecrate,

while she remembers
tissue, perfume, chains — there
where the herds of night emit their
dangerous cries to ignore :
the exacerbation that they
gave to this;

rips open, scratches, burns :
whose representation corporeal
became interdict

«*these gestures that animate*; detouring again
from a tiny trace on the breath»

trembling before their nullity; our parole
diverges in a cart, the last moat to the
day incertain   this
that oscillates

Charles Bernstein

the indistinct remonstration verging on angle

                                                        hazard holds

    under   a trajectory

«*blanched, she obliterates
he attenuates*»

at this rite where images dissolve
avers a tear;   in
a grasp, remembrance like
if one were walking in exhaustion at the
day's break

        or abstracts the object; divvy the gesture that
          cracks the geste, face to the nourishments
        that name in the extreme; an avidity of offering,
                      sacrificed paroles

    «*then adorns the moldering image, a disparity*»
     «*she engendered his son in the muteness of
           a figure of style*»   and one
memory fitted to unravel at the lesser twisting
           in the vowels, an abstraction of origins; his
    face reflecting the homonym of a pert antecedent
the replicas
    this archaic episode accentuates

        the law of succession of the blanching of
    signs a distance veritable
      they have blemished
and braised such logic

Anne-Marie Albiach was born in 1937 and lives in Neuilly-sur-Seine on the outskirts of Paris. Her major collections include État (Mercure de France, 1971; republished 1988), Mezza voce (Flammarion, 1984), Anawratha (Spectres Familiers, 1984) and Figure vocative (1985; reissued by Fourbis, 1991). Claude Royet-Journoud writes that, for him, the 1971 publication of État "changed the 'face' of poetry." Jean-Marie Gleize's Albiach is the first book on her complete work to date; it will be issued by Éditions Belin (Paris) in 1995. In the United States, essays on her work have been written by Keith Waldrop, Paul Auster, Benjamin Hollander, Geoffrey O'Brien, Joseph Simas, Norma Cole, Michael Palmer, Alan Davies, Rachel Blau DuPlessis, Gale Nelson, Rosmarie Waldrop and Cole Swenson.

Albiach has been fortunate in her American translators. Keith Waldrop worked for twelve years on État (Awede, 1989). Mezza Voce (Post-Apollo, 1988) was translated by Joey Simas in collaboration with Lydia Davis, Anthony Barnett and Douglas Oliver. Vocative Figure (Allardyce-Barnett, United Kingdom, 1992) was translated by Anthony Barnett and Joey Simas.

Rosmarie Waldrop has published a translation of "Travail Vertical et Blanc" in her Série d'Écriture (#4, Spectacular Diseases, 1990).

Anne-Marie Albiach gave me a copy of "Travail Vertical et Blanc" on a visit Susan Bee and our daughter Emma made to her apartment in the summer of 1989. On this very bright summer afternoon, the shutters were completely closed, but at Emma's insistence Anne-Marie let the light in so Emma could play on the balcony. Sitting in the apartment, I immediately began to scratch out English versions as a way of reading the poem. The title of Albiach's poem is the last line from "Le drap maternel," a poem of Royet-Journoud's that I had translated as The Maternal Drape (Awede, 1984) — "drape" rather than "sheet," just as "work vertical and blank" rather than the conventional "vertical and white work," which gives some sense of the modified homophonic approach I took to making an "American" version (as the French say) of the poem. By a modified homophonic approach I mean that I give precedence to the sound and word order of the French without completely departing from the "lexical" sense of the original. Working with Olivier Cadiot on our collaborative adaption of his Red, Green and Black (Potes and Poets, 1990), I found the rhetorical style and humor of the original was best expressed by finding substitutions and equivalences for passages of the original, while focusing somewhat less on homophonic crossovers.

Sitting at Anne-Marie's apartment, I thought again about the difference between a thin translation, one that is correct but lacks the linguistic density of the original, and a thick translation, in which the loss of semiotic and sonic reverberation is countered by the creation of compensatory poetic value. Surely, there is no formula for thick translation, but the irony of poetry that is dense and intractable in the original reading "smoothly" in English is too common to think of as anything but the product of an institutional standard that needs to be challenged. I am also drawn to translations which mark the incommensurability with their source languages by retaining traces of the untranslatable. (Lawrence Venuti has written persuasively on these points.) Then again, multiple translations and "reworkings" of the same poem, like multiple readings, are the ideal situation; the more versions the better.

In the case of "Work Vertical and Blank," while I have gone well beyond the permissions of translation as conventionally understood, inevitably I have stayed quite close to the original; certainly I am reassured that Albiach has expressed pleasure with the results.

— Charles Bernstein

Seven Poems
Ishihara Yoshirō

— Translated from Japanese by Hiroaki Sato

STRUCTURE

On what sort of day was there joy. Or suffering. Except for the structures of joy and suffering. That in whatever freedom it was chosen, what was chosen was neither freedom nor agony, but always the structure of either. That a story transmitted is no more than its structure, and that what encouraged the structure has remained an origin no one would ever visit and will remain so — it will be necessary to acknowledge this at least once.

Therefore, what must be transmitted is always not the structure that forced it, but the structure that was forced on it, the structure further inside that keeps forcing upon itself the results of having been forced. There is only one person who transmits the fact that in that structure there was a silence in which one forced the structure as it was upon oneself, and there is only one person to whom it is transmitted.

It is simply because of this that we could be at peace with structures.

HORSE AND RIOT

When two horses run inside us
another horse runs between them.
When we go out to riot
we run with the third horse.
It's this horse that goes out
with us to riot
not the other two beside it.
Therefore what runs off from us

215

when we halt
is the one horse
not the other two beside it.
When two bandits run inside us
another bandit runs between them.
When two hollows run inside us
still another hollow runs between them.
What goes out with us to riot
is this last bandit
and this last hollow.

NIGHT ROBBERS

When they realize it's no longer evening,
one rises to his feet
and strangles a chicken,
one rises to his feet
and strangles a pillar,
one rises to his feet
and twists up his own arms.
According to the depth of night he schemes,
each of the night robbers
will be a night robber.
For example, the one who steps on the back
of a prostrate night robber and runs, is also
called by custom a night robber.
The distance night robbers run through,
from beheading to whipping,
no matter how short,
the daybreak that seems to cut off
equally concerns all the night robbers.
When fire bells clanging, whiskers burnt,
something like reason
pressed on his back,
when he flees home through naked noon,
the one who catches up with him
must also be a night robber.
On occasion, supported by logic,
a night robber runs past

a night robber.
Something like an apple
that the night robber bites and tosses away,
something like a rope
that the night robber tears and tosses away,
these things concern
the morning of the fleeting run.
The boulevard like a bread board,
washed by a shower,
is the distance to broad daylight.

MYTH

Indeed, that morning had no succession at all. It can be said that it was limited to a single generation. For there was finally neither afternoon following the morning nor evening dusk following the afternoon. The morning was there with no clue, by itself, a morning. We all awoke at once and had nothing to do. Between a quieter sea and a far quieter coast, in the vivid silence after those with courage to escape had all escaped, we carelessly, merely exchanged greetings. Were the greetings then any different, for example, from the way the two shells of a clam close? After raising our voices as in a chorus, with no hope of putting in greetings, we fell into a further silence. We bundled hay, pulled down the lever-iron, and in that posture could only wait for the time to have ourselves cut down. Unless cut down, the morning would have to remain merely a morning. In truth, we hoped for it. That the morning in its mediocrity be a morning. If in the end there was nothing to come after that, we would already be able to be vegetables. In any case, before the morning was a morning, we ourselves had to be a morning. We did not wait single-mindedly for our first years, we were not promised a next generation. We waited for the ennui between breaths — for the time when the serene repetition of water and shore would finally, unrelatedly mature into a myth.

217

Ishihara Yoshirō

SONG OF THE RINGING IN THE EAR

The man I left behind likes
for example the ringing in the ear.
Likes for example the small cape
in the ringing in the ear.
Likes the smoky smell of a matchlock.
And the sky is always
on this side of the man.
With a chest where stars stir like a wind
the man is ashamed of me like a medal.
When ringing begins in my ears
suddenly the man begins.
In the distance the wheat sings in his hair
as he firmly looks around.
The man I left behind likes
for example a stuffed donkey.
Likes for example a copper horseshoe.
Likes a sunset that resembles a gong.
Just as a whip meets the flesh
so he forces me to meet the future.
When ringing begins in my ears
he is perhaps the man that begins
but when he begins suddenly
there is another man
that begins, all the other men
that revive at a stroke
and at the end of their line-up
a tower stands gently
like a scarlet stick.
Doubt my ears if you like.
Way beyond the illusory ringing
nevertheless the tower stands
gently
and the man I left behind
still believes firmly
that it stands there.

Ishihara Yoshirō

MIST & TOWN

I wouldn't say night with mist is
particularly free.
No matter where we happen to meet you
there's no line between you and us,
in this town leveled splendidly
by crossfires of accusation,
wherever a man walks
is a boulevard,
but when if rarely an honest wound
peers into your eyes
over your shoulder,
the night with mist, or without,
makes a difference
to the haunting guilt.
In the festival-drunk, witch-hunt town,
only its gravity pushed to the top,
even that bastard
passes as a Jacobin,
but if the stone hammer, striking,
sparks the same color, anywhere,
if a gold coin, whoever flips it,
turns the same face or back,
mist, don't hesitate
to come down in the town
where whip and spur collude!
I wouldn't say night with mist is
particularly free, but even if
the petty thieves
who haggle and get their wayward shadows
leave the fair
and pennies wet with lamp oil
disperse into distant pavements,
even if the bastard
who's placed the night on a whetstone
whirls off in a gust,
until the day breaks
unexpectedly
between your legs blocking the way,
the mist is the one

that comes to draw the line
to this faceless town
where daybreak repeats daybreaks,
where sunset repeats sunsets.

FIGURE

I kept thinking that wind was a first will. That a will always concerned itself with a first figure. That it did not concern itself with the flow of things. I was probably I when I willed, and after that I was violently abandoned. At that moment, I was watching the way I, who was supposed to turn into a wind, turned into a wind, but it is possible that I was watching the way water froze. On which side was what could be called a will? The wind and I, or water and ice. To which did the will belong: wanting a figure, or leaving a figure? At that time too, the rainbow should have risen. But it did not rise.

Several months after Japan was defeated, Ishihara Yoshirō (1915–1977), formerly an intelligence officer of the Japanese army, was detained by the Soviet army in Harbin, Manchuria. In 1949, he was charged with war crimes and sentenced to twenty-five years of hard labor in Siberia. On Stalin's death in 1953, he was released on amnesty and returned to Japan.

Of his experiences in the Siberian concentration camps and his motive for writing poetry, he said:

> *"If you are a human being, I am not. If I am a human being, you are not." This was my friend's last statement to his prosecutor as he was investigated at a concentration camp. He has died since, and I have been left only with these heavy words. These words are neither a challenge nor a protest, but a recognition of facts as they are. Even after I began to write poetry, the words remained*

alive in me and in due time spawned in me the incomprehensible idea of "enemy."

Probably we still live in a kind of dailiness where as soon as a confrontation begins, one of the two parties ceases automatically and quite arbitrarily to be a human being, and where such relations are being continually expanded and reproduced. I can say that it was this dailiness that abruptly thrust me into poetry.

After Adolf Eichmann, a mass murderer of Jews, was convicted and executed in Israel, in 1962, he wrote "The Indictment of Eichmann," and began the article this way:

When I wrote in an essay that I had no wish to make any statement on Hiroshima, I was asked why. Briefly, my first reason is that I was not an eyewitness of Hiroshima. We should not make an indictment on the basis of information. The act of indictment is permitted only to the one who stood there, barefoot — that's what I think.

My second reason is that I feel extremely uneasy about what forms the basis of the idea of Hiroshima — the understanding of "genocide." I cannot accept — can only fear — the notion lying behind Hiroshima: "Not just one or two people were killed. Besides, they were all killed in one second." Is it all right if just one or two people were killed? Are they saying that for someone to be killed slowly is all right? Did not the war bring us a little bit closer to the truth because it allowed us to manage to escape such a quantitative way of thinking?

Ishihara's first book of poetry, Sancho Pansa no Kikyô (Sancho Panza's Homecoming), was published in 1963 when he was thirty-eight years old.

— Hiroaki Sato

From Speech's Hedge Where the Honey
Peter Cole

1. SPEECH'S HEDGE . . .

where the honeyed
    combs of light resolve

onto a couch's blue upholstery,

   shifting with wind:

like spirit
    flinching in thinking

      as though in a gem,

or Byzantine dome,

but the onlooker backing off — unsure to his day.

And orange
          slits of escape nasturtium
          jutting his
       Persian wall of withdrawal.

Not images served,

   but shards of an image —
      breakage's throne —

reflection's
    text as homage,

recording the thrusts of linkage attempted,

    as place curiously home.

        •

Nerve bridles
    before such a future floor

as though in the spooked
    childhood house

forever   on the wooded hill:

    planks
giving way to the story below
    and basement finds —

    the trap of stairs

        and libidinal
swill of spiral
    unknowing

or a corner turned

onto the
bevel of weakened roof

    forced by fear to climb —

for the forecast view to the jagged city,
    small   in the distant haze . . .

    Hives of midday light

through a window's invisible weave —

and a barely registered

breeze
            on the skin,

lifting attention —

annealed,

ornamental,

2. LIPS FOR AN ETHIC

Idols that eyes
        model in mind
border a common space
        of sound,
    and the sound, in turn,
a feast where meaning roots
or lapses,
            lips for an ethic:

an offering of every man
    of willing heart,

of beaten work —

for the light.

•

Make all things
the book of subsistence
            advised,

in accordance

with the pattern shown you
        there —

whose ground was the ground
        dust of eaten gold

of beauty diffused through the dwelling
        denied —

through clasps and loops of blue,
through cups and knops and buds,

the altar acacia covered
  with brass for the body
    and gold for the soul,
      to be borne by
  rings cut like a lentil
  (or food for a liver,

shame to them clinging like fat upon it,

and its lobes coiled
        like the serpent memory rides.

3. "SO THE SOUL . . .

> *. . . without extending and living in its object, is
> dead within itself. An idle chaos of blind and con-
> fused powers."*

                      — Traherne

This was love in the day —

•

the eyes' ray along
                    an iron rail
laced and white as the park
          brides in their hopes and veils

guiding my climb through the air

               toward the bolted
                         double doors
               and rooms below —

Siennese, or like Escher

— so as not to slip,

over the landscape of kingdom and savior —

of blood in the alleys and open sewers,
          of summer flies and trash,
          or Melville's wash of bone —

and hyssop fields overturned,

          or bulldozed
               groves of olive;

a fortress of knowledge and tact
          on a far off hill . . .

          This was love
                    in the will,

          the eyes' line along
                    an iron rail
          laced and white as the bride's
          prospect and veil,

guiding her climb through the air.

4. FOR ONE WHO WOULD FALL

A prayer for reduction,

or release through the opulent vision
    of vermian scarlet and purple
        and insult blue:

    a sign

    to rinse him of signs

      or hollow a place in the day
            for mirrored sight to enter,
                and exit not as meaning
            but set against nothing seen

— by which the world is hung —

    in relief,
          like a kite:

a seat of mercy, with hammered cherubim facing:

a prayer for construction — or recalibration

    — for one who would *fall*
        from fealty to light.

8. THE MUSIC ROOM

Vaulted study arches,
    ersatz Spanish chairs,
        and drinks
    on a brass tray cut with tracery,
            bluing,

talk like *laying a tune on the air*
of Gould's contempt,
         latitude, career,

eyes catching
   the courtyard hibiscus,
      a square
where roses for the child were uprooted
         and sand put in,
    comments on friends,
family and failures
    of nerve, the pauses

bent toward hope
   and loyalties evolved,
      giving out,
not in,
   discussing indulgences,

     virtue and applause,
the cowardly purist,
      the flexible hero

the tomb of reason
   and the graveyard of things:
splitting the hair and not finding a thread
  — response to the needs of the soul,
    so that I go blindly
      as though pursuing
the beauty of something before me
    but unclear—

not to spotlight alternatives
but to resist by form alone the course of the world
  which permanently puts a pistol
    to people's heads.

Better colorless than crude.

•

Where is my music, where—
of Sion they used to sing—
and how should one intone
in an alien land the sweetness of air?

Remembrance of what is good
arose from the changes of things,
and I saw that the good which was past
hadn't been pleasure but pain—

and things which were far away
by dark for dread were sung.

11. (TUNING) HOOKS

All the little
    links involved,
my non-existent
    psalter said—

all the little links involved
would rot away
    in precious time

and leave a taste
    in thinking's air
a shape impressed
like loops and hooks

in precious time

and ingrown love

all the little
    links involved

like must on feeling's tongue,

like must on feeling's tongue.

12.   THE POEM UP THERE

Ornament is nurse of pride.
Pleasure measure love's delight.

—Dowland's *Songs or Airs*
Anonymous

Nursing pride

in pride of place,

  a trope's
loop of
central occasion—
  equipment
(a slap in the face
  to patricians of theme
 and persuasion,

or civil (Horatian)
 representation.

Unlaureate:

the poem *up there*

in the air of

 any beholder:

the painted vase
a useless favorite
 aunt bequeathed,

accessory,

and not our cup
    of tea,

— her dominance —

defined our living
(warmest) room

in time,

   defines my life

with wife and loving

abstract lack and decor —

   not cure —

the offering of sweet
    savor exceeding prayer —

in the volume of splendor
I read)

   *To forge links
     and make light,*

   like Law,

defines a practice.

20. INTO DELPHINIUM

A psychomachia
       for mercurial things,

for future affection and faith
in speech's reflection of Eden's bequeathal
or reef-like thrust —

which further a
soul's landscape
into delphiniums'
white and blue through dusk,

or black-eye's
blue by night,

by day on a bench
(by blankets of infant's blue-eyed-leadwort backed)
a man helping a
beaten-up beggar
with a sandwich
under a Syrian pine   and scarlet
woodpecker gash and black/

defining a slum's

slow retrieval

maybe to gentrification,

like kindness weakening
into a fear of its lack
or possible rival,

against a thought in executive heads,
and one's own ear —

was ex-post-human

unmillenarian

Spirit War for Survival.

"No country will more quickly dissipate romantic expectations than Palestine," wrote Herman Melville on his trip there in 1857, "particularly Jerusalem. To some the disappointment is heart sickening . . ." The poetry of Peter Cole might be considered an elaborate marginalia to this diaristic comment of Melville's, marginalia wherein optimistic disillusionment, or religious realism, takes shape.

Following out a poetic hunch, Cole first went to Jerusalem in 1981, to study Hebrew. For the better part of the next seven years, he stayed there, while the bulk of Hebrew scripture and literature crashed full-tilt into the wealth of Western — and particularly Middle English — poetry already in his head. The encounter produced a buckling upward and within, and several years later his first book, Rift, a collection of planar asperities inscribed on the ground-zero of Judaism. Words in these poems were "denatured" of their habitual associations and raked up into vast lexical spires and belltowers that rang with a music new to American poetry — equal parts Louis Zukofsky, August Roebling and something else entirely. His project was abstract, even devotional by nature, yet the poems were starkly sensual. Both in its serial poems and the more traditional constructions, Rift worked the emotionally charged spaces of betweenness — those that elude us between Scripture and spokenness, loss and gift, eye and world.

When he returned to America in 1988, Cole carried with him the Jerusalem landscape and a honed slant on Hebrew, and in the best Diasporic tradition, created a Sion of the mind, dispatching his thought and feeling all the way back to eleventh-century Spain, the golden age of Spanish Jewry under Moslem rule. It was in San Francisco that he began his project of translating, in the deepest sense of that fraught word, the poetry of Samuel Hanagid (993–1056 A.D.), a writer of notoriously knotty and glorious Hebrew, who has always loomed large as one of the great untranslatables. The resulting manuscript exhibited a kind of transhistorical perfect pitch, but it was an act of salvage as well, rescuing someone so intricately barnacled with the paraphernalia of Academe that he was in danger, in the various extant translations, of never being "seen" by readers of poetry again.

Speech's Hedge, his latest book of poetry, bridges that project with his return to Jerusalem in 1992. Grounded in his immersion in medieval Arabic and Hebrew poetics, the poems have a newly relaxed amplitude, sounding within a wider range of variation. In

233

Peter Cole

the beautiful title poem sequence, short canto-like lyrics climb upwards along a fifty-page spiral armature, seamlessly conflating background and foreground, commentary and invocation, and producing a charmed relativity in the head of the reader, in which unlikely juxtapositions abound. In a conscious echo of the medieval Arabic tradition of inlay, quotations are laced throughout, from sources as disparate as Pentagon spokesman Pete Williams, Arnold Schönberg and the eighth-century Arabic poet Abu Nuwas. The key issue of ornament is explored directly, and psychological sense is released into the figures of the work, spilled, reconciled and gathered back.

— Eli Gottlieb

The Blue Dove
Paola Capriolo

— Translated from Italian by Lawrence Venuti

ON THE EVE OF THE BATTLE, the great Los could not fall asleep. The city too was awake, and it counted the hours.

Los left his house and wandered through the narrow alleys where every light burned. In the reddish glare of the torches, men and women were confiding hopes and fears in whispers.

As Los passed by, the women bowed their heads, the men rose to their feet, but their lips were sealed. Great Los responded by keeping the silence of his people. All around him quivered in expectation: only his eyes were without fear, and hopeless.

When he reached the poorest quarter of the city, a woman's lament came from one of the straw huts built against the walls, and it tore him from his thoughts. He approached:

"Enter, great Los," said the voice.

He looked past the threshold and saw an old woman huddled on a pallet, covered with a hempen blanket. Only her face was visible, furrowed with wrinkles, contracted in pain, and her white hair, scattered across the pillow.

The old woman lifted herself up a bit. "Sit with me, and do not be ashamed if your eyes encounter misery. No dishonor comes to the powerful who keep vigil in this house, since before dawn it will be visited by a still greater power."

Los drew near and sat at the foot of the pallet. "I shall keep vigil with you, if you wish. But at daybreak I must leave you, even if the guest you expect has not arrived."

The woman's lips parted in a faint smile. "If he does not arrive, I shall wait alone, and you shall reach your army. Yet these few hours that separate us from dawn move more slowly than the others: many things may be spoken before the light comes."

"What must I say to you, old woman?"

"You are restless, great Los, but not because of the battle. Your gaze holds no anticipation."

"I don't know you," he replied, disturbed. "Who taught you to read my eyes?"

"Many things are learned at hours such as this. But don't fly into a rage: even if I do manage to snatch a secret from you, I shall soon forget everything. Trust me as you would yourself."

"Let me go," said Los, rising from the pallet. "I left my house precisely in order to bury my thoughts. I sought a wine merchant, or a girl's sweet smile, and instead I found you . . ."

The old woman's body started beneath the hempen blanket. "Don't worry," she said, grasping Los's robe with her thin fingers. "The guest I am expecting is not far away. Stay with me a little longer."

"I shall stay, if you promise me . . ."

"I shall not ask you questions. I am no longer a girl, but if you are thirsty you can take the golden flask on that table and fill yourself a glass."

Los hesitated for an instant, then approached the table, poured the wine, and drank it in a breath.

"Now sit here," said the old woman, "and hold my hands."

He obeyed. The woman's hands trembled, grasped in his, but it was a gentle and caressing tremor, and in the nocturnal silence it beat a slow, sweet tempo.

The minutes began to move more slowly for Los as well, lulled by that cadence of death, and soon his spirit was calmed.

Meanwhile the old woman had closed her eyes. "Tell me a story," she suddenly murmured, "like the ones told to children."

Then Los commenced his narrative.

There is an island, far from here, in the midst of the sea of sand. It is a very small island, but once upon a time palms grew there, and broom flowered. Thus it once was, and thus it still is, if the spring whence it drew life isn't parched.

On the island, surrounded by palm trees, stood a straw hut, as poor as yours. In the hut lived a magician, who was wise and expert in every mystery.

The magician didn't live alone in the hut, on the island in the midst of the sea of sand. With him lived a boy. He grew up there, with the magician, from whom the boy learned all there was to learn of the world. Only his origins remained unknown to him.

Twenty palm trees grew on the island, and to each the magician had assigned a name, so as to distinguish it from the others and to command its spirit in spells. But there were only two men, the elder and the boy, and they had no need of names. So the boy grew up, and became a man, without knowing what he was called.

And when the boy grew up and became a man, the magician said to him: "It is time for you to depart. As the heir of all my knowledge, you are the wisest of mortals. Hence, be not afraid: go forth in the world and find your way."

But the young man replied: "You taught me the twenty names of the twenty palms that grow on this island. You taught me to recognize metals, and the species of plants, and those of animals, and on the ancient maps you showed me the thousand islands in the great sea of sand, and of each you revealed the name. My name, however, you never revealed to me, nor my origin, nor my destiny when I leave the island and venture alone into the world. Tell me this too, and may it be the last thing I learn from your lips. Then shall I truly be the wisest of men, and depart without fear."

"Follow your path," snapped the magician," and you shall find answers to every question. I have already told you enough."

And since the young man insisted, refusing to depart, the magician pushed him outside and bolted the door.

Yet at sunset, when the magician left to gather herbs for his potions, he found the young man sitting on a stone before the hut. "What are you still doing here? I told you you must leave."

"I shall not leave until I know my name and destiny," replied the young man. But the magician shook his head, gathered his herbs in silence, and, as soon as he finished, went back to lock himself in the house.

The sun disappeared. A sea of darkness swept over the sea of sand, and the palms on the island were drowned in that dark wave.

The young man sat on the stone, sad and solitary, gazing at the warm gleam of the fire that filtered through the windows. From the roof issued a plume of smoke, and the young man's mind was flooded with images of many nights spent inside there, on the wooden bench, while the magician brewed his potions, and one memory merged with another in a single nostalgia, as if his life on the island, close to the old man, amounted to one interminable day, rich in discoveries, and one very long night, warmed by the heat of fire.

Thus spoke Los, clasping the old woman's hands in his, lulled by their slow trembling, while she listened to him with half-closed eyes.

And Los resumed his narrative:

Finally the fire too was extinguished, leaving the island prey to the dark, and the last hours of the night arrived, the longest and most arcane.

At those hours men abandon themselves to sleep, and the night remains alone to keep vigil. For this reason, they say, he grows generous and bestows the gift of second sight upon the few who can stay awake with open eyes, staring into the darkness.

This happened then as well: the young man's mind turned limpid as the water from a spring, and all his knowledge flowed before him effortlessly, interweaving in constantly new figures. He let them flow, without attending to their play, until one appeared that surfaced suddenly from a long oblivion. The young man grasped and recalled it.

In his gaze appeared the image of a small flower that grew on the fringes of the island, amongst the broom bushes. The petals of this flower were transparent as crystal, and bewitched: so the magician told him, one morning many years ago, as they strolled together in search of herbs.

"If one day you would like to know something," he said, "and the person who can tell you refuses to speak, remember this flower. Whoever knows its name commands its spirit and has at his service its magical powers."

And the magician picked the flower and put it in the boy's hand. "This is Traue, the flower of confidence. Its petals are invisible, and they dissolve in wine. Whoever drinks it cannot pass in silence over anything he knows."

The young man remembered all this and waited impatiently for daybreak to set off in search of Traue.

He found it amongst the bushes, while the dawn traced a golden border between the sky and the sea of sand.

And in the golden light the young man slowly pronounced the name of Traue, the flower of confidence, and seized its spirit. Then he hid it in the folds of his clothing and headed towards the hut.

Hearing his knock, the magician leaned out a window. "What do you want now?"

"The night has been a good counsellor," the young man replied, "and it persuaded me to depart in obedience to your wishes. Pardon my stubbornness, therefore, and bless me."

"Draw near," said the magician more sweetly. He stretched an arm out the window and with his hand grazed the young man's head. "Now you can go."

Thus spoke the old man, but the other responded: "Do you want me to depart without bidding farewell to the hut where I grew up? I beg you, let me enter one last time, let us embrace one last time and drink the cup of parting."

The young man's entreaties touched the heart of the magician, who removed the bolt from the door and allowed him to enter. Then he took two cups, placed them on the table and nodded to his companion to be seated.

The wine of parting was sealed inside a golden flask. The magician filled the cups to the brim.

"Bring a bit of bread as well," said the young man, "and break it with me, for the last time."

While the magician went to search for bread in the pantry, the young man tore a petal off Traue, the flower of confidence, which he kept hidden in his clothing, and dropped it into one of the cups. The crystal dissolved at once, emitting a slender thread of vapor. But at the magician's return the vapor had already dispersed in the air, and the young man's hand grasped the other cup.

They sat at the table, one facing the other, as they had sat so many times. The windows were shuttered, dulling the morning light that penetrated the interior of the hut. In the dimness the two broke bread and lifted the cups to their lips. They talked in low voices, and their eyes bespoke the sadness of parting.

When the magician emptied his cup, his eyes were misty. "Come," he said, "let's rest beneath the palms." The young man helped him to his feet and led him out of the hut.

The glare of day assailed them violently, like a saber thrust. The magician staggered and raised his hands to his eyes to shield them from the sun. But the young man served as his support, guiding him slowly towards the shade of a palm tree.

They sat, their backs leaning against the trunk, their gazes lost in the sea of sand as far as the distant horizon.

"This light is blinding me," the magician groaned. "Let's go back inside."

"If the light blinds you, close your eyes."

The magician closed his eyes, and the young man watched him sink into a strange torpor. Then he realized that Traue had taken possession of him, and he started to interrogate the old man about his name and his destiny. The magician responded submissively, revealing all he knew.

"I once taught you that if men must travel from one island to another to buy and sell, they do not venture alone into the sea of sand, but form numerous companies, and the most experienced travels ahead, beating a path amidst the dangers, while the others follow him in single file."

"I remember," said the young man. "You spoke to me of horses with thick hooves that navigate the sandy trails in procession. You spoke to me of houses with silk walls which travellers build at sunset in the sea of sand, creating multicolored cities, and at dawn they demolish them again and resume their journey."

"Men of that kind," continued the magician, "arrived here one day and built their silk houses on the fringes of the island. I therefore went to visit them, as custom commands, and we exchanged gifts of friendship. I saw that amongst those hardy people, accustomed to the thousand trails in the sea of sand, there was a child a few years old. That child was you. When dawn broke, from my hut I saw the silk houses collapse to the ground one by one, as if their spirits had suddenly left them. I understood that the moment of departure had come, and I immediately went to the foreigners to beg them to leave you with me. For the days are long in the sea of sand, and the nights even longer, and knowledge does not suffice to conquer solitude. But you remained, and from then on I was no longer alone, and aging was sweet to me, watching you grow."

"But those men must have told you who I was. Was perhaps my father amongst them?"

The magician shook his head. "No one knew you. A few days earlier they found you wandering alone in the sea of sand, wearing a silver medal on your chest, the one you still wear. You must know that mothers whose lot it is to be separated from their children, before leaving them, append to their necks medals of this kind, whereon they inscribe a name. In the name is sealed a love charm which protects the child and guides him on his path through life. Hence, when those men found you, they removed the medal and raised it to their eyes to read your name."

With a slow, somnambulant gesture, the magician lifted a hand and sought the young man's chest. He clutched the medal and pressed it in his fingers, all the while keeping his eyes closed.

"The silver is smooth," he murmured. "No name is inscribed there."

The young man removed the magician's hand. He rose and began to pace back and forth, absorbed in thought. The silver medal, warmed by the midday sun, burned his chest.

Finally he returned to sit beside the magician. "No name is inscribed there. Tell me what this signifies?"

"It signifies that you must seek your name by yourself, on the paths of the world."

"The world has thousands of paths," the young man sharply replied, "and often they are confused, like the trails in the sea of sand when the tempest passes."

The magician smiled. "But only one is yours, and no tempest can erase it. Believe me, you won't lose it."

"If no one guides me . . ."

"Someone is guiding you, never fear."

"Who can this be, if even my mother didn't want to protect me, and denied me the charm of love?"

"You must know," said the magician, "that an invisible blue dove flies over every man's head from the day of his birth to the day of his death. That is his fate, and it guides him always, without his notice, and sees that he keeps to his path, in good as in bad, so that what was ordained for him comes to pass. It is she who leads you to victory or to ruin, and when we choose, it is she who chooses for us, the blue dove that flies over our heads."

"But tell me," asked the young man, "how do you know about the doves? Who told you about them?"

"A most ancient book preserves this mystery."

"You've never shown it to me. I thought I knew all your books."

"Yes, all the books I still keep. But the one whereof I speak is read only once in life, and then thrown into the fire. What is learned from its pages is never forgotten, but it can't be revealed. We who know of the sky blue doves are few in the world. When two of us meet, we recognize each other by our glance and embrace like brothers. Yet we keep the secret."

"So can the mystery of fate be learned only from the book? Has no one ever seen his own dove?"

"Only sometimes, near the end, in the hours preceding death, does she become visible."

"Only then? Are you certain?"

The magician jerked, as if he tried to rouse himself from the torpor. But the spell was still too potent, and with a sigh he slumped back against the trunk of the palm tree.

"Whoever wrote the book, whether god or man, obliterated the last page by covering it with a veil of ink. But I know every spell, including the one that causes vanished characters to reappear, and thus I could read the secret lines. After he who wrote them, I believe I am the first and only mortal to rest his gaze there."

"Tell me what was on that page?"

"It spoke of a remote island, in the midst of the sea of sand. No man has ever reached it, neither those who blaze trails on their thick-hoofed horses, nor the hermits who wander on foot in search of wisdom. On the maps I showed you the thousand islands of the sea of sand, and I revealed each of their names to you. But that island is not indicated on the maps, not even on the most ancient, and its name is a secret no one knows. There, on the nameless island, flows a spring of the purest water. It has flowed from the beginning of the world, and its stream will never end. There all the fates gather, at the hour of sunset, arriving on the wing from every corner of the sky to drink the waters of the spring. Then they become visible."

"And tell me," asked the young man, "what else was written on the cancelled page?"

The magician jerked again.

"Tell me: was the way to reach that island described there?"

And since the spell of Traue was still potent, the magician slowly passed a finger over the sand and traced the route that leads to the island of fate.

For three days and three nights the young man walked, following the trails the magician had shown him.

On the fourth day he glimpsed a vortex of sand on the horizon. It rose into the air, tall and compact as a column, and revolved furiously, although without changing its shape.

The young man was surprised at first, since the sky was serene and not a breath of wind stirred. Then he understood that the golden sand, dancing to the rhythm of an invisible tempest, preserved the mysterious calm of the fateful island, hiding it from human eyes.

And so he advanced, determined. As soon as he drew near, the movement of the vortex slowed down, and the sand scattered.

When at last the tempest completely subsided, a round hill appeared, covered in the whitest gravel. From the top gushed the eternal spring. The water ran through the gravel in silver rivulets, and the young man felt he was contemplating the face of the moon, mutable and quiet.

Then the water sang, gurgling from the soil:

> *If once you taste me, you'll never 'scape me,*
> *'Less you dare the dark threshold to cross.*

Those incomprehensible words irritated the young man. "Are you jesting with me? What does this nursery rhyme signify?"

But the spring laughed and at every new gush repeated its refrain.

"What threshold do you mean? Can it be found here, on this island?"

The spring fell silent, then resumed gushing, although more slowly:

> *Where and when you wish to cross, it's up to you to start,*
> *Because you'll find it always lies deep within your heart.*

"Tell me," asked the young man, curious, "what is beyond the threshold? And why do you call it dark?"

> *He who crosses there, in dark must navigate,*
> *And deaf he'll be forever to the song of fate.*

"Then it won't do for me. I've come this far precisely because I want to know my fate."

The voice of the spring turned derisive.

> *The water flows and quenches him who lets it be,*
> *But if you try to stop it, from you it will flee.*

"Leave off your sing-song," said the young man.

> *Take heed of my words: this place you must fly;*
> *You came here to drink, but you shall leave dry.*

Thus sang the spring, but he was no longer listening. Night was approaching, and the horizon welcomed the rosy tints of the sunset.

From every corner of the sky the blue doves arrived on the wing, just as was written in the book. The young man hid behind a rock and stayed to observe them without making a move.

The spring wept:

> *Flying here together, they formed one great mass;*
> *Ready for departure, they will be one less.*

"Hush," whispered the young man, "and let them settle. I won't do them any harm."

And the doves lit on the gravel, one after another, creating a wide circle around the spring.

"What is happening to you, mother?" asked one of them. "Tonight your gushing sounds like sobbing."

> *The water flows and quenches him who lets it be;*
> *The prettiest of my children nevermore will leave.*

The doves looked at one another anxiously. "Let us drink quickly, sisters, and leave this spot."

But at that moment the young man issued from his hiding place. The doves immediately took wing and fled, raising a din in every corner of the sky. Only one remained near the spring, in the burning light of sunset, and she stood motionless before him, staring with sad eyes.

The dove's beak and claws were the color of ivory, and her blue feathers glistened as if they were bathed in silver.

The young man approached slowly, so as not to frighten her. From the spring came a plaintive murmur:

> *The daughter I most favor,*
> *nevermore will leave,*
> *but he who is her captor*
> *now must learn to grieve.*

He was not listening. Having inched close to the dove, he suddenly bent down and caught her.

He heard a shrill, heartrending cry. It was so shrill and heartrending that he felt stunned and had to close his eyes.

When he reopened them, he was holding a young girl in his arms.

The girl was very beautiful. She wore a light tunic of blue silk, embroidered in silver thread. Her hair was the golden brown of ripened dates, and her skin was the color of ivory.

She was weeping desperately. "Ah, what have you done, what have you done!"

The young man was confused. "I wanted to know my fate. This is why I came here."

The spring wept as well:

> *Trust the judgment of mortals at your own cost:*
> *They believe all is theirs, when all is lost.*

"What is she saying?" the young man asked the girl. "Have I not, perhaps, found my fate?"

"The spring speaks the truth: you lost your fate precisely when you believed you found it. And you have caused my ruin. You came to learn your destiny, and I must reveal it to you. But then you will no longer need me, who keeps watch over your steps, who guides you down the paths of the world."

> *The prettiest of my children nevermore will leave;*
> *Now she is forced to suffer what makes humans grieve.*

245

"Do you understand the spring's words? I shall be a woman like all the others. Like them I shall know old age, and death."

But the young man was enchanted by the girl's beauty. "If you must be a woman, be mine, and continue to follow me as you have always done. I shall lead you amongst men and teach you to share their sorrows and glories."

The spring burst into laughter:

> *Poor is human glory, false is human gain:*
> *Joy is always fleeting, all that stays is pain.*

"Don't listen to her," said the young man. "Come with me."

But the girl stood apart from him. She stopped weeping, and her face grew severe. "I have long flown over your head, and I know all your joys: those you already experienced and those that still await you. Whether living amongst mortals is good or bad, I cannot say, but I do know that one must yield to fate. And fate says I must not follow you."

"You shall follow me, and whatever happens will be our fate."

"Whatever is our fate will happen," insisted the girl. "I shall not follow you."

> *If once you taste me, you'll never 'scape me,*
> *'Less you dare the dark threshold . . .*

"Be quiet," shouted the young man angrily. "Ever since I arrived on this island, you've done nothing but torment me with your incomprehensible sing-song expressions."

"Yes, mother, be quiet. Don't point out the paths that are best avoided."

The spring's gushing became subdued, and the girl took the young man's hand.

Now the sky was the color of violets, poised between day and night.

"The hours move slowly on this island," said his fate. "Many things may be spoken before the light returns. Lie down on the gravel and close your eyes. I shall sit beside you throughout the night, and reveal your destiny. But at daybreak you shall take the path that leads towards the east, and I the one towards the west. You shall cover a great distance and finally arrive at a large island that rises at the border of the sea of sand. There grain is cultivated, fruit grows, and animals of every kind are raised. There stand three great cities, each inhabited by a different clan, and from time immemorial the three clans have been at war amongst themselves. Your steps will lead you to one of the cities. The leader who governed it recently died, killed by his enemies in a bloody battle: you will be asked to take his place. Under your rule, the city will acquire great power. The two rival clans will form an alliance against you, and move you to war. A tremendous battle will be waged, starting at dawn and ending only at sunset. Many men will fall, on both sides, but with the courage of a lion you will lead your soldiers into the fray and gallop through the enemy ranks, sowing death. No saber will wound you, because thus it is written, and you will return unharmed to the city at the head of a victorious army. The enemy cities will be at your mercy, as the spoils of war, and you will become lord of the entire island. Upon your head will be placed a golden diadem, priests will come to anoint your body with holy oil, and thus you will reign in peace for many years, with your subjects fearing your saber and loving your justice. And when you die, your death will be late and painless, and you will leave the kingdom to the favorite of your children. For many women will live in your house, whoever you desire, and they will bear you abundant offspring."

"And you?" asked the young man, turning his gaze towards the girl's sad face.

"I shall not live in your house."

"But will I see you again?"

"Yes, it is written that we shall see each other again. But it is also written that you will not recognize me."

He laughed, "How could I not recognize my fate?"

"Starting tomorrow, time will move differently, for you and for me. And you will no longer have a fate."

Thus spoke the girl. Then she bent over the young man and with her lips delicately grazed his forehead and eyelids.

That kiss infused him with an irrepressible languor. The face of his fate, bent over his, slowly vanished as if swallowed by mist, while the spell of sleep enthralled him, more and more powerfully.

He awoke when the sun was already high, and found himself alone. The girl's footprints were lost in the sea of sand, towards the west.

Tears filled his eyes as he followed those faint, uncertain traces and imagined his fate wandering in the sea of sand, wrapped in a blue tunic, prey to heat and thirst. He imagined her trudging over stony trails, she who was accustomed to flying on the wings of a dove. But very soon his sight faded in the immensity of the sea of sand, and the golden dust rose to obliterate everything.

The tears parched the young man's throat, so he climbed to the top of the hill and drew his lips close to the spring to slake his thirst. But at once the gushing ceased.

> *The daughter I most favored never will return:*
> *Should my waters quench you, or rather let you burn?*

The young man lowered his eyes. "Forgive me, mother. I wish I had never come to this island."

The spring abruptly resumed gushing, and the young man drank. As he bent over the water, the silver medal slid out of the folds in his clothes. He lifted a hand to his chest and began to tuck in the medal, but when he grazed it with his fingers, he noticed that the silver was no longer smooth. He slipped it from his neck and raised it to his eyes.

Near the spring, on the island of fate, he read his name on the medal: "Los."

"And so I set forth on the path towards the east and reached the great island whereof my fate had spoken. What happened from the moment I entered the walls of this city is known to you as well."

The old woman nodded.

"Everything," continued Los, "unfolded exactly as my fate predicted. And tomorrow's battle will also unfold as predicted. With the courage of a lion, I shall lead my soldiers into the fray and gallop through the enemy ranks, sowing death, and at night I shall return to the city, unharmed, at the head of a victorious army."

He cut himself short and sank into a deep silence. His fingers played distractedly with the sick woman's hands, abandoned in his.

Finally he spoke again. "Do you now understand, old woman, why there is no anticipation in the eyes of Los, the fateless? My heart is devoid of hope and fear, and in my actions there can be no courage."

Thus he spoke, and released the old woman's hands as he brusquely stood up from the pallet. He paced the room in great strides, from one part to the other, like a caged animal. The rhythm of the night ceased to lull him, and the words rose rapidly to his lips.

"Why should I care about tomorrow's battle, the victory, the kingdom awaiting me? The golden diadem crowns me before I have won it, and my body is already anointed with the priests' oil. The women I desire are already mine even before I desire them, and already I see the crowd of heirs pressing around the throne I do not yet possess. Why should I care about what happens? Everything is written for me, everything has already happened. It happened that night, on the island of fate, while in the darkness my lost dove whispered to me the words of destiny."

"Calm down," said his old companion. "Sit here beside me."

And Los went back to sit on the pallet, near the ailing woman.

"Tell me," she said, "do you truly anticipate nothing?"

"No," Los replied, "there is one thing, one last thing. I expect to meet my fate again, my blue dove, as is written."

"If it is written, you will certainly meet her. But you won't recognize her: this too is written."

"Let me find her again, and I shall know how to disobey destiny."

Los's eyes were wet with tears, and the old woman sweetly brushed them away. "Remember the words of the spring:

'Less you dare the dark threshold to cross . . .'

"I don't know what this dark threshold may be," Los responded. "I know only that I have lost my fate, and I want to find her again."

She smiled. "Time has changed the sky blue dove. Many moons have passed since your paths diverged, and you won't recognize her."

"However much time has changed her, her beauty isn't the sort that withers. And her brown eyes shine with an unforgettable flame."

The old woman's dry lips parted in a mute, joyless laugh.

"I haven't come here to let myself be mocked by the dying," said Los, suddenly springing to his feet. "In a little while the sun will rise, and it's time I go. If the story diverted you, I am pleased: perhaps you will find it less difficult to await your guest alone."

Thus spoke Los, and then hurriedly left, heading down the poor alley flanked by straw huts.

At the first light of dawn, the silence of the city dissolved into songs and cries of war. The alternate rhythm of clogs scattered the quiet of the alleys, and the bronze armor clanked. The women leaned out the windows to watch the army pass and greeted their men with weeping in their voices.

Great Los rode at the head of his soldiers, dressed in a white tunic. He refused the bronze armor which the priests had blessed. He trusted in his fate, he told them, and in the saber strapped to his side.

Very soon they arrived in the vicinity of the walls where the straw huts were built.

Before one of them a small crowd had gathered. There were women, children, old men now too weak to brandish a saber. They spoke in low voices, as the humble do in the presence of the powerful. Every so often they turned their eyes towards the threshold of the hut and shook their heads.

Great Los halted his horse. "Go see what happened," he ordered a soldier.

The soldier left and returned to report. "It's nothing, great Los. Someone died there, shortly before dawn, and now they're arranging the funeral."

Thus spoke the soldier, but Los nodded to his men to wait and dismounted. Seeing him approach, the people who were gathered around the hut stepped aside.

Before the threshold to the hovel a catafalque had been erected, and on the catafalque lay a corpse entirely covered by a hempen blanket.

Great Los drew close to the corpse and raised a corner of the cover to reveal the face. It was an old woman's face, furrowed with deep wrinkles, framed by a shock of white hair. Los gently brushed it back with his fingers. "Your wait wasn't long," he said softly.

The soldiers observed in silence.

Suddenly, the blanket slipped to the ground, fully discovering the old woman's body. She was wrapped in a light tunic of blue silk, embroidered in silver thread.

Disconcerted, the soldiers witnessed their leader throw himself to his knees beside the corpse and bury his face in the sky blue silk. A convulsive movement shook his shoulders, but from his lips nothing issued, not even a sob.

He stood there, embracing that body, as if time had stopped. From a distance the gallop of the opposing army could be heard.

Finally Los rose, and his men saw his face. No one dared speak to him. The war songs died in their throats. Only the neigh of the horses broke the silence now and then, and the noise, increasingly closer, of the enemy forces.

Los took a few steps towards his army, but suddenly stopped. He let his empty gaze run over the soldiers, and they all bowed their heads to avoid meeting it.

There was a loud bang, a metallic sound. The soldiers lifted their eyes and saw the great Los passing through the gates of the city on foot. His saber lay on the ground, abandoned.

The army was disoriented. "We are lost," several shouted. "All we can do now is to negotiate a surrender." But others shot back: "Wait. Let's request a truce, instead, and send a patrol to search for the great Los. Perhaps we can convince him to resume the command."

And so it was decided. The three eldest soldiers left the city, and when they were in sight of the enemy forces, they threw their sabers to the ground and raised their arms in a gesture of peace.

The leaders of the two rival clans approached them and listened to their request for a truce.

"He's right," one of the enemy said at last. "You can't fight without a commander. Therefore we agree to the truce. Send out your patrol. But don't expect great Los will return to lead your troops: he isn't the man he once was."

"How do you know?" asked a soldier. "Do you perhaps have spies in our city? Or have you seen him?"

"I shall tell you everything," said the other enemy leader. "A short time ago we were positioned down there, arrayed for battle, and we saw him appear before us, great Los, in person: he was on foot, in the open field. He came towards us, staggering and tearing at his clothes. 'Great Los,' we said to him, 'are you so confident of your fate that you are unafraid to challenge an entire army alone?'

Paola Capriolo

"He did not respond. His eyes stared without seeing, like a blind man's. Then we understood that he was no longer there; and since the mad are holy, and it is wrong to touch them, we commanded a herald to take a tour of the army and order that no one should raise a saber against the man who once was great Los.

"But there was no need: the soldiers instinctively stepped aside to let him pass, and so he crossed our ranks with the courage of a lion, or rather with the unconsciousness of a sleepwalker. He left unharmed and headed towards the west."

The patrol too turned their steps towards the west, scouring fields and villages in search of great Los.

Every so often they encountered a shepherd slowly leading his flock, or a farmer reaping grain, or a woman loaded with kindling. Then they stopped and asked if anyone had seen a man in torn clothing bearing the signs of madness on his face.

"Yes, he passed by here," they replied. "A holy man, as you say, a madman. He was walking like someone who drank too much wine, and he was having long conversations with himself, in a low voice."

And they always indicated that the madman was heading towards the west.

For three days and three nights the soldiers followed the tracks of the great Los, and at every hour the hope of leading their leader back to the city grew fainter.

The fourth day was celebrating its farewell when they reached the border of the island, where the sea of sand began.

They halted the horses. In the distance they could see the figure of a man trudging towards the burning line of the horizon.

They remained at length to observe him, without saying a word, in the light of sunset. The white tunic hung from his limbs in tatters. He staggered at every step, and yet he advanced determined, penetrating ever deeper into the sea of sand.

The soldiers' eyes followed the path of the man who once was great Los, but no one thought of calling him.

"Look," said one, lifting his arm. "What strange bird can that be?"

"Which do you mean?"

"That blue bird, down there, flying over his head."

But the man was too far away at this point, and the others could not see a thing. They spurred their horses and set off for the city.

I discovered Paola Capriolo's writing in Milan during the summer of 1988. Her first book had appeared that January, a story collection entitled The Great Eulalia, *and over the next few months it received enormous attention in the press, which was now renewed by the announcement that she had won a distinguished literary prize. My curiosity was naturally aroused, since I seem ever on the lookout for interesting work to translate. Yet when at last I opened the pages aboard the train for Venice, I was hardly prepared for the spell they cast. Suddenly I was transported from a stifling compartment crossing the Lombard plains to a land that was vaguely recognizable, but so obviously remote and magical.*

Capriolo's prose was the first hook: very lucid and concise, supple in its movement, full of subtle changes in tone and nuance. And the narrative was richly suggestive. The long title story, for instance, follows a farm girl who abandons her brothers to join a company of travelling actors, at first serving as their attendant, gradually assuming roles in their productions, finally becoming a renowned performer. Her success is linked to her mysterious relationship with an elegantly dressed man who lives in her wall-length mirror. He later appears at one of her performances, throwing her life into crisis, causing her to withdraw into the mirrored room never to be seen again. This enigmatic tale scrutinizes the illusion of reality in art, but especially as it imprints female adolescence. The girl conforms to the male gaze, which becomes her own.

What fascinated was the revolt against realism. Since realistic fiction remains the dominant form in Anglo-American culture, and I do not wish my encounters with the foreign to be guided by any cultural narcissism, I tend to gravitate toward Italian writing that is diametrically opposed: I favor the speculative and fable-like, with eccentric characters that worry the hallowed ethos of individualism by exposing the shaky foundations of the self. Capriolo is reminiscent of Kafka, Isak Dinesen, Angela Carter or, closer to home, Dino Buzzati, Italo Calvino, Anna Maria Ortese. Like Buzzati, she can represent the unsettling eruption of the fantastic into everyday life; like Calvino, she can use a deceptively simple tale to frame a complex reflection on the nature of artistic representation; and like Ortese, she is interested in the relations between desire and gender. Yet what I find most unique about Capriolo's fiction is the pace: measured, suspenseful, even ritualistic, a slow accumulating of resonant detail, capable of working simultaneously as engrossing story and sophisticated symbolic meditation.

In the several novels that followed her first book, she has refined her techniques and themes. Her latest, I Live for Love (1992), is a brilliantly inventive historical novel that rewrites the libretto of the Puccini opera Tosca, while drawing on the Gothic tradition and Sade. Capriolo's new wrinkle is to cast the narrative as the diary of Baron Scarpia, the reactionary official who aims to quash democratic subversion yet grows fatally obsessed with the singer Tosca. The result is a probing study of religious belief and conservative politics pushed to an extreme of repression and cruelty, a truly chilling read that is not merely an informed comment on the Napoleonic period, but a timely intervention against the right-wing thinking on the rise in Italy.

"The Blue Dove" is quintessential Capriolo. It appeared in The Girl with the Gold Star (1991), a collection of stories designed for children. The intricate narrative, part fairy tale and part Oriental fable, opens up another, adult dimension in which Capriolo continues to explore the vagaries of human identity. The Italian text was sheer joy to translate, requiring an English discourse that was both simple and allusive, a combination of current usage and archaism. My intention was to transport the reader to that distant place where I found myself upon first reading Capriolo — a place whence you return wanting to read more.

— Lawrence Venuti

Pairs, Passersby
Botho Strauss

— Translated from German by John Zilcosky

A MAN IN A GRAY, undersized suit, sitting alone at a table in a restaurant, suddenly shouts "Psst!" into the chattering crowd, so loudly that after he repeats it twice everyone looks over at his table; the stream of voices halts, nearly fades away, and finally, after one last, vigorous "Psst!" from the man, gives way to deathly silence. The man raises a finger and turns to the side, listening, and everyone listens with him, silently, to the side. Then the man shakes his head: no, it was nothing. The guests stir again, their silly laughter returns, and they make fun of the man who, by admonishing them to listen, transformed the mixed company into a unified, listening flock, if only for a few seconds.

A large circle of young men and women rise from their seats. They pay the bill and make briskly for the door, continuing their lively discussion. But a woman remains seated at the table, thinking back on the terrible thing someone had just said. The others are already standing in the vestibule, and here comes her husband back to her. He noticed, just before the exit, that his wife was missing. But there she is, already standing up and walking past him through the double doors.

At the striking of an uncertain hour, after many years of tiredness, confusion and attempts at separation, two people look at each other in their home with widening eyes. A recognition draws them to each other, a craving, as if, finally, only the incitement of all their sexual energies could, like a revolution, free them of the burden of their shared history by bringing it to an end. A desire to finish things races out of every lane they ever walked down. A desire they experience only as the desire to rebel. They embrace in a violence that condenses the entire substance of their intimacy, their memory, their hopelessly long companionship — and plunges it like a dying star into black nakedness.

Despite and in the midst of a decidedly bad mood, which had come about because of a fight and brought them to spend two days of their trip under the pressure of extreme taciturnity, the woman, who had been poking disinterestedly at her filet tips, suddenly lifted her head and hummed — with loud affection — an old pop song blaring from the bar loudspeaker. The man looked at her as if she had lost her mind and even jumbled the structure of her soul.

All love forms a utopia behind itself. In the dim and distant past, spoiled by happiness and songs, lies the origin of this wretched partnership. And the beginning survives as a frozen, ossified moment in the woman's heart. It is still *illud tempus* inside her, where everything else has changed and deteriorated over the years. From the first, frozen-solid, ice-dusted, not very nourishing provisions.

During their first hour, two people still at the starting line are so late — to meet their families, their spouses — that they must rush through a strange part of the city to catch a subway that will get them home just before their lateness becomes conspicuous. The speed, the wind, the stumbling run jar free the loose confession that, in the silence, did not yet want to come out. And as they run, the woman two steps ahead of the man, he pants it out behind her. Urged on by his calls, which act like the goading caresses of a jockey at the neck of his racehorse, the lover dashes faster ahead, as if the whip gave her happiness. In the mad rush, she can barely turn her head and call back into the air, she loves him too. Then they lose one another in the crowd and don't meet again until the next day.

I'll hear it for a long time to come: the cries of the woman who wanted to throw herself from the top floor of an apartment building. At first, a steady, muffled shouting established itself slowly above the congested street noise and drifted towards me. The apartment building bordered directly on the house where I was staying, so I couldn't observe the jumper herself, only the expectant circle that soon formed in front of her solitary perch. The apartment building measures maybe fifteen, at the most twenty meters to its roof, and it seems questionable whether a jump from such a low height would result necessarily in death; more likely, just the most horrible injuries. Her shouts increased in volume, she was now screaming very loudly, plaintively, almost joyfully: "Help! . . . Help!" Queen of desperate straits, she gathered little by little a small nation, subjects of her reign of suffering, at her feet. The employees in the offices diagonally opposite the building leapt up from their desks and, pushing and shoving against the many windows, rolled their eyes upward. But the vacillating monarch on the window ledge didn't keep her people in suspense for long, for already the police and fire trucks appeared. At the approaching sirens — and this word wavered here once again, back and forth between its old meaning, the song of seduction from the depths, and its present one, the rescue alarm — the woman screamed more and more vehemently, more and more plaintively: "Help . . . Help," and "Now listen to me!" But she had absolutely nothing to add, only "Help, Help" once again. The firemen unrolled their safety net; six of them held it stretched out below the window. But they never really took a good look up, watching instead the crowd of faces gawking skyward and taking pleasure in every glance that happened to linger on their accomplished grips or their poised, sturdy physiques. They performed their duty and scanned the scene. But they knew she wouldn't come. After taking only a fleeting, but experienced glance at the posture, standing position and gestures of the candidate, the men obviously knew that this would not be the scene of a jump. And they were right; a little later she — a young woman, incidentally, her forehead crossed with brilliant strands of blonde hair — left escorted by the police. Strapped to a stretcher, she was towed out of the building and shoved in an ambulance. Saved.

We saw her again in the evening. This edition of the television news introduces us to people who have just survived suicide attempts. We are present when those poisoned with sleeping pills awaken; we live through every second, as their eyes open to a new existence in front of the television.

The impression we gain from the saved is generally disappointing. Describing their condition before the great passage, they are at a loss for words or they talk nonsense. Strange, also, how they take in their surroundings without surprise: they seem to be immediately aware that they are in a hospital bed and not in the realm of the dead. Some go first to the sink to brush their teeth. The young woman who wanted to throw herself from the window of the apartment building now tells the television crew: "Peter, he's crazy jealous. I didn't have no idea where I was. I didn't have no choice." Expressed that way, her lofty cry from the morning, her will to carry out the one, final, the supreme human act, seems suddenly effaced by human, all too understandable and thus meaningless motives. And yet: the real misery is that real misery cannot make a space for itself. It stifles awareness, it doesn't break out. The great sorrow is housed inside the thousands of meaningless sorries. As long as she babbles and doesn't jump, she'll continue to double-cross both Peter and Death. . . .

From time to time, when she feels in the mood, she goes to see a muscular, well-dressed young man, and he is usually there for her. She does not have to pay. Their relationship is purely physical. They know little about each other, nothing profound, only what you can learn about the other's journey through life during a cigarette break, and easily forget. That's how it's done today, exactly as described, even recommended, in thousands of magazines. These two help each other, in a most exemplary way, to live alone and without ties. In front of the house she gives a good-bye caress to the cheek of the man in his white pants. It looks gentle and grateful, worldly-wise, not risqué. A gesture, nevertheless, containing the languid kindness and abundant evasions, wherein loving goes far afield of love. What we have here is a liberal democratic institution, freed from chaos and fear — love subordinated to the greatest good, domesticated, devoted to freedom. Fear belongs to nuclear power plants. No one is forced to endure it these days at its sexual origin. And many seem to succeed in provincializing it, besieging it.

Simply hearing the word *relationship* over and over again dries the sweat on one's palms. Sounding so flatly economic, it resorts to artifice to sober up encounters with love and the real threat they pose, intrinsically, to the general welfare — it insinuates a certain calculability into a sphere that is still man's most native, impenetrable and entangled. Perhaps this will change; perhaps the power of endless possibility, absolute license and consumption will in the long run render all bonds loose and frail. Just as the man without history delights in the cold stagings of the past, the sudden tableaus of Prussians, Hohenstaufens and Pharaonic tombs, so the man without love will find excitement only in tracking down evidence of love. He will be only too happy to find out what a so-called erotic adventure was really like or what a passion looked like when it matured by breaking down traditions, rules and resistances.

For those of us in the cities — mobile, accelerated, of mixed class — partner choice is decided through a "free" game of attraction and repulsion, varying according to our mood and the assortment of stimuli. It seems as if the reality of eros, the external scene of changing opportunities, has developed into a perfect copy of the soul itself, with its snarled, unsettled needs and copious ambivalences. We will never again meet the person we know straight off suits us like no other, the right one. For our way of life, in which we are supposed to become increasingly independent of each other but increasingly dependent on the whole, such a beautiful deception of the heart is no longer useful, and it will gradually vanish from our feelings. But where the soul need obey so few external designs, the power of inner ambivalence emerges all the more unbridled. The talk of bonding — resting uniquely on emotion, no longer responsible for supporting the common social fate — is a complex yes/no, and its unsplittable core is love/coldness. Decisive is whatever pleases the soul at the moment, which won't please it at the next, because, as we know, the soul is a shifty stronghold. The encounter that takes place under the conditions of greatest possible external freedom and irresponsibility soon becomes the maltreated victim of compulsions, of the desiring and destroying moods of the unconscious. In this sphere, where the social (reproduction, the construction of community, the handing down of a cultural heritage, etc.) has forfeited its predominant role, mood traffics promiscuously with opportunity — external stimuli, the new, with the quick change of address — and, out of this wide stream of intercourse, where the wished-for and the given always come together at short notice, no firmly promised bond can lift itself. The stream runs through us all.

She inherited a house, the dainty young woman, employee of the municipal department of transportation, who speaks enthusiastically about her grandmother, recently passed away, and the house, nothing but back rooms! keeps talking at her colleague, already married, but staying at her place for the weekend. Plans, plans. She draws the house for him on the paper napkin and wants to lure him inside. In the reversal of her situation she can barely contain herself, going into ecstasies and frightening herself and more and more insistently offering a strange, silent man a shared future. The man for his part rolls his wedding ring more and more nervously around his finger, smiles in disbelief, lightly shakes his head as though this were all too odd, while at the same time allowing, just once, on a trial basis, a reversal to draw itself in silence from his calves upwards, through his own relationships.

A borough official in his mid-thirties warms up his intelligence in front of his wife, who just sits there, silent and listless. He sheds a critical light on certain incidents at work; yes, he elevates himself to a detached observer of his own office, now, in the evening, out at the bar for a late-night drink. Because neither an objection nor a glance — either would expose his ridiculousness — can be expected from her, he speaks more and more vehemently, boasting about the abuses in the administration, what steps he intends to take against them. And since he's the only one speaking and doesn't have to pay attention to anyone else, he feels his intelligence steadily swelling, and his insight into the connections intoxicates him. Suddenly he also perceives an aspect of the woman; for his own satisfaction he needs her to be somewhat smarter than she is, and he imagines it. Sitting next to him, so harmlessly captive, this person is the best drug he can take for lightly raising his opinion of himself. Although she betrays, now and then, through an incorrect rejoinder, how little she has stuck by him, how little she is on the "same wavelength" — a deficiency in the partnership, because of which the young official has already interrupted, with bitter regret, many flights of intellect. He (in the course of his official upbraiding): "What that costs the taxpayer!" She: "Isn't there another office it could run through?" He: "Of course not! Imagine for one second what that would cost the taxpayer!" And says it more emphatically, almost angrily, so that the woman will finally rant with him. But that's not her nature; she lets nothing and no one launch her into a blind rage. Suddenly, he is silent, and a next question, a further enquiry on her part, is never advanced. The man pays the waiter, and a little bit later both of them stand up. As he holds the coat open for her and they look at each other, an instinctive, ineffaceable shimmer of frivolous compassion rises in the man's eyes.

An alcoholic couple in the department store Source stand in line at the register. The man keeps to his wife's side, looking at the floor and mumbling. She squeezes her right eye shut, over and over again, for no apparent reason, as if sharing a lewd secret with an invisible friend. The jangled nerves perform a short, endlessly repeating dance. At brief intervals, driven by an automatic horror, she snaps her head around and then smiles, as convivial as she is anguished, in a direction where no one is and whence no call came for her. A fickle drama plays across her reddened, bloated, scaly face, set off by the distress of standing in line, by the cramped positioning among strange people. The smile, the shards of a smile appear from all angles to be a friendly defense against excessive distress. The mouth, in a radiant grimace, exposes a row of eroding tooth stumps, getting smaller and more full of holes from left to right. She has shopped for a lemon yellow alarm clock. Why set an alarm? For the first mouthful? I stood at the main exit next to the glass door, holding an unwieldy piece of garden furniture and waiting for a friend, who brought the rest of the set. The alcoholic couple walked out just as we were loading up our cargo to carry home. The woman remarked to her husband that it was of course especially smart of us to decide to pack things up so close to the exit. Although we weren't in their immediate way, it seemed to do her noticeable good to think of herself as part of the order and of us as disturbance, and to point this out. My friend growled rudely at her: "Shut up, old sow." When I heard that, it sounded as if someone gave an accident victim a good kick in the stomach. Because I had watched the course of her fate for a while and could feel nothing but sympathy. When we passed the couple on the street, the woman stopped her husband and said quietly, as if in the presence of someone famous, "Called me an old sow!" "Who?" the man asked. "That guy over there," the woman said and nodded at us. With so many preemptive smiles and ghostly friendships, she tried to ward off everything around her that seemed injurious, and then, in the end, it struck her anyway. Truly troubled, not infuriated, she stood motionless and repeated the affront, and it seemed even more incredible to her.

An American soldier who deserted in 1949 kept himself hidden in West Berlin for almost thirty years. His hideout was the apartment of his German girlfriend, who also provided for him and shielded him from the outside world. Until she died. Only the television and his girlfriend's stories had hinted at an abruptly changing reality. He didn't even dare walk out onto the balcony. The day-to-day occurrences in his neighborhood were so unfamiliar to him that, after leaving his lair, when he wanted to telephone the police in order, finally, to give himself up as a deserter, he couldn't figure out how to use a German call box. He simply didn't know how it was done. A passerby had to show him.

The man beaten down by his job, the woman and the door that does not close. "Take care of that door once and for all!" the woman calls. The utterly despondent grip of the handyman on the door, his inscrutable melancholy while *busying himself* with the door.

He squats on the floor with his knees pulled to his chest, lightly rocking across the curve of his ass. The woman bends down to him, full of the promises of existence proffered by a pointing, out-stretched arm: "And the sun?" The man shrugs his shoulders indifferently and rocks unmoved. No desire.

"The world is filled with events and is possibly even in a state of upheaval. And you don't do anything, just rock back and forth like an idiot."

What remained of her, fragments of a frustrated erotic sovereignty.

A woman stands in front of a house, right leg raised, foot pressed against the wall, knee stuck sharply out; defenses readied, readied.

A woman photographs you, spreading her legs, jutting her pelvis, receiving-conceiving you, click-castrate.

A woman, who, after three quiet days of reflection and ruthless self-scrutiny, lashes out all around her and shouts: I don't want you! You I do not want!

A woman runs ten spread fingers through her hair at the moment you want to embrace her.

A woman startles you with thoughtless hands, pressing her fingers from behind onto your eyeglasses and calling out: Who am I?

A woman points at you with an outstretched finger and commands: You! Think it over!

A woman remains standing in front of you, not moving from the spot. She uncovers the insolence of your heart through your benevolent gaze.

Strange, unpleasant even, how one, as the years pass, grasps straight away, almost compulsively, the essentials of a person met only fleetingly. The attitude of a finger, the countenance of a gait, and at once "experienced supposing" (Heidegger) sets in, through which we can calculate — often feel internally forced to — with the help of a few looks, a few sense data, the entire behavioral sphere of a person; we play out an arbitrary sequence of possible situations, bringing the person authentically before us, how he stands there, how he speaks.

The arrogant intelligence of the Professor of Education, in his late thirties, a reader of the left-wing Berlin daily, whose big thing is to go on and on ("like the common man," you know) about engines, excellent restaurants, dream trips. "They've got new test results out on that model, it gives you 250 horsepower easy." One glance, one eavesdropped sentence records so many value-added particles of character that you can also, actually in the same moment, see how this man uses his nail file or hear how he responds when his wife calls him a liar.

Searching for her room along the bewildering corridors of the hotel, the girl discovers a man in a white shirt and black pants standing at the end of a narrow, dimly lit hall. The backs of his hands are pressed against his hips, and in each of the hands are three plates. From time to time he lifts up the plate-filled hands and looks at them, as if hands with the plates in them did not suit him; then he turns them over and props the backs of his hands (with the plates) on his hips again. Maybe he's a juggler who's lost his bowling pin. Maybe it's just a person who has never before had to hold three plates at once in his hands. In any case, he doesn't know what to do, on this hallway of closed doors left and right, holding these plates. He doesn't seem to know how the plates got into his hands, or better yet, how he himself — with the plates in his hands — got into the hall not knowing what to do. The light bulb, which was hanging from the ceiling, falls without losing its glow and pops on the floor, forming a puddle of light, a footlight that suddenly illuminates the man from beneath.

The daughter of the head steward smiles at this and thinks, yes, now you see, there's really no choice but to become an artist.

When Aeneas, the hero of Troy, landed at the port of Carthage, he discovered scenes from the legendary war he had just returned from carved into the marble of a temple, and beneath the warriors, he found an image of himself.

A., only a party member, a mere "supporter" of the Nazi regime and now an old man, sits in the front row of a movie theater when suddenly, in an old newsreel or a Hitler documentary, he recognizes himself among the screaming masses — sees himself, a shouting young man, in close-up. Yes, he thinks, feeling anonymous to the tips of his toes, I was there, I screamed, I was one *volk* — one scream. Now I sit alone in a dark theater among all these young people — this pack of critical minds that can only be "surprised" at our scream — who even break out into a roar of laughter over it, feeling no reverence at all for the evil.

A stroll through the Tiergarten. Frost and sun. Ducks along the icy edges of the Landwehrkanal. Skaters on the small lake. The old Spanish embassy and its somber pomp of ruins. At the rear of the building, like the imprint of a fossil, the walled-up chapel arcade, a stone crucifix. Silent, empty castle of fascism behind an overgrown garden. The century's excesses age, too, contrary to a pitiful Romanticism.

Nevertheless: Preserve, keep everything! Tear nothing down!

The judge asks the old man, concentration-camp guard Fuchs, for his present view on the facts surrounding the extermination of the Jews. The man, who has a heart condition, answers according to the paradigm of incorrigibility: "The Jews should have been deported to a deserted island." The judge: "And what would you say if the State decreed that all people with the name Fuchs be deported to a deserted island?" Fuchs, sheepishly: "The Jewish question should have been solved in a respectable manner." The pedagogical judge: "What do you call respectable?" The Nazi, thus driven into a corner, finally says very quietly what one wants to hear from him: "The Jews should have been left in peace."

Nietzsche's hatred of anti-Semitism: "It is one of the most morbid swellings of absurd and unjustified, imperial German self-ogling." By now we know republican German self-ogling only too well and know that it gets vainer the more economic prosperity falters, and that, consequently, hostile stirrings toward too many foreigners in the country increase again. Certainly, in the rest of Europe, in France and England as well, protests — sometimes more violent but also more open — are led against the influx of foreign workers; but regardless of the economic justification of these self-protective instincts, they coalesce in this country really in no time at all into the old familiar suckers, too long left empty, of racist desire. When one notices the sudden revival of hatred — no rarer in the very young than in the older, tested racists — one could gain the impression that German emotional life has, for a long time, consisted essentially of a void; nothing that arrived from the colorful potpourri could fill it, nothing stirred it; only when the race-hatred arrives, one senses immediately: it fits! The feeling feels again, something central is committed to it again.

"Wouldn't want to know how many Turks were there," says the Berlin housewife in the Edeka store, the morning after shop windows were broken and stores looted during a squatters' demonstration. (Of course the panes of the Turkish stores in Kreuzberg were not spared the violence.) Obviously one can again call the ethnic scapegoat — responsible for all abortive developments in social life — by its name, and the conspiracy theories will not be long in coming. But there are still thousands of prescribed sensitivities, punctually inserted moral shudders in the mass media (such as *Holocaust*), and just as punctual, after a considerable while, emotional-pornographic relaxations through Nazi revues and period-picture nostalgia. A well-nigh inescapable, fundamental dishonesty and lack of freedom run through the entire so-called "overcoming-the-past" movement — which is partly enlightenment, partly glorification of the nation, the German subsoil in each of us; this miserable ambivalence, these nonreimbursable inner reparations, could altogether, in conjunction with an actual worsening of material conditions, lead to the stooped German soul stretching itself hastily to its full height, simply shaking off the undigestible ballast, the phantasm of a lasting guilt — curing itself of evil by wanting and doing evil anew. And beginning again by spraying its poison all over the foreigners in this country. It is, in any case, no longer the hour to trust liberal democracy, with its simple fringe-center thinking, to cope permanently with the parapolitical and most negative needs of a people. And permanence will be a close call anyway. We should be prepared for a future in which abrupt events arrive much more quickly than in the past thirty years — where blocked currents can converge and burst forth, and the fuses of modern rationality could, "at overloaded capacity," quite suddenly, without much warm-up time, blow.

Botho Strauss

A German friend gave me Botho Strauss's Pairs, Passersby in Berlin in November 1989. "Everyone's reading it," she said. "As antidote" (I assumed, to the fever of reunification). I had known Strauss, in the seventies and early eighties, as an absurdist playwright, a creative critic of bourgeois culture on a par with Peter Handke and Luis Buñuel. But Pairs (1981), a loose collection of observations — part essay, part fictional vignette — established him as the cult writer of the liberal left, a "must" for the skeptically well-informed. I began reading Pairs, expecting to find Germany's contemporary critical voice. But Strauss, in the spirit of Adorno and the Frankfurt School, deflected me at every turn. He presents appearances, not depths; insights, not arguments. Snippets of people's lives and fragments of cultural criticism, coupled strikingly, parade past the reader. Demonstrators against realism, these passersby are relentlessly empty yet mysteriously akin. They demand a reading strategy, and I searched for a way behind their façades.

Pairs contains, according to the Frankfurter Rundschau, the complete "physiognomy of our times." Strauss, Germany's physiognomist, weaves himself in and out the text, sometimes as actor, sometimes as disdainful commentator. He studies, appropriately, his nation's faces: "A., only a party member, a mere 'supporter' of the Nazi regime," sits alone in the front row of a movie theater and spots himself shouting among the masses in a Hitler documentary; a woman, "queen of desperate straits," screams from the sill of her Berlin apartment building, gathering a crowd below her but refusing to jump; a borough official in his mid-thirties "warms up his intelligence in front of his wife, who just sits there, silent and listless." As physiognomist, Strauss hypothesizes an essence from these surfaces. He fixes every character — each one's constitutional flaw — somewhere between particularity and stereotype. One by one, or, better, pair by pair, they suffer the narrator's type-casting gaze. He nails them, freezes their telling twitches, and we cannot look away.

The narrator's self-acknowledged "compulsive" stereotyping is simultaneously diagnosis and symptom. It is, for Strauss, the sign of a society without history — a postmodern culture in the throes of différence and posthistory — trying to identify itself, pin itself down. The prognosis is bleak. The "data salad" of postmodern German life enervates the individual and scrambles memory. Consciousness, splintered and fragmented, does not play and replay itself ecstatically; rather, television reassembles it into nifty "delusions

266

of totality" — as presented in historical dramas, special reports and mini-series. But just as television falsely contains collective histories (Strauss notes Germany's mandatory "moral shudder" during the airing of Holocaust on public television in 1979), the contemporary writer produces sham personal histories. He functions like a data bank for narratives, obsessively creating memories from a "spree of stereotypes."

Strauss's elastic German syntax supports (more elegantly than English) an overload of temporal adverbs ("again," "once," "then"). Fragments of longing, these markers repeat Strauss's desire for an authentic German past (both collective and personal) — for a "now" that relates to a "then." But Strauss's search, my search, always ends at National Socialism, the hole in the postmodern hypertext. An old man, an ex-party member, sees himself screaming on film. . . . The "real" persists, but is embalmed within a "static, ahistorical epoch." And postmodernity — the flattening of memory — reveals its specific German meaning: it is a poetics of repression. The repressed subject — the individual without history — cannot communicate, and like Strauss's narrator, who is at home in isolation, the modern German passes us by.

— John Zilcosky

Five Prose Poems
Semezdin Mehmedinović

— *Translated from Bosnian by Ammiel Alcalay*

GLASS

1. Standing by the window, I see the shattered glass of *Jugobank*. I could stand like this for hours. A blue, glassed-in facade. One floor above the window I am looking from, a professor of aesthetics comes out onto his balcony: running his fingers through his beard, he adjusts his glasses. I see his reflection in the blue facade of *Jugobank*, in the shattered glass that turns the scene into a live cubist painting on a sunny day.

2. In the evening, I listen to the news along with the glazier, the Old City's master glass-man. At the mention of place names during dispatches from the front, he appends his own lively anecdotes, the recollections of a man whose work took him all over Bosnia: here, he did the glass for a school; there, an auditorium or an arena . . . I listen to him like a student listening to a teacher. After the news, I experience Bosnia like a huge glass warehouse crackling through the thin wires of a transistor hooked up to a car battery. The homeland shatters brittlely in the ears of the glazier, her true president.

WHITE DEATH

When snow falls on Sarajevo, when pines crackle with frost, the bones underground will be warmer than us. People will freeze to death: a winter without fire is coming, a summer without sun has passed. The nights are already cold and when someone's dog starts barking on a balcony, a chorus of strays answers back, howling in sorrow like children crying: even Irish setters, usually so filled with glee, bark sadly at night in this town, like Rutger Hauer in the last scene of *Blade Runner*. Snow will bury this city just the way war has buried time: what's today? When is Saturday? I don't know. The daily rituals are dead, just like the yearly ones. Who, in December, will print a calender for 1993? There is day, there is night: in them are people prepared for the end of the world, well aware that existence in its plenitude would be all but lost were they unconscious of global cataclysm. That's why they burn a small light at the first sign of dark: the wick pulled through a ball-point refill, a cork wrapped in tinfoil to keep the oil in the lamp made out of an empty beer can burning on the surface. And in the small, clear blaze they can see that intimate objects and faces have an earthly glow, and that there is no grief, until *aksham* falls, at the sunset call for prayer.

A MARTYR'S RESTING PLACE

A body just about to be buried. I see a soldier on his knees: still a kid. His rifle rests in his lap. You can hear the guttural murmur of Arabic voices. Sorrow gathers in circles under the eyes; the men pass their open palms across their faces. As the rites continue, I feel the presence of God in everything; when this is over, I shall take a pen and make a list of my sins. Now everything in me resists death: as my tongue passes over my teeth I can sense the taste of a woman's lipstick. No one is crying. I keep quiet. A cat jumps across the shadow of a minaret.

CURFEW

After curfew, Tito Street is dead. The sound of wind in the glass-less nylon windows. When it stops blowing, you can hear a cat walking on the asphalt. Then, out of the dark, a man calls: "Who are you?" The narrow beam of his flashlight searches for my iden-tity papers. They meet, signaling to each other with their lights: the black-helmeted driver of a Jeep without any windows, and a pick-up completely covered with iron panels — "Dobrinja" appears on it in yellow letters. When I turn into a narrow street, I think

269

about how someone must be preparing to make a set like this for a science fiction film somewhere. An extra in that film is less mortal than Sarajevo. Less real. I walk the main streets carefully, afraid that, in the dark, I might get tangled up in the fallen trolley wires. There aren't any on this street but, nevertheless, I keep on my toes. You can't see a thing but I know that, to my left, there is a kiosk. The glass is broken, the doors have been removed, and its insides have been cleaned out. The ripped-out shelves hang off the walls. From what was left, someone made a *precise* installation. On exhibit, behind no glass, a row of color photos of Sarajevo is hung over a piece of silk with clothespins. It's been that way for days already. The creator of this installation remains anonymous. It would be enough to simply reach in and take the postcards; it's quite strange that hasn't happened yet.

LION'S

The former municipal cemetery, brought back to life by the war. A trenchdigger shovels out new graves; he digs in advance, counting on the dead bodies. When the shells fall — and they often fall on this cemetery — the trenchdigger's driver and the gravedigger helping him jump into the freshly dug graves. "Forced" trench: for an instant, something in death's domain serves life.

Semezdin Mehmedinović was born in 1960 and is the author of four books. Sarajevo Blues (from which the texts in this issue of Conjunctions *have been selected) was the first book in the* Biblioteka *"egzil-abc" series. Published in Ljubljana, "egzil-abc" has provided a forum for Bosnian writers and translators, either under siege or in exile, to continue publishing their work. In the scale of things, the books themselves are "small" productions: 4 x 6 inches, between twenty and seventy pages and printed in editions of one hundred to two hundred copies. Each has a lowercase letter on the cover; to date, books a through x have appeared. Mehmedinović, active throughout the war in Sarajevo's artistic resistance, has been chosen to represent Bosnian writers at the 1994 Frankfurt Book*

Fair; if circumstances permit, he will exhibit works published by Bosnians during the war. When actually holding these books (both those published in exile and those appearing, one way or another, during the siege in Bosnia-Hercegovina itself), you begin to understand what Semezdin Mehmedinović (still a citizen of Sarajevo, where he continues to "live") means when he writes that "writing is, finally, quite a personal thing that doesn't make much sense unless you are practicing for the last word." For those Bosnians still under siege or in exile, whether in this world or the next, these "last words" remain intimate possessions, one of the last bastions left against the commodification of tragedy. At the same time, by translating this work, we take both the risk and the responsibility of giving these words another life, of turning the "last word" into "literature," and providing their possessors a path — however tenuous — back into an indifferent world such words no longer seem to have anything to do with.

— Ammiel Alcalay

Two Poems
Pascalle Monnier

— *Translated from French by John Ashbery*

PARA SIEMPRE TERESITA? PARA SIEMPRE RODRIGO

> "It is written of her that as a child she was co-
> quettish and full of pride, but that prayer and
> the rigor of a Spanish, Christian upbringing suc-
> ceeded in taming her character . . ."

Then a servant girl told him
Oriane was the most beautiful of all
they called her The One without Equal
the Queen gave her the Squire of the Sea
My Pet this is a squire who will serve you
I like him replied Oriane

hence, Galahad, son of Lancelot of the Lake
clothed in gold brocade by the angels
placed a crown on her head
and a ring on her right hand

Palmerin de Oliva, illegitimate child
abandoned on a mountain in a wicker cradle
suspended from the branches of an olive tree

as an adolescent she tried to seduce her cousin
she kissed him on the lips
despite the duennas and etiquette
the cousin was then dispatched to the Indies

and so as not to marry she chose the convent
she mourned her mother's death
her brothers' departure

one must pray a great deal
I pray
how do you pray?

she journeyed across Castile
staying sometimes in the houses of princes
more often in tents and in grottoes

a *determinacioncilla*
to flee
to flee by night

It's the nina
the nina
who's responsible

she knew how Amadis was consigned to the oceans
Elisene, his mother, launched him in a skiff resembling a coffin

chivalry is what causes no wrong
you must swear that you'll die in combat rather than flee
the defender of each damsel equally

already the knights are leaving for Seville
in a single day 14,000 baptisms were performed
and precious stones rolled around like pebbles

the world is vanity
life is short
having decided to enter the convent
I am afraid of myself
I am afraid of being weak

above all your mother will come
to recall your past life for you
from the day down to the present hour
although your mother
although your father
I have gone out of my father's house

He promises to deliver
a bed, coverlet and quilts
six linen sheets, a pillow
two mattresses, two cushions
as well as a novice's habit and liveries

first we kiss his feet, his hands
we give him a kiss on the mouth
their soul has slept in the arms of the beloved
he stays close to me

writes to his brother Lorenzo
had married wealth in Quito
give me 40 piastres
I am leaving for Toledo
my presence is requested there
I am entering the house of princes
the wind is too faint
they must live from their work
renounce palaces
Cordovan leather, marble, ivory, mother of pearl and silver

LOCATIONS

The garden hose hoses down the gardener, the Cliff, Cliff Villa, atop
    a cliff:
a terrace with a small rose-garden, a garden hose, some sun.
The little girl bites into the bread, the stray dog, one night,
in the pavilion; the sisters return from Barcelona.
The skirts are too short, especially one with a big floral print;
on a bench, three tanned people gaze in the direction of the cliff.
There: learn to swim, bundled in a blanket,
102 degrees, very hot, throat sore, Leonore,
take care of oneself, injections, medication, someone who's even
    sicker.
The newlyweds' trip, back from the trip; for: the landlords' daughter
will get the same illness (the same year at the latest).
Here: a female bridge champion, in the shed, geraniums in the
    greenhouse

(the cliff, sea-urchins, a fork, shoes,
the Australian crawl to swim as far as the rock).

Aquatic flower, the old town, near the school,
back from the trip, the Scottish dolls, this house,
unwrapped under the stairway. This house has a freshwater name,
insipid, the small garden, in front, the stairway under the stairway,
      three floors at least,
with the name, the Scottish dolls, the proximity of the school
where: the brothers give fountain pens to the students, the church
— there, everything happens under the stairs.

Silver coast, in the square, farther on, on the Corniche route,
more Parisian, richer, a girl, the lawn raked with a fine-tooth comb,
the shoe-factory, yogurt at the beach, the outboard motorboats.
Us: a boat and Françoise the doll. Them: a red Ferrari,
then yet another car where it killed the other brother.

The little chair, on the porch, for meals,
in another villa on a lake with no special name.
Melon-seed necklaces, the old man, near the toilets
— mushrooms and dances on the porch.
The same woman is dead, farther north, much later, on a legal holiday.
Him: he's become the brother-in-law of her who has become the
      sister-in-law
(who is no longer that much of a sister-in-law).
Ruffle on white blouse and macaroons,
in the wood, found with the fishmonger's delivery van.

Elsewhere, opposite, Villa Bonjour, silting up,
(less Parisian, less rich, familial, different)
but: afterwards very rich, Parisian, the beach,
not for everyone, reserved for crabs, shrimp, rocks,

that family's beach or perhaps another family's.
Here: a veranda with broken panes, Virus, the battle, Roseline.
Was campsite caretaker and conductor of the little train, at night,
      during the day,
the low-ceilinged bedroom up above, look at everything through a
      round window,
the same one later on, repainted, occupied by strangers, very expensive.

The name of one of them lost, came a red convertible,
the year of their marriages, shared his room, in the basque style,
white walls and brick-red shutters,
except for that nothing happens.

Another house (shipwreck on the radio) at the top of a hill:
less provincial, play golf, the senators.
There: dry leaves from the tree for smoking cigarettes
and the game of the tradeswomen's garage. The same storm
on land as for them at sea; thus: the shutters slam.
Recherché, they're lost, found, heard
at the top of the stairs. Ill under mosquito-netting, in wind standing.
Looked after by the sister of him who'll become the brother's best
    friend,
watched over by the cousins of her who had lost her little sister
— will be cousins of his cousins (but still later).

Another house, beside the road, very much the orphan:
but protected by a garden bordered by a wall and the trees' foliage.

Another (high up, at the end of a red avenue, on a hill-top).
There: men on the moon and the monkey buried in the garden,
there again: canaries, the circus picture,
in the bedroom, rings tossed down a well, the bike,
there: plaid Bermuda shorts and betrothals
— with the cousin of those who were later called the uncle and the
    aunt.

Another: no name, overlooking a village, very far away,
very foreign, then toward the lake, still sick, ping pong,
migraine, the surgeon, friends of those who had two kitchens,
a tiny outboard motorboat, the daughter found later,
an apartment with converted bedrooms linked together.
Was she too: a girlfriend of the friend
while the father was: the mother's boyfriend
and before: the father's friend, took the kids to the zoo
(found abroad in the city, the same villa, but later).

The other, on the beach, opposite, the first year, without rocks.
There: breakfast and mattress on the beach for sleeping.
Under a porch roof: look at the sea, the dunes,

the channel, then rocks, stairway, pine-tree seedlings protected
(with ropes and signs reading pine seedlings)
then, a kind of trench.
For him, the boat that belonged to the one who was his father's friend.

Much earlier: Joan of Arc, opposite near the pier, in the alley,
(near the small-scale replica of the twin sister's Russian-style villa)
a veranda and the terrace, large, atop the embankment.
Two girls, tanning on the cement flagstones, burning.
Below, docile sea and Mickey Mouse Club. Opposite, shoal visible at
    low tide.
The sister and the cousin are expelled from England: one of the two
    was drowned.
Much later, there were marriages and children, like the other sister
— sister of the one killed in a car crash by the fiancé; he was also the
    brother's friend.
With the name of the fiancé who killed the sister, he the friend of the
    family.
At the entrance to the alley: the tobacconist's, with the uncle.
Dany runs the sailing school, likes boys or girls depending on the day
    of the week
and when during a hurricane keels and barges fly along the alley.
It's the style of almond cookies, other petit fours, sorbets and curds.
Dinner: him on the second floor, downstairs the wife and the friends
but her: love also of him and husband of her: love of the daughter too.
Three to a bedroom, the armoire for undressing.
The balcony collapses, the embankment collapses, the stairway
    collapses.
One night, later, taking a shower, a few villas away,
another summer, about a hundred yards from there (but that, much
    later).

Later: The Hut, another terrace, much bigger.
Greet the uncles, the family (we still retain traces of a decent
    upbringing).
There: front porch, back porch, long dining room.
Vacation over, the children leave for the country;
on their knees, the girls rub the parquet with steel wool.
The two sleep in a glassed-in bedroom,
to the right of the front porch, facing the sea, one sees the sea,
everything is glazed, green and white, quite Norman in style.

277

Pascalle Monnier

To lie down at the top of the embankment. Consolidate breakwater,
Rebuild the embankment, it costs money to maintain embankments:
the embankment separates from the beach, separates
separates from those lying on the beach, lying under beach umbrellas,
near the ice chests, near the roller coasters, near the trapezes,
between the overturned keels, on the folding chairs,
undress behind towels;
the mother or the sister holds the towel.

---

*I first met Pascalle Monnier in 1989, when I was poet in residence
in a program sponsored by the Florida-based Atlantic Center for
the Arts at the Chateau of La Napoule, near Cannes on the French
Riviera. Pascalle was one of five French poets I'd chosen on the
basis of work submitted, and I very soon felt the urge to translate
her poems. She strikes a note that I haven't seen elsewhere in
contemporary French poetry: for instance, the cascading seaside
images of "Locations" with an undercurrent of sinister happenings
remind me more of French cinema (Rivette's* Out One/Spectre, *for
example) than of French poetry. The breathless run-on lines which
don't always add up grammatically are a surprise: avant-garde
French poetry usually tends to observe the classical norms; hers is
more suggestive of some of today's American innovations.*

*Some of her colleagues in France are the poets Jean-Jacques
Viton, Olivier Cadiot and Anne Portugal (the latter was also in the
group at La Napoule), all of whom have embraced a newly experimental mode in France. Her first collection will be published in
late 1994 by the pioneering French publishing house, Editions POL.*
— John Ashbery

The Howling Twins
John Tranter

THE TWINS Marilyn and Stanley and their friend Charlie Rugg had stopped at the top of the hill, propped against their red bikes. They'd come rocking along to the farm at Rockaway Junction to see if they could find their pet cat named Snowball. Snowball had been rescued from Uncle Daniel's farm a dozen times, but no good had ever come of it. They'd looked and looked, to no avail.

"Well, I guess Snowball has given us the cold shoulder again," Marilyn said. "She hid in her own kitty heaven, a heaven in the underbrush. She would have heard a dog barking, should a dog have barked. Hey, don't you two want me to pick some apples while I'm here? I'm hungry. Maybe she'll turn up, while we're waiting. Maybe somebody has already found the little tyke."

"Sure, and maybe a bunch of guys grabbed the critter, and took her as sacrifice to their dreadful god Moloch," Charlie replied scornfully, "guys who had seen Snowball but who said nothing, nothing at all!" He burst into tears. Marilyn comforted the poor fellow, who was now dreaming of the breasts of the boys, sobbing after they had been crushed by the stone god.

In the quiet country morning there were sounds of many animals. Stanley's acute hearing trapped the other sounds, and sorted out their pet's bickering meow. "Cats hear more than we know. I hear one meowing now, up in the branches."

"Uh-uh. I don't see a cat rescued from the branches," Marilyn said. "Not by us, at any rate."

It was fun at Uncle Daniel's farm, but that was a vacation, not employment, which is each day suffering money burning in wastebaskets. The one symbolic escape is amnesia, and the only escapees are those who watch from the place of forgetfulness.

Marilyn listened to the spiritual sounds on the old metaphysical telephone. Lots of static. Then Death spoke, and said he was coming to get the boys. What was their crime? Looking upon Death himself. How to escape him? Look upon Life.

"To look upon Life," Marilyn said, "we could visit dives in the city and from the anonymous dark watch the incomprehensible jazz criminals perform with their flow of semen, or so Charlie once proposed. If I felt like it I could accuse Charlie of something awful, something to do with his body."

"Marilyn, I'm sure you would accuse the stoops off a building if you could," snapped Charlie, who had overheard. "I don't give a damn if you worry about my body. I don't know what to do next with this body, which is more than I can say for you. I've been places, remember."

Marilyn remembered Charlie had gone to find out what was happening on the West Coast, and Stanley had claimed to be the True Consciousness and said he didn't need to go there to find out. But he did go, and he found there the three old shrews: the stunned government of Insulin, Xanax and Electricity.

Stanley, who wept for the boys the starry-spangled shocks of harlequin speech had led astray, Stanley, climbing the stairways of sin in empty lots, Stanley who jumped into the void of insulin, Stanley who lounged hungry and speechless and said "Kiss the ass of war, the monster whose fingers inscribe the terror." Stanley, who is still cursing at the harpies of the poem of life, burning a light in his naked room as a shrine. Stanley thought of Cocks and their monstrous Bombs. In the evening sky, the two twins were visions.

In his dream Stanley finds Snowball and flings the last radio of hypnotism into the East River.

Uncle Daniel said the children could have been bothered on several occasions, and no call for the police. Stanley smiled, happy with his bottle of months. "Bothered?" he thought to himself. "They don't know the half of it." He fondled Marilyn.

"I love you," he said, insincerely.

"I do too," said Marilyn. "Switch that light on, will you?"

"As the godhead illuminates itself," Stanley said, flicking the switch, "so imaginary walls collapse, and the skinny Legions rush outside to be sick. What you are, you are, that's the wisdom. The ghostly boys build harpsichords in jail, and the players are waiting when an angel's voice calls out *Boys, stop that!*"

When Marilyn told Charlie about this rave he said that Stanley was turning into someone weird and wiggy, and said that a wig of blood is like a debt always running up.

"You never repay that debt," he said. "Back in sixty-eight you twins were all wiggy, and we were expelled from San Francisco, known as the Lower Realm of Demons. There were innocent kids in the street asking for their shoes to be filled with free steam heat."

"That's tragic," Marilyn said. "No one gets shoes full of steam heat. Not in America."

Charlie remembered Snowball's epiphany: "Snowball was so high in the estimation of the angels that the hospital illuminated her hair like electric snow. Can you imagine that? Are you jealous?"

"Yes," Marilyn cried out. "I can well imagine that! A lost angel! Oh, Mother, I'm with you in Rockland! Where fifteen or twenty miles along the highway a shuddering winter midnight glows, and off in the Bronx I'm shaking with shame, rejected yet confessing, but prepared to go out whoring with the machinery of this invisible madman. Let me pay for luncheon at a restaurant, let me record the final doom of the machinery of Moloch whose loveless tasks and Peoria bone-grindings show us the last sad light flashing above the parks! Moloch, whose soul rushes out from its body, whose robot apartments expelled from their pilgrimage a little sister — what shall we do?"

No one knew exactly what to do next.

Suddenly Charlie's bleeding hand, where Snowball had scratched him, showed a sign. They had looked long enough for forgotten animals. Charlie had already found Snowball, and then lost her again. Charlie had moved Moloch's stone heart to beat, whose skyscrapers crush pederasty, and what good came of it? The sign writhed and pointed to the west.

Charlie felt he had to explain. "It's like watching the Empire State Building shift and waver under the shade of the granite cocksman," he said. "You try, you get somewhere, and then nothing happens. Or it's like trying to understand the Chinaman of Oklahoma discoursing on the rhythm of the cross-country jazz jam, seventy hours into the woods and the music just beginning, the rhythm still clicking. Very few can do that. This means, go west. That's all it means."

"May the Spartan Dioscuri be with you," said Uncle Daniel. "At least, half of the time."

Fine, but where to find salvation? Where your old cat is burying her skeleton treasuries, where dolmen-realms of leaden verse persecute you? Ask the angels who wander around Uncle Daniel's farm in the fever of spring, ask them where the forgotten animals disappear, follow them through the iron dreams of backyards and movie houses' rickety rows, follow on from Bellevue to Museum to the Hudson under those heaving genitals, past demonic industries scattering bleak phonograph records of time, those angels with their holy yells who float off the ground and fall into the lake, angels red-eyed and angry.

Uncle Daniel's friend the Brilliant Spaniard asked if he could come around, and brought a catch of sardines wrapped in a clean handkerchief, and a draft of his forgotten novel stained with animal soup.

The theme of the novel was the need to escape the horrors of the mundane world, and it made Uncle Daniel think. "I'll tell you what, old Dago pal," he said. "Let's put an advertisement in the paper, inquiring after the secret of illumination. As soon as we see who answers, and it's bound to be the F.B.I., we'll go straight to Mexico, leaving no indication of where we've gone. They'll never find us there. Unless we go broke," Uncle Daniel added.

"May the Heavenly Twins forfend," said the Spaniard, and crossed himself.

"There in Mexico the archangel of Third Avenue dreams his iron dreams," said Uncle Daniel, his voice rising, "with a flush of remorse, confessing out of the branches. There we'll be in the streets of sorrows, praying to the same archangel in the shadow of dungarees and undressing by his shrine as the wind bothers the trees."

The Spaniard spoke. "You and I, we should open a store," was his opinion.

So Uncle Daniel decided to open an antique store in Mexico and they went, leaving tears and sobbings, joyfully hearing over their shoulders the twins calling them to come back.

Marilyn said with no uncles it would be starvation in the morning but prepared a delicious supper nonetheless, and after that ran up a flight of stairs and found Snowball stranded in a limousine filled with sparks and flame.

"A limousine full of electricity? And is Harlem crowned with the sparkle of it?" Stanley asked Marilyn. "In the congress of public parks the cosmos instinctively vibrated, for sure."

"The car was unloaded around about here, wasn't it?" Charlie asked. "I can't remember any electricity. Is the cat all right?"

"No," Stanley said. "To find what we need to find, it's time to drive!" and in the blowing wind and in the answering eastern night the twins and their pal were followed by madness, starting in fear as each bough crashed on the roof, aiming for Denver — offering joy to the fleeting time, yet putting down roots. A glimpse of small-town ecstasy: out back of the roadside diner, in the dusky parking lot, a lonely petticoat fluttered.

"Petticoats," said Stanley, his hands guiding the wheel. "Of the goddess Isis, fond of many petticoats, it is reported that her heroes were only driven mad when sudden Manhattan struck them, and then they sat through the tales of the children to hear the holy name in the sure and certain hope of being healed, for children unknowing have that gift." So Stanley said to Charlie. "Nobody can leave my little sister when she speaks, when she prophesies with flashes of genius. She entrances them, Manhattan strikes them, and they know nothing more. The people there, they say *petticoats*, they say *breasts*, until they grow dizzy. Their conversation is destroyed by unbearable flashes of consciousness."

Stanley's sister cried out in her fit of prophecy, excited now she was lost in this new experience, a vision of a dozen naked angels eating lunch with glowing pacifist eyes, enduring hallucinations and then running outside.

"What is Manhattan but a catalogue," she said, "a variable measure of poor human prose and immortal verbs? As a city it shouldered its own despair, as an idea it crawled out from under the fashion of the fifties and the madmen of Los Alamos wailed, who ate fire in paradise alleys aiming for New York, the whole boatload of lost animals." She recognized something in the style of that hallucination, and at once thought of Mr. Bobbsey. She quickly checked, and sure enough, he did it.

"I did that hallucinating," he admitted, reaching for Marilyn's breast. "I did it for you."

"We'd better go home, don't you think, dear?" Mrs. Bobbsey asked. Charlie said yes, they'd better.

"You guys are certainly smart," Marilyn said, when the adults had gone. "Why, I once caught Mr. Bobbsey doing things he shouldn't do. He was not in a Turkish bath when he said he was. We twins, we had been driving cross-country seventy hours from Denver. To keep awake we mixed Dexedrine and hot spirits with orange juice and chili peppers. That was nothing. Once we crossed the continent without a break, Methedrine sodas our salvation. Everywhere, suburban tracts like lobotomies."

"Aw, you'd think only junkies have feelings," Charlie said. Charlie owned shares in a condo in Malibu.

"All losers have feelings," shrieked Marilyn. "The boys and girls in empty lots, kids with sparkling eyes and intelligent brains and lots of opium, losers who drank nitroglycerine and whacked their heads against the wall! You think they don't have feelings?"

"Oh, give it a break," said Charlie.

Lost on the Jersey Turnpike they came unto Manhattan again, and stumbling pedestrians in tatters. Stanley and the others started to check it out, but their strength was insufficient. Then the little sister got up to trouble in some huckleberry bushes by the pike messing around with guys. It wasn't too serious, they weren't Mafia, but it was decided nonetheless that her loveboys were bad news, magnets to the wild eyes in passing cars sexy in the vibrating air trembling in oblivion, who followed them and saw it all.

Marilyn jumped up and down in their minds: new loves of a mad generation lying down on the ground at midnight by the highway and staring up at the constellations, their philosophy a hunch welded to a list of saints. They went to find her and were greeted by madness, starving human seraphim, the last door closed, locked and barred, and plotting the end of the world.

Oh Marilyn, I remember your family, your mother gone crazy, but while she was with us we hugged her and tears flowed. We didn't think then of boys sobbing because of their lobotomy, boys who now watch the lawn grow the poisonous grass of capitalism and are paid to mow it, boys who drove trucks into the river and who drove the black locomotive to Harvard laughing.

"Well, no response from the academies for the epiphanies and despairs of ten years' freakouts and root beer insights," Charlie Rugg complained.

"Maybe we brought them down, with our bad poetry," Stanley said.

There was a timid knock on the door. "Don't tell me, it's Uncle Daniel back from Mexico, isn't it?" Charlie said. He was disgusted by now. Uncle Daniel, who hiccuped endless hooch and bop eternity outside the highway diner, who collapsed and went to jail. There are great suicide minds in jail, but just as many loonies.

Elsewhere in the endless western night lost souls await the clear signal to awaken, up early and high, their minds smoking from lounge to bar to motel washroom leaving genitals and madness behind. They bade farewell to their brains.

But it wasn't Uncle Daniel, it was the twins coming home from the hunt for Snowball, bleak with despair.

Then they found the basket in the laundry. In the basket was the cat. Charlie gaped at the beast. "Motionless in Moloch," he said, "the cat whose fate ran through my dreams and so I stumbled and sobbed all night! I shall build it a monument, I shall make it into something magnificent."

They linked hands, the power kicked and flowed between them, and it seemed they were walking in the streets of love, where dream spirits read the stanzas of their brains and visionary angels crazy in the public parks shouted their fond agreement to the end of time.

––––––––––

The process of writing "Howling Twins" was rather like jazz improvisation, though in some ways it was the reverse of Charlie Parker's modus operandi. A jazz musician starts with a melody, takes it apart and puts it through the blender of his art, practicing what Viktor Shklovsky called ostranenie, *the making strange of the familiar.*

This piece began with an analysis of the frequency and distribution of letter-groups in two pieces of writing: Allen Ginsberg's Howl *and the first fifteen pages of* The Bobbsey Twins on a Bicycle Trip *by "Laura Lee Hope," a pen name of the indefatigable Edward Stratemeyer. The analysis was concerned only with the letters of the alphabet and a dozen punctuation characters, and not with grammar, syntax or meaning.*

Then came the construction of a new text based on a mingling of the data and index tables of these two letter-group analyses. The result was a heap of dreck: twenty pages of fractured letters, words and phrases among which was buried a tale of lust, ecstasy and a lost cat. It has been vigorously reworked in the interests of the reader's enjoyment, and among the eleven secret herbs and spices I stirred into the recipe are a sense of fun and a liking for melody.

John Tranter

I usually do maybe a dozen drafts until a piece feels right, but this one needed more than that. It was so scrambled when I began that I thought I'd never make it whole. The experience put me in mind of a bad dream about an accident in the Transporter Room of the USS Enterprise: the members of the exploration party have had their molecules mangled as they were being beamed up from the planet surface, and I'm Bones, the ship's doctor, charged with the job of making out of this mess something — not necessarily human — just something that can walk, speak English and operate the phasers.

You might guess that such writing is not common in Australia, and you would be right.

— John Tranter

From The Babel of Iconoclasts
J. Rodolfo Wilcock

— Translated from Italian by Lawrence Venuti

ARAM KUGIUNGIAN

INNUMERABLE ARE THE BELIEVERS in the transmigration of souls. Of these, not a few have proven themselves capable of remembering their previous incarnations, or at least several of them. Yet one man alone maintains not simply that he lived, but that he lives, at any precise moment, in many bodies. Foreseeably, the largest number of these bodies belonged to well-known people, some quite well-known, and this fact rendered him particularly famous in narrow circles, esoteric as well as Canadian.

He was called Aram Kugiungian. As a child, he fled Turkish Armenia with his father, who was obliged to reach a rather well-off brother in Rioja, Argentina, but through a fortuitous concurrence of circumstances, he instead reached a very poor uncle, actually a tatterdemalion, in the vicinity of Toronto. The uncle arranged a ride for them on a vegetable cart bound for the city, where Aram's father, as at Erzerum, immediately went to work in a cobbler's shop.

The shoes in that country were so different from their Turkish counterparts that virtually his only qualification for practicing the primitive craft was the habit of remaining seated before a shoe. Mr. Kugiungian possessed a limited idea of the real dimensions of America, but he quickly grew weary of asking which train would take him to Rioja. They both learned a simulacrum of English. Aram was disconcerted by the fact that people could be Jewish, Turkish and Christian simultaneously. This astonishment pushed him from the agnosticism he originally held towards theosophy. The plurality that others attributed to him planted deep roots which one day would send forth unexpected branches. In the meantime he frequented a Toronto-based group known as "The Karma Wheel."

J. Rodolfo Wilcock

One April evening in 1949, on the sidewalk of a dirty street heading towards Lake Ontario, Aram Kugiungian noticed for the first time that he was also someone else, or indeed that he was several others. He was then twenty-three years old. He had not yet finished learning English, and there were in fact girls who claimed that he spoke French: America was undoubtedly a continent suited to being different people at the same time.

His father managed only to be his father, dedicated to accumulating minute sums of money inside an old victrola, which he kept underneath the pillow when he slept. His father's uncle, however, chose not to be anyone, or more exactly, he was no one, since he had not made another appearance in the past decade.

As for Aram Kugiungian, the wheel of his karma began to spin uncontrollably, as it seemed, perhaps to arrive prematurely at its fixed terminus. The fact is that at intervals of approximately every two months Aram was born again, while continuing to live in other bodies. Obviously, arithmetic is useless with souls: a soul divided by a thousand always yields a thousand perfect souls, just as the Breath of the Creator divided by three billion yields three billion Breaths of the Creator. Aram knew he was the Armenian boy of whom it was said: he wished to know who he might be.

He sought advice from his friends in the Karma Club. He made clear that he was not suffering from a case of double or multiple personality; he knew nothing at all about the other people. There were just occasions when, seeing a name or photograph in a newspaper or publicity poster, he experienced the acute sensation of being that someone else as well, whoever it might be. These abrupt encounters had already happened with a young actress, apparently English, named Elizabeth Taylor; with a Catholic archbishop from New York on a visit to Quebec and with a certain Chiang Kai-shek, who was clearly Chinese. He did not know whether he should contact these people, even if by letter, and explain to them that they were all his reincarnations.

His friends were quick to understand a case of this kind, although it was the first to occur in Toronto. They listened to him with interest, with wonder, with the respect that the supernatural inspires when it departs from its usual daily routine. They told him that if he wrote a letter to himself, he risked getting no response. So their counsel was that he read the newspapers more often to see whether he could trace his identity in other people and compile a list of them for publication in the club's monthly bulletin.

The bulletin, like the club, was entitled "The Karma Wheel." In the October 1949 issue, an enthusiastic note by a certain Alan H. Seaborn commented on the singular velocity of Kugiungian's soul. The list of his previous incarnations — he did not recognize the subsequent ones, evidently a question of boys and girls still too young for fame — comprised, apart from the people cited above, Louis de Broglie, Mossadek, Alfred Krupp, Eleanor Roosevelt, Olivier Eugène Prosper Charles Messiaen, Chaim Weizmann, Lucky Luciano, Ninon Vallin, Stafford Cripps, Eva Perón's mother, Vladimir D'Ormesson, Lin Pao, Arturo Toscanini, Tyrone Power, El-Said Mohammed Idris, Coco Chanel, Vyacheslav Mikhailevic Molotov, Ali Khan, Anatole Litvak, Marshal Tito, John George Haigh, Yehudi Menuhin, Ellinor Wedel (Miss Denmark), Joe Louis and many other personalities who have since sunk into oblivion (the vampire John George Haigh, meanwhile, had been hanged in England).

His fellow club members often asked him how it felt to be so many people at the same time. Kugiungian always replied that he did not feel anything extraordinary, in fact that he did not feel anything at all, or, at the most, a vague sense of not being alone in the world. In reality, his corporal multiplicity came to be the first refutation of the so-called solipsistic thesis *in corpore vili*. Kugiungian, however, thought that Berkeley was a cricket field near Hamilton, and solipsism a form of refined vice. Several of his fellows questioned the strange coincidence that all of his simultaneous reincarnations were prominent figures. But Kugiungian prudently countered that in all likelihood his epiphanies were very frequent because, lacking the means to inquire into the little known, he was forced to limit himself to the most conspicuous.

At this point, a young Steinerian advanced the hypothesis that perhaps Aram Kugiungian might be the entire world population, which in that period was rather enormous. The idea was seductive — a freewheeling soul can complete a great number of revolutions per second — and Kugiungian was flattered by it. But here he had to confront the resolute opposition of the other club members, nearly all of whom obstinately refused to think of themselves as the Armenian's embodiment, whether as a reincarnation or a preincarnation. Only one young lady responded favorably to the proposal. The others took this gesture for what it certainly was, an awkward effort to flirt, on the pretext of a shared soul.

Nonetheless, Kugiungian continued to recognize himself in

newspaper photographs and subsequently on television as well. From one of his statements in the *Journal of Theosophy* we must infer that ten years later, namely in 1960, apart from the people cited above, he had also become A. J. Ayer, Dominguin, Mehdi Ben Barka, Adolf Eichmann, Princess Margaret, Karl Orff, Raoul-Albin-Louis Salan, Sir Julian Huxley, the Dalai Lama, Aram Kachiaturian, Caryl Chessman, Fidel Castro, Max Born, Syngman Rhee, Elvis Presley and Anita Ekberg.

He currently lives in Winnipeg, and although in recent years he has multiplied himself exponentially, he has never wished to meet any of his incarnations in person. Many of them do not speak English, others seem to be very busy and, to tell the truth, he wouldn't know what to say to himself.

JULES FLAMART

In 1964 Jules Flamart went to press with his dictionary-novel, which he shrewdly entitled *La langue en action*. The idea was this: since standard modern lexicons, however diverting or licentious they may sometimes prove, are virtually without exception unsuited to sustained, systematic reading — which alone justifies the continued existence of a given work — the author proposed to compile, with Flaubertian patience, a new type of dictionary that would wed the utilitarian to the adventurous, providing the definition and usage of each word like a garden-variety dictionary, yet accompanied not by the pleasant observations and erudite divagations that lighten (or used to lighten) the old encyclopedias, but rather by brief narrative passages linked in such a way that, when the reader is finished, he has not only learned the correct use of all the words constituting the language, but has also been amused by following the intricate development of a plot whose busyness rivals its naughtiness — i.e., the sort of plot usually found in a pornographic spy novel.

The foregoing description does not of course suffice to give a true idea of this work, which is probably unique in the world and yet strangely neglected. It will therefore be necessary to present an excerpt, selected at random from its eight hundred and fifty pages, while seeking to obviate the fact that the dictionary is, after all, a dictionary, and, moreover, a French one. Let us open to page 283:

Enfoncer: to thrust deeply into; to penetrate. Arthur *enfonça* her.

Enforcir: to reinvigorate. "The president's television speech will *enforci* him," observed the witty Ben Saïd.

Enfouir: to bury; to stash. When Géraldine opened her eyes again, she protested, not without irony: "But where have you *enfoui* it?"

Enfourcher: to stick with a pitchfork; to pierce. "You should rather say *enfourchi*," explained the subprefect's secretary between mouthfuls of baba au rhum.

Enfourchure: crotch. "Alastair, grab him by the *enfourchure* and try to pull him back," implored Fauban.

Enfourner: to put in the oven; to book. "Not for nothing do they call him the *enfourneur*," added the phony nun with an air of authority.

Enfreindre: to shatter; to violate. "Do you like Benjamin Britten?" asked Ben Saïd, suddenly *enfreignant* the respectful silence.

Enfroquer: to put on a monk's cowl; to masquerade as a monk. Beyond the door a chilling voice could be heard shouting, "*Enfroquez!*"

Enfuir (S'): to flee; to escape; to leak out. Géraldine parted her knees and let him *s'enfouir.*

Enfumer: to smoke; to fill or stain with smoke. Slipping her panties over his head in the guise of eyeglasses, Alastair *enfuma* them by means of his peculiar breathing and lay down beside the subprefect's secretary.

Engadine: Engadine. She reeked of *Engadine.*

Engagé: hired. "Why that week-long *engagé* look?" the little nun asked him sarcastically as she threw herself into the armchair, on Fauban's lap, in order to reach the button with her right foot.

Engageant: attractive. The door suddenly opened, and Géraldine saw a not very *engageant* St. Bernard enter the room.

Engagement: pledge; promise. The nurse who was following him headed towards Ben Saïd. "I have kept my *engagement*," she announced, smiling ambiguously, and with a swift gesture she inserted the needle of a large hypodermic syringe into his left ear.

Or else take page 577:

Personne: person; anyone; no one. The captain entered the shaft and said: "*Personne!*"

Personnellement: personally. The aspiring parachutist dared to put forward a timid objection: "I, *personnellement* — " The other man hissed and darted out his tongue: "Wearing nothing but those flimsy pants, cut out of the evening newspaper?"

Perspective: perspective. "That's a matter of *perspective*," bellowed the boy. "Yours, however, are made of cheap silk."

Perspicace: perspicacious; shrewd. "You are *perspicace*," observed the captain, shoving him into the darkness.

Perspiration: slow transpiration. Michel was covered with *perspiration*.

Persuader: to persuade. Something in the loud tinny noise at the end of the corridor did not *persuadait* him.

Persuasion: persuasion. But suddenly, on his delicately haired leg, he felt the slippery barrel of a pistol and a silent hand coldly determined to brush aside any compromise in its work of *persuasion*.

Persulfure: persulphate. A stench of *persulfure* assailed them.

Perte: loss; waste. "And this?" the officer finally asked, without releasing his victim. "Is this a *perte?*"

Pertinace: persistent. La Condamine's colleagues in Counterespionage — not to mention his numerous enemies in foreign Secret Services — knew very well how *pertinace* he could be.

Pertinent: relevant. "Do you really think that's a *pertinent* question?" said the boy, removing his finger from his nose and immediately stripping off his undershirt. "It belongs to me," he added, "and I'm keeping it to myself."

Pertuis: hole; opening; perforation. "It really isn't so large," mumbled the officer. "Here's the *pertuis!*" he abruptly exclaimed, licking his moustache.

Perturbation: perturbation. The neophyte's perspiration began to metamorphose into *perturbation*.

Péruvien: Peruvian. "Do you hear that tinny noise down there?" whispered his guide. "It's the *péruviens*."

Pervers: perverse. "They say they're terribly *pervers!*" murmured the adolescent with a shudder.

Pervertir: to pervert; to deprave. Without making the slightest move to detach himself, the captain dragged Michel two more meters into the dark tunnel. "Worse still," he said between his teeth, "they're *pervertis!*"

Pesage: weighing. And with an absentminded air he started the *pesage*.

Pesant: heavy. "*Pesant?*" asked the boy, suddenly inquisitive.

Pessaire: pessary. "I shouldn't have left the *pessaire* in the Jaguar-

Morris," cursed La Condamine.

Pessimisme: pessimism. A new stench, more violent than the first, swept away his *pessimisme:* this time it was a question of a semipublic lavatory, probably communicating with the cinema.

Peste: plague; damn (it). "Here we are," he said. "*Peste!*" exclaimed Michel. "How do I dry myself now?"

And so forth till the blazing finale, hinging on an orgy of *zythum* (zythos), ale of the ancients and particularly the Egyptians. Didactically impeccable, especially suitable for youth and students in general, Flamart's work is one of those dictionaries — so rare, alas! — that compel one to read breathlessly and without pause from the first to the last page, dictionaries born with the sign of epic on their brow.

CHARLES WENTWORTH LITTLEFIELD

With the mere force of his will, the surgeon Charles Wentworth Littlefield succeeded in making table salt crystallize in the shape of a chicken and other small animals.

Once, when his brother endured a deep, self-inflected wound in his foot and lost some blood, Dr. Littlefield got the idea of reciting a passage from the Bible, and the hemorrhage immediately stopped. From that day onwards, Littlefield was capable of executing the risky interventions of major surgery, adopting as a coagulant his own mental power assisted by the same Biblical excerpt.

At a certain point, the doctor decided to study more methodically the secret cause of his thromboplastic power. Littlefield suspected that the salt content of the blood provoked the coagulation. Consequently, he dissolved a pinch of table salt in water and put the solution under the microscope. As soon as the water evaporated, the observer softly repeated the surgical passage from the Old Testament while contemplating a chicken. Much to his surprise, he witnessed the tiny crystals slowly form on the slide and arrange themselves in the shape of a chicken.

He repeated the experiment a hundred times, always with the same result: if, for example, he thought of a flea, the crystals settled in the shape of a flea. The report of the research can be read in a book by the same Littlefield, *The Beginning and Way of Life* (Seattle, 1919). It is a profound study of the subtle magnetism that renders crystals docile to the control of the human mind. In the preface, the author thanks St. Paul, St. John the Evangelist and the English physicist Michael Faraday for dictating chapters to him from the other world.

ARMANDO APRILE

Armando Aprile possessed the consistency of a ghost. He left nothing behind, except for a name that sounds fake and an address that didn't belong to him: both were printed on a poster that appeared one day in the streets of Rome. Ephemeral utopian, he proposed an order to the world, but the world seems not to have wanted it. The poster read as follows:

ATTENTION!!! A VERY IMPORTANT MESSAGE. Launch date: 1/12/ 1968. I swear I shall enforce the following laws, if and when the world population joins me in wearing certain identifying signs, such as their watches on their right wrists or the initials "AA" on a visible part of their persons or clothing. We shall adopt green handkerchiefs, uniforms in a uniform color, white or blue, and black shoes, in case of mourning. Our flag will be white and/or blue.

These laws serve to establish an equality among six ward divisions. The major ward is reserved for the first thirty-six Managers of the World. Second ward: for the next 36,000 Managers of the World. Third ward: for the Judges. Fourth ward: for Scientists, Doctors, Commissioners, Engineers, Lawyers, Generals, as well as officers and administrators of various sorts, including brigadiers in the Carabinieri, theater directors and producers, and coaches and trainers. Fifth ward: Treasury, Admiralty, Carabinieri, Police, Students, Military, Clerical, et cetera. Sixth ward: children, from birth to twelve years of age, and Prisoners convicted of homicide. The capital criminals will work ten hours a day; the other convicts will be paid wages and hence will work free for eight hours a day, until they have finished paying for their crimes. And any of them can take advantage of our good conduct policy. Those who are released will work no more than five hours a day.

4. The unemployed will receive a daily wage as if they worked.

5. Retirees, whether because of age, accident or illness, will receive a daily wage as when they worked, in addition to hospitalization, medicine and housing — gratis.

6. Every youth regardless of height and sex may carry the flag, unless they have been convicted of homicide.

7. Wherever possible, every workplace will be air conditioned, fitted with the latest furnishings, maintained in maximum cleanliness, et cetera.

8. Whenever any citizen reaches twenty-one years of age, they will have the right to a new lodging, free of charge, in the town where their profession permits them to be resident.

9. We shall speak a single language. Dialect will be punished by fine.

10. My new regulations for automobiles and other motor vehicles will allow us to avoid 90 percent of all accidents.

11. Taxation will cease, since everybody will be a dependent of World Management.

12. Deserts will be inhabited and cultivated. (My simple plan will allow us to avoid disagreements between the North and South of every Nation.)

13. Divorce is permitted. Hence, it is better simply to avoid marriage.

14. As soon as possible I shall cause volcanoes to be extinguished since, apart from their sheer danger, they burn such an expanse of subsoil as to prove useless to our evolution today, and perhaps tomorrow.

15. It is most likely that I shall succeed in removing the water from the seas and leaving only what is necessary for irrigation, since they pose a great danger to the planet Earth. What if someone, for example, immersed gigantic blenders in the seas? We would all die in the wink of an eye.

16. I promise immortality with a 90 percent success rate — i.e., youth can remain young, and the aged can regain their youth.

17. Whoever agrees with these laws should assist me financially in whatever way they can by sending a donation to this address: Aprile Armando, c/o Giglio, 243 St. Nicholas Ave., Brooklyn, New York 11237. Help me spread this message in every possible language throughout the World, while hindering the false laws that our enemies spread in their turn.

18. My identifying signs are: a height of 1.54 meters, shoeless and hatless, thin, dark-haired, florid complexion, scar on the right

side of the thorax, a small wart near the right ear, face divided in half by a natural, nearly invisible line, surname and name: Aprile Armando, born 29/12/1940.

JOHN O. KINNAMAN

In 1938 John Kinnaman visited Sodom. On his return to England, he published *Digging for Truth* (1940). In this book, he describes finding a site that contained a considerable quantity of columns and pyramids of salt. His discovery rendered rather difficult, not to say impossible, the task he had initially set for himself: ascertaining which of these protrusions might be Lot's wife. He writes: "There are too many of them. Who can say at this point which are the remains of that unfortunate woman?"

The surrounding area yielded a compensation. He unearthed the house where Abraham lived and, in the house, a stone whose surface was incised with the patriarch's signature: 𝕬𝖇𝖗𝖆𝖍𝖆𝖒.

A. DE PANIAGUA

A pupil of Elisée Reclus and friend of Onésime Reclus, A. de Paniagua wrote *The Neolithic Civilization* to demonstrate that the French race was originally black and emerged in southern India, although without excluding the fact that in an earlier epoch the French emerged in Australia, given the linguistic ties that according to Trombetti join Dravidic and primitive Australian. These blacks abandoned themselves to continuous migrations. Their first totem was the dog, as the root "kur" indicates, and therefore they called themselves Kurets. Since they travelled everywhere, one finds the root "kur" in many place names throughout the world: Kurlandia, Courmayeur, Kurdistan, Courbevoie, Corinth, Curinga in Calabria and the Kurili Islands. Their second totem was the rooster, as the root "kor" indicates, and therefore they called themselves Corybantes. Place names that begin with "kor" or "cor" — Korea, Cordova, Kordofan, Cortina, Korca, Corato, Corfu, Corleone, Cork, Cornovaglia, Corno d'Oro and Cornigliano Ligure — can also be found throughout the world, wherever the ancestors of the French may have travelled.

Such a migratory passion is explained in part by what seems to be a verified fact: wherever Kureti and Corybantes arrived, whether in Scizia or in Scozia (evidently the same word), Japan or America, they turned white, or yellow, if need be. Hence, the original French split into two large groups: the Kur, who were properly called dogs, and the Kor, who were roosters. Ethnologists have often confused the latter with dogs: unfortunately, observes Paniagua, the reductive spirit tends to impoverish history.

Dogs and roosters traverse the steppes of Central Asia, the Sahara, the Black Forest, Ireland. They are noisy, gay, intelligent — they are French. Two powerful cosmic forces move Kurets and Corybantes: the one to see where the sun rises, the other to see where the sun sets. Guided by these two impulses, opposed and unstoppable, they wind up circling the globe unwittingly.

Towards the east they withdraw, raving and frolicking, planting their menhirs along the road. They reach the Kurili Islands; another step, and they are in America. For confirmation one need only find the name of an important place that begins with Kur. The most obvious is Greenland, whose true name, Paniagua explains, must be Kureland. It would be mistaken, however, to believe that "Greenland" means green earth, since Greenland is white, from whatever side one looks. Yet the ethnologist's winning card is a photograph of two Eskimos, evidently taken in the infinite polar sunset: they are in fact almost black.

Other Curets and Korybantes, they too leaping and jostling, they too dressed like dogs and roosters, set out towards the west. They venture up the Ister (today, the Danube), driven by a most sublime ideal. Deep in the dark blood of the race they already feel the joyous impulse to found France. As for their skins, upon passing through the Balkans, they turned white, even blond. At this point, they decide to assume the glorious name of Celts, so as to distinguish themselves from the blacks they left behind. The author explains that "Celt" means "celestial worshipper of fire," from "cel," celestial (an immediate type of etymology) and "t" (fire in Dravidic, a mediated type of etymology).

While the new whites navigate up the Danube, Paniagua praises their patience and courage: so much travail, so many rivers and mountains to cross, all in order to lay the first stones for the edifice of light and splendor where the profound soul of France dwells immutable.

On the way, the Celts dispatch exploratory missions here and there, founding colonies that subsequently become illustrious — for example, Venice (the original French name is Venise), from the Dravidic "ven," white, and from the Celtic "is," down. It is difficult to find an etymology more exact, comments Paniagua. Yet another migratory break, and the Tyrolean are torn away from the principal branch to establish themselves permanently on the coasts of the Tyrrhenian, as the root "Tyr" indicates.

One more thick branch, losing patience with Switzerland for obstructing its path, sails down the Po and founds Italy (the original French name is Italie). The etymon is rather immediate in this case as well: "ita" comes from the Latin "ire," to journey, and "li" from the Sanskrit "lih," to lick. This means that the Kuret dogs do not only bark, but lick. Hence, "Italy" signifies "the country of migratory licking dogs." The point becomes even more evident if one thinks of the Ligurians, that mysterious people: "li-kuri," or licking dogs par excellence.

La Civilisation Néolitique (1923) was published by the firm of Paul Catin. Other volumes in the series include *My Artillery* by Colonel Labrousse-Fonbelle and *Hellas, Hélas!* (memories of Salonika during the war) by Antoine Scheikevitch.

BENEDICT LUST

The inventor of zonal therapy was Dr. William H. Fitzgerald, for many years the head otorhinolaryngological surgeon at St. Francis Hospital in Hartford, Connecticut. According to Fitzgerald, the human body is divided into ten zones, five on the right side and five on the left, each of which is directly linked to a digit of a hand and to a corresponding digit of a foot. These linkages are too subtle to be detected with a microscope.

In 1917, Fitzgerald and a disciple by the name of Bowers published their fundamental treatise, entitled *Zonal Therapy*. The authors affirmed that it is always possible to relieve the body of pain, and in many cases the illness itself, simply by pressing one digit of a hand or foot, or else some other peripheral area linked to the infected organ. This pressure can be applied in diverse ways. As a rule, one must bind the digit with a rubber band so tightly that it turns blue; a clothespin can also be used. In certain special cases, it suffices to press the skin with the teeth of a metal comb.

Fitzgerald's theory was developed in a rather obstinately entitled manual, *Zonal Therapy*, the work of the esteemed naturist, Dr. Benedict Lust. Lust's text, a useful supplement to Fitzgerald's homonymous treatise, offers detailed explanations of which digit must be pressed to overcome most of the illnesses that afflict humankind, not excluding cancer, polio and appendicitis. To cure a goiter, it is necessary to press the index and middle fingers; but if the goiter is so large as to extend to the fourth zone, the doctor would achieve the best results by pressing the ring finger as well. With disorders of the sight, and of the eye in general, the index and middle fingers are likewise pressed. Deafness is cured, however, by pinching the ring finger or, better yet, the third digit of the foot. An efficacious method for combatting partial deafness consists in wearing a clothespin constantly attached to the tip of the middle finger, that of the right hand for the right ear, that of the left for the left ear.

Nausea is eliminated by exerting pressure on the back of the hand with a metal comb. Childbirth is rendered painless if the woman in labor firmly grasps two combs and squeezes them in such a way that the teeth press against the tips of two fingers simultaneously. The prospective mother will feel almost nothing at all if she takes the further precaution of tightly binding her big and second toes with a thin rubber band. With the same method, the dentist can forgo anesthesia: it will suffice to apply a rubber band tightly around the digit of the patient's hand that is anatomically linked to the tooth to be extracted.

Hair loss can be combatted with a system that Lust calls simplicity itself: quickly rubbing the nails of the right hand against those of the left hand for brief periods of three to four minutes. The operation is repeated several times a day for the purpose of improving the circulation of the blood and reinvigorating the scalp.

HENRY BUCHER

At the age of fifty-nine, the Belgian Henry Bucher was only forty-two. The reasons for this temporal contradiction can be read in the preface to his memoirs, *Souvenirs d'un chroniqueur de chroniques* [*Memories of a Chronicler of Chronicles* [Liege, 1932]]: "Having obtained my degree and embarked with all the impetus of my green years on the delightful study of history, I soon realized that the task of locating, translating and commenting on the entire corpus of medieval chroniclers — the obscure precursors of Froissart and Joinville, of the great Villehardouin and Commines — which I had set for myself as an absolute and preeminent pledge, exceeded the anticipated limits: perhaps one life would not be sufficient for me to bring it to a conclusion. Omitting the chore of searching for lost texts, in large part already completed — and admirably — by my revered teacher, Hébérard De la Boulerie, the mere process of translating from Latin to French (from an often bastard Latin to the elegant French of our days) would have required the entire arc of years that presumably the Fates were still reserving for me. To this must be added the annotations, concordances — yet in this specific case it would be much more just to call them discordances — the typing, as well as the various tasks relating to publication, proofreading, introductory essays, polemical exchanges, correspondence with various Academies, et cetera, not to mention the inevitable contingencies, and the reader will understand with what embarrassment and perplexity the young man I then was, on the threshold of twenty-five years, contemplated the enormous labor presenting itself to me, and the urgent need for a rational plan of work.

"The whole group of historical chronicles to be translated and annotated, excepting new discoveries which were unlikely at this point but always possible, I already knew quite well and had acquired. Furthermore, I had imposed an additional limitation, that of concerning myself exclusively with works compiled between the ninth and eleventh centuries. The twelfth had already been mastered, perhaps a little too brilliantly, by my colleague Hennekin of Strasbourg; of the eighth, the Church was avariciously guarding the most promising pearls in its catacombs (*dans ses caves*). Even so, those lean three centuries would have cost me — according to calculations that were perhaps generous to a fault — at least thirty years of translation; if to this were added the remaining tasks, I would not succeed in crowning the work before I reached eighty. To an ambitious and impatient young man, the static condition of an octogenarian can at times appear, I should say without any rational basis, scarcely attractive, and without luster the laurels that unfailingly — but not always — adorn it. Thus things seemed to me then; I therefore excogitated a way, if not to conquer time, then at least to restrain it.

"Already I had acutely observed that for a particularly active person, a week was not sufficient to fulfill a week's obligations; the deferred tasks accumulate (replying to letters, filing papers and sorting socks, proofreading writings for the voracious press, without forgetting trips, weddings, deaths, revolutions, wars and similar wastes of time), so that at a certain point it would be necessary to halt the cataract of days in order to give one's complete attention to neglected duties. After which it would be reasonable to set time in motion again, rid of arrears: free, revived, agile, without aftereffects.

"And so I did, with the aid of my personal calendar: on any given day, let us say a 17 July, for example, I finished translating the Third Book of Ottone de Trier. I stopped the date; ipso facto I was free to type the manuscript, correct the proofs for the First Book, participate in person at the Conference of History at Trieste, draft the Notes to the Second Book, leap over to the Sorbonne to foil an Apocrypha, bring my correspondence up-to-date, push on as far as Ostend by bicycle — and all this while holding firm the date of 17 July. At a certain point, no longer subject to obligations or constraints, I took up the Fifth Book and resumed my work. For other people, nearly two months had elapsed, and autumn was commencing; for me, in contrast, it was still July, precisely 18 July.

"Little by little I experienced the distinct sensation, corroborated by the facts, of lagging behind in time. When the Prussians invaded our beloved provinces, slitting the breasts of pregnant women and, what is worse, the electrical power lines, I was still fixed in 1905; for me, the war of '14 ended in 1908. On the day that I finally reached '14, my poor native land arrived at 1931 and passed through what they describe as an embarrassing economic crisis. I in fact noticed that every time I stopped the calendar, the price of paper took a huge jump upward. In any case, thanks to this process of taking my time, I did not grow weary; I feel young, in fact, I am young; the historians who are my contemporaries are almost sixty, but I have only recently crossed the threshold of my forties. My simple expedient has proven itself to be doubly effective. Another ten, twelve years, and I shall have completed the work, the entire edition in fluent modern French, with an equally fluent commentary, of 127 chronicles from three centuries. At merely fifty years of age, I shall taste, if not glory, then the admired astonishment of my colleagues and — why not? — of ladies."

J. Rodolfo Wilcock

SOCRATES SCHOLFIELD

His existence has always raised doubts. The problem has occupied St. Thomas, St. Anselm, Descartes, Kant, Hume, Alvin Plantinga. Not the least of this group was Socrates Scholfield, holder of the patent registered with the U.S. Patent Office in 1914 under the number 1.087.186. The apparatus of his invention consists of two brass helices set in such a way that, by slowly winding around and within one another, they demonstrate the existence of God. Of the five classic proofs, this is called the mechanical proof.

The more I learn about J. Rodolfo Wilcock, the more intriguingly eccentric he seems. Starting with the curious name: it signals his motley cultural makeup, part Spanish, part Italian, part English. The "J" stands for "Juan."

Wilcock was born in Buenos Aires in 1919 and later emigrated to Italy, where he died in 1978 in Viterbo, a city just north of Rome. In Argentina he associated with the group of innovative writers that included Jorge Luis Borges, Adolfo Bioy Casares and Silvina Ocampo. In 1940 he contributed a story to their anthology of fantastic literature, and over the next two decades he published poetry and prose in Spanish. His sojourn in Italy seems to date from 1960, when he started to write a torrent in Italian: poems, plays, journalism, theater criticism, many volumes of fiction and many, many translations from English, French and Spanish. He translated the writing of his Argentine associates, but he published these translations under a pseudonym, "Livio Bacchi Wilcock," a double who was both ancient (the translator Livius Andronicus introduced Greek literature to the Romans) and wryly mythological (the god of wine). Livio occasionally collaborated on Juan's other books, assisting, for example, with an Italian version of Virginia Woolf's A Room of One's Own. Juan in turn contributed a preface to Livio's anthology of Catalan poetry.

A partial catalogue of Wilcock's translations reveals the dazzling range of his literary interests: Aubrey's Brief Lives, Beckett's English poetry, Black Elk Speaks, Edward Dahlberg's Because I Was Flesh, Rider Haggard's She, excerpts from Joyce's Finnegans Wake, the collected plays of Genet and Marlowe, Macbird, Flann O'Brien's

J. Rodolfo Wilcock

At Swim-two-birds, Shakespeare's Richard III and *William Carlos Williams's* In the American Grain.

Wilcock was deracinated, an émigré in transit between diverse languages, periods, styles, but his roots were clearly modernist. He nurtured an experimentalist's fascination with classical and Renaissance literature, the American oral tradition, pop romance, topical satire. And these interests inevitably animated his fiction, perhaps nowhere more strkingly than in The Babel of Iconoclasts (1972). It consists of thirty-five chapters, each focusing on one character, always a man engaged in a weirdly imagined discovery or project, often with the potential to bring about cultural and social change, sometimes on a global scale. The tone shifts between hilarious ridicule and caustic irony, at once funny and disturbing. Here Wilcock is a learned critic of the political uses to which specialized learning may be put. The writing is sometimes reminiscent of Ionesco's plays, particularly The Lesson, that macabre tutorial session in which a professor browbeats a pupil into learning nonsense and finally murders her. There are also traces of a grimly amusing satirist like Jonathan Swift: among the wonders of Gulliver's Travels is the floating island of Laputa, where scientists apply themselves to extracting sunbeams from cucumbers and building houses from the roof down.

Wilcock was a rarity on the Italian literary scene (although his influence may be detected in Umberto Eco's latest work). There is certainly nothing quite like him in English. This is the first reason to translate him. The second: his remarkable invention is matched by a stylistic variety that reflects the different projects, personalities, disciplines and aspirations of his "iconoclasts." He offers a translator a rare opportunity to write with a more intense self-consciousness, to range over various dialects and discourses, conventions and genres, to play the arch mimic. Yet Wilcock is infectious: the translator who catches him forever feels a strange detachment from writing, an acute sense of its irreducible otherness — despite the labor of bending it into self-expression. Like this essay: part potted encyclopedia entry, part belles-lettres appreciation, describing a figure who belongs in a book entitled The Babel of Iconoclasts.

— Lawrence Venuti

Table of Matter, or, The Completely Lost Letters of Frédéric Chopin to His Friend Titus Wojciechowski

Friederike Mayröcker

— Translated from German by Rosmarie Waldrop

August 21
without skylight/highlight

Dear Tycio,

my diminutive comes down (or in handy) like the half-moon, two pastoral curtains —

my languages blustering like musketeers / musketooters, but I have only two arms and steadfastly fend off the child with the cornucopia she comes to empty over my head, I turn away and around, look behind me for some *ersatz* oil portrait, because: can she really mean me? (or: surely I can't really be the one she means . . .?)

but let me start at the beginning and tell you everything in order :
I have looked in the eye of the hurricane and, shepherd of a time signature / pardon the Polishism / in such a way that this event seems to mark the extreme point of a course which a confusing net of preparatory conditions may have made it necessary for me to follow — and has put me so *beside myself* that I ponder, with melancholy, not only how it must vanish with time, but also how it is hardly possible to hold on to such *audacity,* even though memories pursue me day and night, threatening ruin — and no sooner has it become visible than it is already waning like the moon I just pushed in front of your eyes / suspended above the city, her half-moon-shaped vanity / or like a storm, its gusts breaking on the stronghold of a roiling sea, a grainy mirror: springtide and WORLDS IN MOTION / blustering half-ears / hearts of stone (Fr. sweethearts?)

REBUS / that even things can finally be used to shed light on a

theory : a first reader, the torch, the *fidibus* I lit for *her* —
I still see myself hurrying toward her, through the long hall of
the salon, with the flickering chip of wood (please do not go out
in my fingers!) and so coming into dangerous proximity of the
searing flame *of her imagination* / while she, reclining on a bed
of red silk cushions on the Turkish parquet, *attends* to me with
one of her *devoted looks,* so that the rhythmic tidal wave that
laps at the deepest roots of my heart must soon flood it completely; and while out of various tropics small flocks of pigeons
restlessly lifted off and resettled (their field gossip! what vulgar
hustle and bustle in my head!) I began to wonder whether this
challenge of fate was not all my own doing : having dared the
fatal descent into the deep well / *of her eyes* I am now punished
for it —
(abyss of birds?)
[. . . . . .]
she was crouched, propped against the black Pleyel grand, with
her knees drawn up, her round knees like a jolly young huntsman's, and gently blew the smoke from her Indian pipe upwards —
the reed of the speckled mouthpiece with stuffed gray swans, gypsy
fumes? or : small windharp aeolus harp between her teeth ghost
harp (any gateway / sensation of keen radiance, that is, seeping
away into the white magnesium glow of the night)
and alternately lowered and raised her head to the *figured moon* /
rough moon / beyond the six-beat curtain [. . . . . .]
her Turkish trousers her puffed leggings (feathernettles?) the sun
in her deepest forest — but she is a blade, a terrible pied piper
then we sat in the house for about two hours while outside the
most glistening storm came down / how unmolested a hell! this
transgression of movements — steep flank and water-chamber,
nature aflame with thunderbolts and flashes of lightning (every
three out of four breaking in a cloudburst!), wind-clock and tor-
rents for the end of the world / and, in each other's arms, accompanied the satisfying bluster of the spectacular with an occasional
look at the window : a distraction we might have explored within
ourselves, in navigating our surges, just as we tried to draw the
most amazing connections between lightning catching in the air
and the driving roar of the water —
the torrent outside our windows : silvery armies of lurching fishes
sea monsters (sea angels?) *to wit descending pitches* : seemed eager
to lure us inside the inaccessible *roaring waterfall* inside the

Friederike Mayröcker

crystal heart of its riffling glittering halls / *phallus* until duller
rumblings and fainter sheet lightning announced : the raging sky-
machine was coming to rest, the bleeding of mimetic music
stanched, the thinly brushed blue waters / of her net of pulsing
arteries had seeped away and a lucky star finally risen for us : TIME
HAMMER : ARTAUD's poems which we read as if he, ARTAUD,
revolved above us, a heavenly pillar of writing, as if he, ARTAUD,
wrote his most grandiose heavenly thoughts here, above our heads,
as if he, ARTAUD, performed such giddy heavenly acrobatics in
the unfettered distance that it would take effort to keep up with
his travel speed : the disconcerting details incrusted in his imagination, the parts jutting out of his shading effects, the traces of his
feathery *nervous processes* —
(milkywhey / Marienbad) —
[. . . . . .]
could this flash from the flaming sword of her eyes this zigzag gust
of ripping light really have been meant for me, and blindly, as it
were a boundary mark of heaven?
the last of the trios so her hand would not notice I had grasped it
nor her foot (fingerskin of utmost porousness) — must I now fear
that a *secret* change of mood in the course of the most various
emotions has made her forget what happened? that her demeanor
will again, as so often before, take on that forbidding severity comparable to one single gesture of defense and cast me down in the
DUNGEON to STARVE? that her turning from me will again
plunge me into that state of violent torture that empties my head
of reason and blasts my heart / with unquenchable desire?
fuel-port DUCHAMP : on a staircase, this *foot stuck* while walking or standing, indifferently as it were, in too large and white a
woman's shoe
handguide "outwardsounds" (the idea of teaching her pretty fingers)
showerguard / of her footwear that her footwear must needs have
taken on the form of the foot enclosed : stroked the most delicate
ankle and did not exempt even the sole of the shoe from my caress :
and right after crashed, dear Tycio, crashed down an octave : the
hand I had grasped withdrew, the tender foot-team
[. . . . . .]
said she had feet huge enough / for a statue two quails on careful
pilings how unusual a sight : tongue-tolerance in her head a sea
hardly for weeping / and no one, she protested again and again,
must be excluded —

her capering green eyes a two-bird-cage / beaks and bracts the oval table of a dream : her right arm in the sun in a large remote room or arbor the sun would reach later, her arm in the sun in a park or garden where she said she would wait for me, in the sun, and I asked her how far the sun would actually reach? as if I must fear not to find her (an endless movement / pedaling her foot by the foot of the table —) : and had just now had one foot each one pair of feet each — I mean we were playing two pianos : one foot each one pair of feet each braced against the base of the small oval antique table which, like a magician's obedient tool, would totter wildly as soon as we began handling the tea cups, which seemed bliss to us (and *all aflame* : "IT'S LIKE NEW YEAR'S! IT'S LIKE NEW YEAR'S!" in my ear, her whisper touching my ear)

so while the stupendous storm was raging outside and all dams threatened to burst it went likewise with the two of us here in the house : she pulled at the white threads of the sugar-candy and with a wink granted me a look / from the dining divan / from my distant youth / through the wide open door panel into her bed chamber where her large brass bed, leaf bed, oyster bed, stood with its head toward me : fossil of a house (and crackling / *cloudbed*)

musketeer? *Muskat* tea? nutmeg tea? we drank out of small earth-colored cups and while strokes of lightning climbed our Faraday cage — *a roof and among pygmies:* — I saw in the layered mirror her white face half bird of prey half sea monster (calamus? and smells of extinct stones? fly agaric? subterranean arteries?) or cinnamon, shriveled faded fallen petals of the tiger lily on the mantle / winter tidings: got up and rushed off without a word

even the idea / of a word and me beside myself at the interruption : juicy stew stewing in my own juice "elkfishkingcarp"

and moves through the sleeper (me), taller by a head, as if walking on stilts, leaves in a hurry and me behind : *a stranger to myself* and step by step BY STEP 1 bushland or as Mendelssohn put it: "... he (I!) seems to be in great distress ..." wail and woebegone / as if he (I) had slept on the bare ground and on waking felt an impulse to pick the whole universe up by the armpits like a tender child and whirl it high into the tough air, high into the *apprehensive* air (so flinging a child in the air half-all right child of what spirit / and *lucky teeth*)

my attempts to entangle her in questions so that she would have to stay were, however, foiled, and she did not return until the salon had filled with guests, then pressed her album on her friends,

and on me too — but what I wrote (miracle of palimpsests?) soon caused me shame (*so that I was ashamed and deep in self-pity, even called myself a dolt*) : "BECAUSE I LOVE YOU I KNOW / TO READ YOU : INTERWOVEN WITH LIGHT / THE LETTERS OF YOUR HEART / CAST INTELLIGIBLE / SHADOWS OVER MY WORLD" — and a different hand added later : "FROM HOHLEN-WALDE / GREETINGS FROM YOUR / MAJESTY / MIRROR PAINTING / AND SHINY / HOPE CHEST"
obliteration and nerve-spectacle : so many variants : that even with the windows closed the white curtains seemed to billow against the inner panes, in the bleak woods in my head such a storm in the bleak woods / so much harm and *unruly* / stress on the door as closing, the two pomegranate trees in our garden : without vowel marks : petal-shaped DEFICIENCY, the even patho-logical condition of such REFUSAL : *listening, thus, with spell-bound ears, for the withdrawn voice* : all this seemed to effect that my already disastrous detachment from myself took a turn for the worst or, as Mendelssohn said : ". . . he seems to be in great distress so that his cry of pain . . ."

September 10
(water cannons?)

as certain events of the recent past assail my inner ear, inner eye, in the form of memory images and even return as doubles to tor-ment me, they seem to reveal a secret meaning : HALFWAYS questioning she covered him (me) with snow / repeatedly : "and could he then stay with her?" invoking the somber narrow room, "the tea leaves in the cup . . ." — in any case, she parried, those did not mean good luck, but rather cliché and seastar, transalpine radionist, such littlegod, buckling Central Alps, but the only blue ball of the abacus : an amulet effective against the evil eye (Hirsch Ilya Schlimowitz, Hebr. 1870, scroll on Esther as a bear)
[. . . . . .]
while they (we) rested *for a moment* he broke off a branch of syringa and laid it in her lap, and she immediately *bedded the sick flowers* ("weary beasties") *on her knees*, and he realized with violent emotion that she was beginning to arrange the berries and leaves *on her knees* in a manner that made them appear signs of a secret script decipherable only by her, and only through this process, / what tidings

[. . . . . .]
burr-spun sky like ENSOR light leaf light body / *stolen branch* /
and STEP BY STEP she said, the *sick flowers* ("weary beasties") of
a pair of blue very beautiful and witty eyes, pioneer flower and
silently forking —
drummed away on the white drum, my one peacock sonata, with
bent fingers, or planted congenial flowerseeds like Schubert's "Die
Sterne" — that scream of blood!
random scabs and (hybris) a feeling of being incessantly flung at or
into the heavenly earth, which grew into a sensation of extreme
pain, or the violent desire, after dinner, to be swept through the
fireplace up into the sky / owes much to Cubism
with such audacity, dear Tycio [. . . . . .] I would like
[. . . . . .]
and, most of all, to vomit several times a day —

                                        September 14 (recognize my
                                        sister's eyes in the eyes of
                                        the girls here)
for the moment, my platonic life in the shadow of a bird's wing or,
putting it theoretically / marked by death / : it is less a problem of
inspiration than of preserving an irrevocable *vulnerability* : which
means one must not want to put on armor against the world,
much as one might sometimes like to . . .
till it is time to CRACKTHECOCOON (chainmail vest) toward
the end of summer, dear Tycio, the great heat, the *sick flowers*,
and although our temperaments — hers and mine — are very different we nevertheless are as alike as two drops of water; also, at
times, I think we have gone beyond the stage of mere unpremedi-
tation, as proved by the exhibits of anticipated future in my phantasies, I mean I dreamed rather pleasantly (had stuffed my pillow
with fresh ferns!) of green lance tips (gladiolas? : which she does
not like!) or green ears of corn in higher and multiple stages, which
turned their daggers against, but could not harm me (for false conclusion an initiate gullet and stuffed with her *angelic facts* (REBUS)
/ about to discharge, any moment, a veritable angelic cannonade
over me and the whole edifice of the world)
and while we are walking side by side I feel all sorts of wishes rise
within me (1 white Wienzeile, dear Tycio) : we wandered through
somber mixed forest (Devil's Bog?) on paths sloping gently downhill,

stopped frequently to look through radial clearings down into the valley, a treat for nostril and eye, and it seemed to me that both winds and sedulous time held their breath, as did we in our rapture, *while the hand of the storm* (legendary cool forest: raising motley trees into a semblance of a roof) *shook* the top of an isolated pale *linden shoot* down in the dry creek-bed and while, likewise, a dark silent magic born of the dazzled forest scattered our attention in all directions and banished it to the deep ivy-covered ravine that embodied our thoughts grazing at great depth : in comparative forest time and leaping alternately up and down : repetitions, roebucks, flower service : back to the creek-bed, the ravine between the crumbling old walls, that is, back to the hand of the storm shaking the top of the linden shoot, whereas farther up the hill we saw leaves motionless on their branches / as if inside a palm-house on fire so that thick ash /

and we began to worry and consult our watches as if time in its *audacity* had caught up with us after all (while the linden twigs (temporal!) while the sudden storm while the leaves on their branches) [. . . . .] : *so that it finally seemed as if our mouths could discharge both cold and warmth at the same time*

even the cook even the stoker, between midnight and the new morning, and under the coroner's (Grandville's?) watchful eye that holds me, turned to stone —

for, dear Tycio, not even in this steep green world can I any longer escape the death rattle : a frantic clatter and racket as unsettling as it is uncanny — I mean, it follows me everywhere, and my ears ring with booming clanging whirring droning blaring trumpeting — my *ears and eyes* at the mercy of this dull barrage of clustered dissonance : flag hoisted by the *exclamatory subproxy* : a changeling *ersatz dream* : I EMBRACE SOLANGE whereas in truth I want to embrace ONLY HER ONLY HER ONLY HER —

a gloomy procession, dear Tycio — wandered through bogs crossed the sea plowed the ocean / to wilt the lead sinkers

I shall go by express / I think I'll start tomorrow on my journey to death / my traveling bag is packed : but you will not be able to follow me into despair, dear Tycio . . .

I do understand : small lead sinkers sewn into the hem of my coat — no weight any more, everything would dissolve (to wilt the lead sinkers)

funereal, down the dark valley / minor third : now stones piled under my piano and HER A STONE'S THROW AWAY : BUT

UNATTAINABLE FOR ME — [. . . . . .]
Grandville, that balloon that friendly life-mask figure of reference :
I can hardly bear, in this overwrought state, having to deal with
indifferent people : in fact, the constant effort required by her act
of withdrawal drains me so completely that even meeting friends
is difficult and not unfrequently turns into pain — moreover, anyone as much in need of comfort as I has no strength left to give
comfort to others who might also need it
still most bearable when SOLANGE flits through (*Atlas always!*)
out of my window the evening sky the half moon; the larches a
golden yellow — as for you, I think you stand firm like the ivory
tower and the gates of heaven . . .
last night went on another long solitary ramble through the streets /
stubble fields / ran into Grandville, gracious fellow! his new hobby :
he casts pet horoscopes! what a friendly dickiebird complete with
frock-coat and melancholy
talked merrily at me, but my mind was you know where, and it
cost me an effort to follow him even for moment / but I also caught
myself *not wanting to understand a thing* he said
(how good it feels to play deaf and plunge into fog and, if the many
possibilites are not a dream . . .)
that is, last possible delay / and out of snow : icewater hollow between chest and shoulder muted broken emotion a terrible scattering, dear Tycio, while my *delusion, my stubbornness dare not
go near the smallest conviviality,* but rather bind me more and
more tightly to the place of error without any possible escape
hatch [. . . . . .]
and with a heavy heart I watch *her* and SOLANGE disappear in
the sky

(?) 15, winter tidings
because I sometimes try to *block out* the truth that devours my
reason by revving up my fancy, I aggravate the fatal evil, my
divided mind / tint tincture knife in the shirt, *the only prong,*
sticking out of her open jacket —
she disapproves of the idea that I spend time being with her in my
thoughts (the more I lack a world? the rarer the occasion to touch
the most tender and violent *world of her thoughts?* tuft of hair
mere human chaff this self-deficient feast / variable theaters / exchange and aberration into dreams)

and, recurring every night, this dream would seem to announce
my ruin : robinia panicles fanned out against the white flaky sky /
of an Artaud / hard black morning shadows on the slant roofs of
the houses opposite / like quiet flags of mourning / silent and un-
armed by her side, hankering for her touch like a thirsty man for
water, walking along a prospect of woods flooded with light, the
banks of the Elbe? with cedars? that is, minted in bird tongues
minted / a closed system of delusions as if breathless and could not
go on and : *repeated outbreak of disturbing factors* — and exclaim,
utter prayers : that we might remain hidden from the world!
but they descend on us, sneering, in a porous whirl of flakes, of
artfully copied mirages, evil phantasies, parallel languages, nerve
extracts, memorable pantomimes : they snow down from above,
they rise up from the ground, in groups, singly, crippled dwarfs,
massive giants, limping, hiding their extremities / jutting cudgels /
under loose wraps — *a roof and among pygmies* : my eyes my ears
splitting out of snow collapsed lungs and hope chest / a frivolous
bout of fever as if he (I) felt ever more closely watched as if bleeding again : though his restless imagination forbade him to [. . . . . .]
so natural a trumpet
(and which the DRY LEAVES : EYE LEAVES conversation lines in
the waxen shield of her forehead) as if she had, a reading-groupie,
sunk up to a thousand poems in the Main river — REBUS / that
even things
[. . . . . .]
but what has remained for me the most incomprehensible and
enigmatic event of the past night may, dear Tycio, seem quite understandable to you : on my return home around midnight I found
the floor covered with one-sou pieces (reed pen? winter tidings?)
and likewise winged letters : the PALM OF YOUR HAND! too, as
if you had delivered your own, quickly dropped it off in passing,
or as if the mailman had, against his usual habit, stuffed yours
and all the others through the crack under the door (which occu-
pies me, crowds me, gives me a feeling of dismay all around) all
those letters from back home, from you, from Louise, my parents,
Jan . . .
so I strongly clasped the bundle to my chest and, having once more
read the names of the correspondents on the front to increase my
pleasure of anticipation, finally withdrew to my bed and stretched
out in order to read in comfort : your letter with its beautiful regular (wavy!) hand I wanted to open first, before all others : which

312

seemed however frustrated by a sudden noise outside, possibly a knock at my door (chatte? chien?) :
while I, startled, vault out of bed, push aside *those letters dropped out of the sky* and rush to the door to see who it might be, there seemed to occur in the room, which I left ever so briefly, the most mysterious excesses of a hellish master plot (the culmination of a wily bird-snare) :
(hell has opened, dear Tycio! and my naked eye / dry karst mountains . . .) :
to wit, in some inexplicable manner this, your, letter must have slipped (been slipped?) between the sheets, must have hidden — chatte? chien? like Melmoth when he crawls under the covers with me — so that I found it only on waking, in the morning, crumpled and still unopened under my pillow —
but that I should not have noticed it was lacking while I read all the other letters, that I should not have missed it, the main attraction of the postal cornucopia, the exclusive aim of all my longing thoughts, this seems to me unfathomable, incomprehensible indeed!
(I had even tried to soothe my impatient expectation, to anticipate some of its contents by holding it up to the lamp to begin deciphering it through the envelope!)
but once out of sight! and our thoughts run wild and pull us *off on a journey* (dazzled bagpiper, and before the wind sweeps us apart forever!)
? and which hung by 1 nail?

September 16/17 / prim light, the ears of Reykjavík or : there is no wind let go of my ears! there is no wind!

. . .

and rapturous greetings, *Ch.*
(POSTSCRIPTUM PLACED AT THE BEGINNING : after renewed dangers won back her affection tonight / and rapturous greetings, *Ch.*) [. . . . . .]
world of backdrops (wrapped around the table leg) / and Jesus / let go of my ears / to wit, acutely stupid thread from heaven : adrenalin rush in the blood thickening veil-tissue — oasis light
ears and eyes bewitched, even my body weight dwindling to the

point where already in the morning I float through the house
like a shadow beyond gravity, and rapturous greetings, dear Tycio,
rapturous greetings : PUT HER TWO HANDS ON MY HEAD
AS EARS : buckled ears to my head with her two hands as if she
wanted to alleviate the noise of the world with these comforting
flute-ears or felt called to NURSE me — this porousness on both
sides, the axis of heaven collapsing — and lifts a glittering stone
to her eye : as if truly all phenomena of this world were to me
but *wandering shadows of her form* / but was also reminded of
SOLANGE's childish gesture when shown the *erratic block* on
the gravel path in Père-Lachaise, section 86, early one morning : a large stone washed smooth, sleek and heavy, with grayish-
yellow veins, and domed and hollowed like a giant auricle — EAR
BUCKLE! she cries, BUCKLED TO THE EAR! claims it is a *left
ear*, holds the stone to her left temple, skips about under the trees,
presses it against both cheeks (WESTFLEET / "had anyone ever
held this stone in his hand?") and anxiously clasps it to her breast
a tender flute-ear
a graveyard by the sea?
animals all the way to the sky
(the last time SOLANGE was here she examined with childish
eagerness all the jutting walls deeper pillars roofs of my house
that might serve to protect a couple of lovers (HOPE CHEST she
laughed) in case of a sudden earthquake —
flaunted a radiant laugh : that, however, THE MORNING SUN
frightened her / hence she rather went for Western light)
[. . . . . .]
we eagerly scraped along / the gravel paths in the warm sun / and
I wonder if I can bear SOLANGE (alone of all living beings) these
days, even feel almost attracted to her, because *that hand that
look that voice* may have been near the child just before I myself
touch SOLANGE's hand, see SOLANGE's face, hear SOLANGE's
voice — and although I cannot help feeling ashamed, even abject
to use SOLANGE as a go-between (as when SOLANGE talks about
her mother, or I ask questions about her, what is she doing, working on, which friends come to the house / as ingenuously as possible and seemingly without too much interest /) I nevertheless
feel something like relief during these conversations, as if I were
to some degree readmitted to former intimacy
(flagstone mendicant monk? stone scar?)
so we hold on to firm and strict form (and pour into it a seething

life more various than we can know) :
so we go through sequences of various contradictory feelings
(nadirs zeniths on the mill of our imagination) : and just as *the
swallow's saliva* (was that relevant?) allowed for copious empathy
with / ordinance of / the unquestioned right of things : so he was
laboring to gather the most trivial findings and cement them with
the saliva of FRENZY and the saliva of FOOLISHNESS — *collage
invention* of a new faith (after these past days of laceration, despair,
velleity, pain)
[. . . . . .]
and would she then light a lamp?
knowing how she always carries a freight of things, dear Tycio, a
breath of anise from the garden, and all over the house a scent of
thyme / but closely tied to thoughts of my end, so that I must
complete the composition of this flood of events (cataracts!) as fast
as possible because I see more and more clearly how imminent
the dissolution of my physical strength
(are graveyard-flowers? drops out, and off: *the white bones of the
mouth*)
[. . . . . .]
and everything leads to *her*, even numbers, syllables, sounds, tools,
veined rock, eyebright, rain and wind, wrapped earth (the medial
bandages of the shrunken head!), a pan-fry (lion), a head turning, a
wink, the dice-dog's snake-dart-and-dust . . .)
but I am also like a sleeper awake, and objects which used to be
only on her side — I mean she had been able to *win them over* —
now are significantly close to me as well so that I sometimes think
I can see reflections of her person in the *mixed occurrences* of
daily life : crossing of borders?
surging, the beloved woman / deep knowledge / bloodiest dawn :
the *spreading* of liquids (littlegod and moves around on 1 table the
objects that move God / lumberjack in front of the house); the
spilling of sugar, salt, soul; *the surging the picturing* of fire (calyx
spice : somber ceiling and how my thoughts tend to break off toward her in a wild gallop)
and what was hitherto without grace : letter calligraphy, spear-
glitter of musical notation : now comes to me as loving tool, soul-
ful authorship (ladle, a shot through a candle flame, reversal of
light values) —
concave sternum, that is, a new Nike (aluminum replica?) or fleeing across snowy fields on the palms of my hands to her / to my

work / and such a maze of a garden anywhere a poet's delight (DeChirico)

made the acquaintance, dear Tycio, the acquaintance of St. Donatus so high / and rank the brushwood of description, that is, fever visions terrible fever — shaken by high fever . . .

what a day! white and yellow day (saffron and turk's head lily) and all day long the eagles above us all day long the eagles / and chained to the needletip of the rhino-rock until finally : EXHAUSTION OF THE EYES!

a tent suspended in the air, dear Tycio, as if suspended in the air, when I look at her —

she had come in so quietly I only recognized her once she spoke [. . . . . .] on dove feet [. . . . . .]

but as soon as I ask will we ever meet again [. . . . . .] and touches her palm to the ice-flowered window pane

? September 17 / what masterful
ambivalence : ours a
smooth indifference between
rough blundering (thundering?)
conversations / and as can
be read in all the gazettes —

I am vague in dating my letters, dear Tycio, I often do not know the day or the hour (quotes of titles, notes from Titania?) : alas, how confused it must all seem to you, what I write, but my perceptive faculty spins around its own center like a top out of control /

silence in this hollow *as if she had felt like crying bitterly* :

reads my music on the (starstrewn) ceiling, *lifts this lopsubsided rock of my body up to new life* (presses the smooth brown *chestnut foundling* from the Bois de Boulogne to her cheek, pensively traces the shape of her lips with it / what vowel marks, threads from heaven, unconscious genesis, looks up at the window and the tree tops in the garden . . .) penetrating these lovers' snow blanket / daily snow blanket and the temptation to get lost in it (broad day wide night giant phoenix-palm pushed to the farthest corner of the room, and at the hour of the Angelus a caressing lingering pat : attachment of her palm) : whole WORLDS IN MOTION, dear Tycio, I mean my mind is in a state of constant extreme agitation, and I wonder how I have ever been able to live without this experience?

but I also wonder how can I go on living this way, constantly under the spell —

and I can already hear my friends exchange worried speculations why they do not get to see me more often, whether my illness has gotten so serious that I cannot leave the house, and afterwards: where had I been the whole time? — and had already prepared an explanation that would satisfy them : namely that he had finally given in to his desire to sequester himself from the outside world and intended to spend the coming weeks and months in HIS DARKROOM and devote himself to work on those LIGHT PRO-JECTIONS whose SENSITIVITY [. . . . . .]

in photo sequences, in plunging lines, in possession of writing ("THE BIRD AS PROPHET" by Robert Schumann ("and would he enter into friendship?"))

: so he had tried to photograph her from her most remote nadirs (via the present tenderest ATTACHMENT) all the way to the zenith of her future old age / zoom delight MEINE SOAP "MEM" / and awakened simultaneous emotion?

September 23, in an unfindable
place / and "eyebright"?

enclosed the list of keys —

bluebottle / sheer pin money / and almost out of joint, dear Tycio, the sun wiped out as well! and out of snow, with 2 notes of music "bequeathed" to so thick a darkness that I felt dizzy / when my beautiful day and night butterfly beats its wings against my fore-head — tender tremors bewitching WORLDS IN MOTION [. . . . . .]

and the trees dripping with rain? and the trees dripping with rain? and the trees dripping with rain?

we leaf through her past together : through albums that picture her tender girlhood (eccentric headdress, of a dream?), the elements I hope fire air and wind, the Masurian lakes my needle toward my pole-star ("exhaustion of the eyes" — "and that she must not look at me this long?"), the events of the last days and nights, her newly attentive manner of receiving me ("and could she receive him today?"), this flood of gloomy associations, enthusiasm, sounds, emotions, concepts, thoughts — whole SHEAVES OUT OF THIN AIR! have brought it about that the significance of *her birth* (as

317

the beginning of a crucial phase in my life) seems suddenly sur-
passed by that other *hidden* period of my life : the many years I
spent on this earth ahead of her, so that I have come to the firm
conclusion that this very *time before her* birth and *of my* early
childhood must (in its quality of porous tenderness) have been so
embracing a time that not a single hour of our actually shared life
could compare with it —
in day-and-night-squalls / non intérieur / she says / SHEAVES OUT
OF THIN AIR *they would not float* she says, the leaves of the
gingko — *they would not swim*, the leaves of the single plantain
in front of her house, *they would tumble and crumble* / plumage
of heavenly sounds . . .
only now, she says, only here, we could see a clinical curve, an
upward curve, a faint scraping scratching sound as if sugar cubes
slid with gentle friction back and forth on the bottom of an empty
china cup / magnetic water?
and murmured to him (for she had sat down at his feet and laid her
head in his lap / while I somewhat apprehensive, uneasy, worried
I would *somehow give offense* / bowed my neck
but he had lifted her face to trace the delicate vestiges of her gifts
and wishes [. . . . . .] heart-line unknown)
then, because the night was mild, he (I) had slept on the balcony
and listened all night to the rain falling; in the morning his clothes
had felt damp and he had looked toward the banks of the Elbe and
the jackdaws steep in the firmament—
sheaf, sheaves of compositions, and huntings, in a remote corner
of the world : THEY WOULD NOT FLOAT, she said, bare sheaves
laurel leaves and evening tea : THEY WOULD NOT SWIM —
well, dear Tycio, I might as well confess : ALL THE BEAUTY
OF THE WORLD BEARS HER TRAITS! : such *chain link* diction, dear Tycio (adjectival!) : a man thinking about madness :
MAGRITTE! / and so overwhelmed by her most recent visit that I
actually forgot everything that might have pleased her, I even
neglected to give her my latest piece of music although I had already written the dedication to her, I neglected to tell her so many
things —
if only she would come more often —

September 29 (?)
("Sheep little Jesus sheep little chick!"/
. . . andante, "walking")
(sleep was sweet if sweet is the word for the calmest happiness)
[. . . . . .]
the faithful gullies were steaming as we, around noon, left the house and walked down the somber lane ("Wienerwandering"), merry, carefree, ambling, determined to *pine,* and puzzled out the world's loose unleashed phenomena, occurrences / and I burst into sudden, quite unmotivated laughs / that the inexplicable bellboy's multifarious nose [. . . . . .]
warmed through by this mental flame we walked hand in hand, or arm in arm, with such a rapturous mien that anybody could have read our condition, walked as far as the Heidenschuss and the Cathedral, losing all sense of time / and circled back, but around a displaced core : the grosse Michaelerhaus, Komödiengasse, Wiener Horn — the sun unsteady and slant, the dark Hoftheater offering an appearance of the 11 apostles *(followers of Jesus?)*
under the influence of this secret ether (of place and occasion)
[. . . . . .]
and could not help whispering to one another — where I am and how I am, dear Tycio, I cannot tell, except that a strangely breathless feeling comes over me when her eyes . . .
and at night when we lean out of the window, intoxicated with the fading colors of the sky, the flimsy cardboard houses across the street seem to totter, collapse or move off into the dark / a subtle style of singing

September 30
(landslide / engraved nameplate?)
so richly elated so on wings (rainy day in the distance?) that I decided at so late an hour to follow up happiness with a musical adventure : went without a ticket to B. to hear W.'s new opera
[. . . . . .]
false coda / piano score closed —
also would have liked to thank you right away, I spend many an hour with you in my thoughts — but my thoughts are perhaps like bird cries over a stormy sea —
outwardly everything runs its regulated course, and, except for you, no one has any idea of my true condition : already old doubts

319

are catching up with me, have I been led into a maze? to wit, a
neighborhood that requires that I observe and ponder all transi-
tions and distances each time anew
finished the major books : chamber choir / Gorkipol (Pushkin's
railroad station) WORLD MUSIC or "kindergarden" (which the
audience receives as harum-scarum or worse! : and would rather
recoil from its ABNORM!)
[. . . . . .]
in any case the strangest things have been happening to me recently — sometimes I think I see you in the street, see you, Jan,
Louise, my parents walking ahead of me : I get extremely excited,
rush to catch up with you, embrace you : scrutinize each face —
but it turns out mere illusion which saddens me more than anything (distorted writing, simulated courier-collages)
away! one tiger (servant) laughs! imagination, that is, and near my
former domicile, so it happens more and more often that my feet
take me there as in the old days — and each time I am freshly confused to arrive in front of the house I used to live in, and only a
kind of embarrassed shyness keeps me from climbing the 2 flights
of stairs to the door with the old engraved name-plate . . .

October 31 / toward imprisonment
(light case of aphasia?)
toward the colt green / colt gray / which is the firmament, and
back with colt leaps, dear Tycio, tremendous backward leaps my
mind (and dancer alla Turca!) takes, perhaps pathological, a syn-
drome of serene raving madness? I rush back, a star at the height
(or depth?) of its course (its pain), or, to be more precise, I am at a
point of my life (singleaves), with an occasional ritardando, even
crab canon — back to my parents, childhood friends, siblings . . .
sedge, the edges cut-glass-green, as if grass of the old compass
[. . . . . .]
and so drawn to her *as if he no longer dared allow himself any joy,*
courier-boots, *corset* : as if he wanted to submerge his pain in ever
more memories out of the old family chest — like his mother sup-
plicating (at the risk of hurting him in the long run) imploring the
doctor even at the last fitting to spare the fragile boy this instrument of torture — and how vivid a feeling of shared pain had been
painted in her beautiful eyes!
her tender attention, and so anxiously concerned with his well-

320

being : ("was he not all too rash in aiming at the highest stakes?"),
her objections, fears : ("he might be hurt, treated unfairly, his
boldness misinterpreted, his work misjudged in such a distant
country . . .")
to enter that now unenterable place, measure that now immeasur-
able time — fossil of a house, Zelazowa-Wola, *gillyflower bay*
(in its lovely familiarity : with its roses dahlias willows / *human
chaff* / its twin cherries cries of swallows lopsubsided stones muted
evenings brilliant mornings / sharp morning smells foretelling fall
in the middle of summer / and the post from town taking three
days to reach us / the clear nights when the piano was carried out
under the fir trees and his playing could be heard in the most remote orchards and they all listened behind the hedges —
and Emilie auguring — her prophecies from random passages in a
book / Bible verses . . .)
it is getting dark, dear Tycio, flakes falling already? in October
March August? and a seeping, a white rustling, in a white night /
something, an unfamiliar noise from the street, kept me from
going to sleep last night
[. . . . . .]
of another dream I have been able to preserve a few tones / elms
yews frockcoats willows / coal flat iron / or stag winterling snow-
heath lungwort [. . . . . .]
and the trees dripping with rain? and the trees dripping with rain?
(the sun wiped out, and out of snow, *Ch.*)

Postscript: for Tycio, for all who sleep with my memories

The first time I met Friederike Mayröcker, she and Ernst Jandl were
on a reading tour in the United States. They came into a party already in process, with students dancing and at first a bit reluctant
to stop and listen to poems. But as soon as Friederike and Ernst
started reading everybody was spellbound. Years later, people
would ask about "those wonderful Austrian poets." Friederike may
come on mine de rien, but she is a powerhouse — and a wonder.
It takes an infallible ear and sense of form to hold together that
"hallucinatory prose."
"I have always avoided making a story," Friederike Mayröcker

Friederike Mayröcker

has said. "I don't see stories anywhere. Even in the course of my life, or other lives, I see nothing resembling a story. And I'm unable to read a book that has a story."

"Table of Matter" is certainly not a story in the traditional sense. The author has looked at biographical material, listened to records, but above all, "looked into the eye of the hurricane."

Friederike Mayröcker was born in 1924 in Vienna, where she has continued to live, first as a teacher of English and, from 1969 on, as a free-lance writer. In the 1960s she was associated with the experimental "Vienna Group," and she often collaborates with Ernst Jandl. In the last two decades she has mostly written prose. She has received many prestigious literary prizes in both Austria and Germany, including the Theodor-Körner-Preis (1963), the Georg-Trakl-Preis (1977) and the Grosse Österreichischer Staatspreis (1982).

— Rosmarie Waldrop

NOTES ON CONTRIBUTORS

ANNE-MARIE ALBIACH is a French poet who lives near Paris. Translations of her work include *État*, by Keith Waldrop (Awede); *Mezza Voce*, by Joey Simas with Lydia Davis, Anthony Barnett and Douglas Oliver (Post-Apollo) and *Vocative Figure*, by Barnett and Simas (Allardyce-Barnett).

AMMIEL ALCALAY's recent books include the *cairo notebooks* (Singing Horse Press) and *After Jews and Arabs: Remaking Levantine Culture* (University of Minnesota Press).

JOHN ASHBERY's *And the Stars Were Shining* was published this year by Farrar, Straus & Giroux.

CARLOS GERMÁN BELLI was born in Lima, Peru, in 1927. His first book of poetry was published in 1958, and he is still publishing today. He currently lives in Lima, where he both teaches and works at the newspaper *El Comercio*.

CHARLES BERNSTEIN's most recent books are *Dark City* (Sun & Moon) and *A Poetics* (Harvard). He is a professor of English and comparative literature at SUNY-Buffalo.

Before becoming the most well known artist of the *cordel* tradition (hand-printed booklets of woodcuts and verse), JOSÉ FRANCISCO BORGES was a farmer, potter, carpenter, toy maker, mason and house painter. His woodcuts have been exhibited in Brazil, Argentina, Mexico, the United States, Germany, Italy, Switzerland, the Netherlands and Belgium.

Born in 1951, CORAL BRACHO studied literature at the Universidad Nacional Autónoma de México, spent time in England, France and the United States, and was a scholar for Instituto Nacional de Bellas Artes. She won the Aguascalientes prize in 1981. Her books include *El ser que va a morir* (1982) and *Peces de piel Fugaz* (1988).

PETER BUSH has translated works by Juan Carlos Onetti, Antonio Muñoz Molina, Luis Sepúlveda and Senel Paz. His translation of *Quarantine* by Juan Goytisolo was published by Dalkey Archive in 1994. Quartet Books (UK) has recently published his translation of Onetti's *No Man's Land*. He also edits *In Other Words*, the journal of the Translators Association (UK).

PAOLA CAPRIOLO lives in Milan. Her first book to appear in English will be *I Live for Love*, forthcoming from Serpent's Tail. Her first appearance in this country was the story "The Woman of Stone," published in *Conjunctions: 18*.

PETER COLE's *Hanagid: From the Diwan of Shmuel Ben Yosef Ha Levi* is forthcoming from Princeton University Press. He recently completed a new book of poems, *Speech's Hedge*.

BEI DAO's most recent book is *Forms of Distance* (New Directions), which appeared last summer. He left China in the late 1980s and currently lives in Ann Arbor.

JOY DWORKIN teaches world literature and writing courses at Missouri Southern State College.

JEAN ECHENOZ received the Prix Médicis in 1983 for *Cherokee* and the European Literature Prize in 1991 for *Lac*. His other novels include *Le Méridien de Greenwich*, *L'Equipée malaise* (published in English as *Double Jeopardy*) and, most recently, *Nous trois*. He lives in Paris.

On the publication of his first book in 1943, FAIZ AHMED FAIZ was recognized as the leading contemporary Urdu poet. He has been translated by V. G. Kiernan, Naomi Lazard, Agha Shahid Ali and others.

Born in Baidoa, Somalia, NURUDDIN FARAH is the author of several novels including a trilogy on African dictatorship, *Sweet and Sour Milk*, *Sardines* and *Close Sesame* (Graywolf). His most recent book, *Gifts*, won the 1993 Zimbabwe's Best Novel of the Year Award. Currently, he is at work on a nonfiction book about Somali refugees in Europe. He lives in Kaduna, Nigeria.

MARK FRIED is the former editor of *NACLA Report on the Americas*. He has translated Eduardo Galeano's *We Say No* (Norton) and José Ignacio López Vigil's *Rebel Radio: The Story of El Salvador's Radio Venceremos* (Curbstone/LAB), as well as Galeano's *Walking Words* (Norton, forthcoming 1995).

AKUTAGAWA FUSEI (1912–1971) suffered, like Araki Yasusada, from prolonged illness brought on by radiation poisoning. He was an apprentice in a cloisonné jewelry business before the bombing of Hiroshima. There are intriguing references in Yasusada's notebooks to a fiction manuscript by Fusei entitled *Epileptic's Scalpel*, which the translators are attempting to uncover.

Uruguayan author EDUARDO GALEANO lives in his native Montevideo. Seven of his books have been published in English, including the trilogy *Memory of Fire* (Pantheon), *We Say No* (Norton) and *Walking Words* (Norton, forthcoming 1995).

FORREST GANDER lives outside Providence, Rhode Island. His most recent books include *Deeds of Utmost Kindness* (Wesleyan) and *Lynchburg* (Pittsburgh). He edited and translated poems for *Mouth to Mouth: Poems by 12 Contemporary Mexican Women* (Milkwood).

ELI GOTTLIEB is a translator and fiction writer whose first novel, *Fad's Eye*, will be published next year.

JUAN GOYTISOLO is the preeminent writer of contemporary Spanish fiction. The two volumes of his autobiography were published by North Point Press. The *Count Julian* trilogy, *Makbara* and *The Virtues of a Solitary Bird* have been published in paperback by Serpent's Tail. His chronicle of the ups and downs in the Marx household and world politics will see the light in the Anglo-Saxon world in 1996 (Faber & Faber, UK).

DAVID HINTON translated *Forms of Distance*, Bei Dao's most recent book. His translations from classical Chinese include *The Selected Poems of Tu Fu* (New Directions) and *The Selected Poems of T'ao Ch'ien* (Copper Canyon).

324

BRIAN HOLTON has translated Chinese poetry into Scots and English, and is working on a Scots version of *The Water Margin*. Forthcoming is *Non-Person Singular* (Wellsweep Press, London), the collected shorter poems of Yang Lian.

NINA ISKRENKO's book, *The Right to Err*, translated by John High and Patrick Henry, is forthcoming from Three Continents Press.

RONALD R. JANSSEN teaches modern literature at Hofstra University and directs the Hofstra Summer Writers' Conference. With Jian Zhang, he is translating Zhang Cheng Zhi's *History of the Soul*.

OZAKI KUSATAO was the only survivor of his immediate family from the bombing of Hiroshima. He was a member, with Araki Yasusada and Akutagawa Fusei, of the Layered Clouds and Oars literary groups. He remarried and moved to Osaka in the 1960s, where he was an executive with a large insurance company.

OKURA KYOJIN is a poet and sculptor living in Hiroshima.

Poet and essayist YANG LIAN started writing during the Cultural Revolution. *Non-Person Singular*, a translation of *Wu Ren Cheng*, a selection of his short poems (1981–1991), will be published this year by Wellsweep Press, London.

CLAUDIO MAGRIS lives in Trieste, Italy. His many books include literary criticism and travel writing, as well as novels and short stories. Available in English are *Danube* (Farrar, Straus & Giroux), *Inferences From a Sabre* (George Braziller) and *A Different Sea* (Harvill).

FRIEDERIKE MAYRÖCKER's novel *Night Train* (translated by Beth Bjorklund) was published by Ariadne Press in 1992. Other work in English can be found in *The Vienna Group: 6 Major Austrian Poets* (translated and edited by Rosmarie Waldrop and H. Watts, Station Hill). Burning Deck will shortly publish *Heiligenanstalt*, of which "Table of Matter" is a part.

New poems by ANDREW McCORD are forthcoming in the *Paris, Partisan* and *Yale* reviews and several more of his translations of Faiz Ahmed Faiz will appear in *Modern Poetry in Translation*.

SEMEZDIN MEHMEDINOVIĆ, the author of four books, continues to work and write in Sarajevo, where he has remained active throughout the war as an editor of the popular Bosnian cultural magazine, *Our Days*.

PASCALLE MONNIER was born in 1958 in Bordeaux, France. In 1983–1984 she was a Prix de Rome resident at the French Academy (Villa Medici) in Rome. She lives in Paris.

TOSA MOTOKIYU was born in Hiroshima, Japan, in 1955. He studied music composition in Milwaukee and Madison, Wisconsin, in the early 1980s. From 1984 through the present he has resided alternately in Japan and Sebastapol, California, and has been engaged in translating and editing the Araki Yasusada manuscripts.

OJIU NORINAGA, from Hiroshima, is a doctoral student in comparative literature. He currently lives in Tokyo, where he teaches English at the Nippon School of Business.

ROSE PASSALACQUA, an instructor at Washington University and at Fontbonne College in St. Louis, is currently working on a bilingual volume of Carlos Germán Belli's poetry as well as on translations of two Colombian poets, Aurelio Arturo and Giovanni Quessep.

MARK POLIZZOTTI has translated works by Jean Echenoz, André Breton, René Daumal, Maurice Roche, Jean Baudrillard and others. He is the author of *Revolution of the Mind: The Life of André Breton,* to be published in 1995 by Farrar, Straus & Giroux.

ABD AL-HAKIM QASIM (1935–1990) was deprived — by exile and humility — of the celebrity enjoyed by many other Egyptian writers of his generation. The excerpt from *Al-Mahdi* that appears in this issue of *Conjunctions* is the first work of Qasim's to be published in the United States.

JOACHIM SARTORIUS is a poet, translator and editor who lives in Berlin. Besides two books of poetry, he has most recently published collaborations with artists James Lee Byars (*The Golden Tower,* 1992) and Nan Goldin (*Vakat,* 1993). He has translated Wallace Stevens and John Ashbery, and edited the complete works of William Carlos Williams for Hanser Verlag, Munich.

HIROAKI SATO has published more than two dozen books, sixteen of which are translations of Japanese poems into English. Among his recent books are *Right under the big sky, I don't wear a hat: Haiku and Prose of Hôsai Ozaki* (Stone Bridge Press) and *String of Beads: Complete Poems of Princess Shikishi* (University of Hawaii Press). Along with Burton Watson, he received the PEN translation prize for *From the Country of Eight Islands: An Anthology of Japanese Poetry* (Doubleday).

English translations of HAROLD SCHIMMEL's work have appeared in *Conjunctions, Partisan Review, The Forward, The Jerusalem Post's Poets Cornered, London Magazine, Delos, Furnitures, Talisman* and *Ariel.*

SIBYLLE SCHLESIER is currently in the master's programs of English-creative writing and German studies at the University of New Mexico.

OLGA SEDAKOVA is a poet and scholar who lives in Moscow. Her work has appeared in leading Russian journals, almanacs and in three books, two published in Russia and one in France.

BOTHO STRAUSS began his writing career in 1967 as an editor and critic for Theater Heute. He is primarily known as a playwright, but has also written several novels and a collection of short essays and vignettes (*Pairs, Passersby*). In 1989 he won the prestigious German literary award the Georg-Büchner-Preis.

NATHANIEL TARN has been doing research on religion in Bhutan. His latest book is *Flying the Body* from Arundel Press in Los Angeles.

PETER THEROUX is the author of *Sandstorms* (Norton) and *Translating LA* (Norton) and the translator of Egyptian, Iraqi and Saudi Arabian novels, chiefly of Abdelrahman Munif's *Cities of Salt* trilogy (Random House and Vintage paperbacks).

Ten volumes of JOHN TRANTER's poetry have been published, the latest of which are *The Floor of Heaven* (HarperCollins), a collection of four verse novellas, and *At the Florida* (University of Queensland Press).

LAWRENCE VENUTI's latest book is the translation of I. U. Tarchetti's novel *Passion* (Mercury House), the basis of the recent musical by Stephen Sondheim and James Lapine.

ANDREW WACHTEL is associate professor of Slavic languages and literature at Northwestern University. He has published widely on various aspects of Russian and East European literature, including the books *The Battle for Childhood: Creation of a Russian Myth* and *An Obsession With History: Russian Writers Confront the Past*. He has also translated much contemporary Russian poetry with the largest selection appearing in the anthology *The Third Wave: The New Russian Poetry* (University of Michigan Press).

ROSMARIE WALDROP's most recent book of poems is *Lawn of Excluded Middle* (Tender Buttons Press). *A Key Into the Language of America* is forthcoming from New Directions. Translations include Edmond Jabès's *Book of Questions* (Wesleyan UP), Jacques Roubaud's *Some Thing Black* (Dalkey Archive), Paul Celan's *Collected Prose* (Carcanet) and *The Vienna Group* (with Harriett Watts, Station Hill).

PAUL WEST won the 1993 Lannan Prize for fiction with his thirteenth novel, *Love's Mansion*. His new books are *Sheer Fiction, Volume III*, just out, *A Stroke of Genius* (January, from Viking), a memoir of illness, and his next novel, *The Tent of Orange Mist*, set in the China of 1937 (April, from Scribner).

J. RODOLFO WILCOCK was born in Buenos Aires in 1919 and died in 1978 in Viterbo, Italy. He wrote poems, plays, journalism, theater criticism and volumes of fiction, and translated works from English, French and Spanish. None of his books has ever been translated into English.

C. D. WRIGHT has just completed a two-year study on Arkansas writers, *The Lost Roads Project: A Walk-In Book of Arkansas* along with *A Reader's Map of the State*. Her most recent book of poetry is *Just Whistle* from Kelsey Street Press.

CAN XUE lives in Changsha, Hunan Province, People's Republic of China, not far from the village where Chairman Mao Zedong was born. Her *Dialogues in Paradise* is available from Northwestern University Press. Regarded as being among the tiny vanguard of Chinese postmodern fiction writers, she is a regular contributor to *Conjunctions*.

The notebooks of ARAKI YASUSADA (1907–1972) are currently being prepared for book publication by Tosa Motokiyu, Okura Kyojin and Ojiu Norinaga. Further material was recently discovered at the home of one of his relatives, including a filmed recording of Yasusada and his collaborators, Akutagawa Fusei and Ozaki Kusatao, reading a series of renga to elaborate musical accompaniment.

ISHIHARA YOSHIRŌ (1915–1977) was a major Japanese poet to emerge from post-war concentration camps in Siberia.

JIAN ZHANG teaches in the Reading Department at Suffolk Community College. With Ronald Janssen, she is the translator of three volumes of Can Xue's fiction.

JOHN ZILCOSKY is a doctoral candidate in comparative literature at the University of Pennsylvania, where he studies twentieth-century literature and philosophy in German, English and French.

Back issues of
CONJUNCTIONS

"A must read"—*The Village Voice*

A limited number of back issues are available to those who would like to discover for themselves the range of innovative writing published in CONJUNCTIONS over the course of more than a decade.

CONJUNCTIONS:1. *James Laughlin Festschrift.* Paul Bowles, Gary Snyder, John Hawkes, Robert Creeley, Thom Gunn, Denise Levertov, Tennessee Williams, James Purdy, William Everson, Jerome Rothenberg, George Oppen, Joel Oppenheimer, Eva Hesse, Michael McClure, Octavio Paz, Hayden Carruth, over 50 others. Kenneth Rexroth interview. 304 pages.

CONJUNCTIONS:2. Nathaniel Tarn, William H. Gass, Mei-mei Berssenbrugge, Walter Abish, Gustaf Sobin, Edward Dorn, Kay Boyle, Kenneth Irby, Thomas Meyer, Gilbert Sorrentino, Carl Rakosi, and others. H.D.'s letters to Sylvia Dobson. Czeslaw Milosz interview. 232 pages.

CONJUNCTIONS:3. Guy Davenport, Michael Palmer, Don Van Vliet, Michel Deguy, Toby Olson, Rene Char, Coleman Dowell, Cid Corman, Ann Lauterbach, Robert Fitzgerald, Jackson Mac Low, Cecile Abish, Anne Waldman, and others. James Purdy interview. 232 pages.

CONJUNCTIONS:4. Luis Buñuel, Aimé Césaire, Armand Schwerner, Rae Armantrout, Harold Schimmel, Gerrit Lansing, Jonathan Williams, Ron Silliman, Theodore Enslin, and others. Excerpts from Kenneth Rexroth's unpublished autobiography. Robert Duncan and William H. Gass interview. 232 pages.

CONJUNCTIONS:5. Coleman Dowell, Nathaniel Mackey, Kenneth Gangemi, Paul Bowles, Hayden Carruth, John Taggart, Guy Mendes, John Ashbery, Francesco Clemente, and others. Lorine Niedecker's letters to Cid Corman. Barry Hannah and Basil Bunting interviews. 248 pages.

CONJUNCTIONS:6. Joseph McElroy, Ron Loewinsohn, Susan Howe, William Wegman, Barbara Tedlock, Edmond Jabés, Jerome Rothenberg, Keith Waldrop, James Clifford, Janet Rodney, and others. The *Symposium of the Whole* papers. Irving Layton interview. 320 pages.

CONJUNCTIONS:7. John Hawkes, Mary Caponegro, Leslie Scalapino, Marjorie Welish, Gerrit Lansing, Douglas Messerli, Gilbert Sorrentino, and others. *Writers Interview Writers*: Robert Duncan/Michael McClure, Jonathan Williams/Ronald Johnson, Edmund White/Edouard Roditi. 284 pages.

CONJUNCTIONS:8. Robert Duncan, Coleman Dowell, Barbara Einzig, R.B. Kitaj, Paul Metcalf, Barbara Guest, Robert Kelly, Claude Royet-Journoud, Guy Davenport, Karin Lessing, Hilda Morley, and others. *Basil Bunting Tribute*, guest-edited by Jonathan Williams, nearly 50 contributors. 272 pages.

CONJUNCTIONS:9. William S. Burroughs, Dennis Silk, Michel Deguy, Peter Cole, Paul West, Laura Moriarty, Michael Palmer, Hayden Carruth, Mei-mei Berssenbrugge, Thomas Meyer, Aaron Shurin, Barbara Tedlock, and others. Edmond Jabés interview. 296 pages.

CONJUNCTIONS:10. *Fifth Anniversary Issue.* Walter Abish, Bruce Duffy, Keith Waldrop, Harry Mathews, Kenward Elmslie, Beverley Dahlen, Jan Groover, Ronald Johnson, David Rattray, Leslie Scalapino, George Oppen, Elizabeth Murray, and others. Joseph McElroy interview. 320 pages.

CONJUNCTIONS:11. Lydia Davis, John Taggart, Marjorie Welish, Dennis Silk, Susan Howe, Robert Creeley, Charles Stein, Charles Bernstein, Kenneth Irby, Nathaniel Tarn, Robert Kelly, Ann Lauterbach, Joel Shapiro, Richard Tuttle, and others. Carl Rakosi interview. 296 pages.

CONJUNCTIONS:12. David Foster Wallace, Robert Coover, Georges Perec, Norma Cole, Laura Moriarty, Joseph McElroy, Yannick Murphy, Diane Williams, Harry Mathews, Trevor Winkfield, Ron Silliman, Armand Schwerner, and others. John Hawkes and Paul West interviews. 320 pages.

CONJUNCTIONS:13. Maxine Hong Kingston, Ben Okri, Jim Crace, William S. Burroughs, Guy Davenport, Barbara Tedlock, Rachel Blau DuPlessis, Walter Abish, Jackson Mac Low, Lydia Davis, Fielding Dawson, Toby Olson, Eric Fischl, and others. Robert Kelly interview. 288 pages.

CONJUNCTIONS:14. *The New Gothic*, guest-edited by Patrick McGrath. Kathy Acker, John Edgar Wideman, Jamaica Kincaid, Peter Straub, Clegg & Guttmann, Robert Coover, Lynne Tillman, Bradford Morrow, William T. Vollmann, Gary Indiana, Mary Caponegro, Brice Marden, and others. Salman Rushdie interview. 296 pages.

CONJUNCTIONS:15. *The Poetry Issue.* 33 Poets, including Susan Howe, John Ashbery, Rachel Blau DuPlessis, Barbara Einzig, Norma Cole, John Ash, Ronald Johnson, Forrest Gander, Michael Palmer, Diane Ward, and others. Fiction by John Barth, Jay Cantor, Diane Williams, and others. Michael Ondaatje interview. 424 pages.

CONJUNCTIONS:16. *The Music Issue.* Nathaniel Mackey, Leon Botstein, Albert Goldman, Paul West, Amiri Baraka, Quincy Troupe, Lukas Foss, Walter Mosley, David Shields, Seth Morgan, Gerald Early, Clark Coolidge, Hilton Als, and others. John Abercrombie and David Starobin interview. 360 pages.

CONJUNCTIONS:17. *Tenth Anniversary Issue.* Kathy Acker, Janice Galloway, David Foster Wallace, Robert Coover, Diana Michener, Juan Goytisolo, Rae Armantrout, John Hawkes, William T. Vollmann, Charlie Smith, Lynn Davis, Mary Caponegro, Keith Waldrop, Carla Lemos, C.D. Wright, and others. Chinua Achebe interview. 424 pages.

CONJUNCTIONS:18. *Fables, Yarns, Fairy Tales.* Scott Bradfield, Sally Pont, John Ash, Theodore Enslin, Patricia Eakins, Joanna Scott, Lynne Tillman, Can Xue, Gary Indiana, Russell Edson, David Rattray, James Purdy, Wendy Walker, Norman Manea, Paola Capriolo, O.V. de Milosz, Rosario Ferre, Jacques Roubaud, and others. 376 pages.

CONJUNCTIONS:19. *Other Worlds.* Guest-edited by Peter Cole. David Antin, John Barth, Pat Califia, Thom Gunn, Barbara Einzig, Ewa Kuryluk, Carl Rakosi, Eliot Weinberger, John Adams, Peter Reading, John Cage, Marjorie Welish, Barbara Guest, Cid Corman, Elaine Equi, Donald Baechlor, John Wieners, and others. 336 pages.

CONJUNCTIONS:20. *Unfinished Business.* Robert Antoni, Janice Galloway, Martine Bellen, Paul Gervais, Ann Lauterbach, Jessica Hagedorn, Jim Lewis, Carole Maso, Leslie Scalapino, Gilbert Sorrentino, David Foster Wallace, Robert Creeley, Ben Marcus, Paul West, Mei-mei Berssenbrugge, Susan Rothenberg, Yannick Murphy, and others. 352 pages.

CONJUNCTIONS:21. *The Credos Issue.* Robert Olen Butler, Ishmael Reed, Kathy Acker, Walter Mosley, Robert Coover, Joanna Scott, Victor Hernandez Cruz, Frank Chin, Simon Ortiz, Martine Bellen, Melanie Neilson, Kenward Elmslie, David Mura, Jonathan Williams, Cole Swensen, John Ashbery, Forrest Gander, Myung Mi Kim, and others. 352 pages.

CONJUNCTIONS:22. *The Novellas Issue.* Allan Gurganus, Lynne Tillman, Robert Antoni, Arno Schmidt, Harry Mathews, Robert Olen Butler, Wendy Walker, Stephen Ratcliffe, Kevin Magee, Barbara Guest, John Barth, Donald Revell, James Surls, and others. 384 pages.

ARNO SCHMIDT

COLLECTED NOVELLAS

Collected Early Fiction 1949-1964, volume 1

Translated by John E. Woods

the first in a 4-volume edition of the early works of Arno Schmidt

"An enormously important talent in the fictional line of cruel comedy that runs from Rabelais through Swift and Joyce."

—*New York Review of Books*

at better bookstores everywhere
or available directly from the publisher:
Dalkey Archive Press
Campus Box 4241, Normal, IL 61790-4241
phone orders: (309) 438-7555
($22.95 plus $1.50 p&h)
ISBN 1-56478-066-X, 440 pp.

An International Conference
University of Liverpool
15th - 16th September 1995

THE LINGUISTIC FOUNDATIONS
OF TRANSLATION

Literary Translation and the Translation
of Sensitive Texts

CALL FOR PAPERS

This two-day residential conference will focus on two specific but related issues in Translation Studies. The subject of Literary Translation will be approached from the perspective of the changes—whether of an aesthetic or an idealogical nature—which occur during the translation process. The topic of Sensitive Texts will refer to situations where defects in translation may have serious consequences, e.g. when such texts are concerned with religious or legal matters.

Invited Speakers Include:

Mona Baker • Basil Hatim • Eugene Nida • Lawrence Venuti

Proceedings will be published. Send abstracts (max. 300 words) to either:

Professor Michael Hoey
Director, Applied English
  Language Studies Unit
University of Liverpool
P.O. Box 147
Liverpool L69 3BX
England
Tel: 031 794 2771

Dr. Terry Hale
Director, The British Centre
  for Literary Translation
University of East Anglia
Norwich NR4 7TJ
England
Tel: 0603 592134
Funded by the Arts Council of England

Closing date: 15th March. All speakers must register for the conference.